VISUAL QUICKSTART GUIDE

QUICKTIME AND MOVIEPLAYER PRO 3

FOR WINDOWS AND MACINTOSH

Judith Stern
Robert Lettieri

Peachpit Press

Visual QuickStart Guide
QuickTime and MoviePlayer Pro 3
Judith Stern
Robert Lettieri

Peachpit Press
1249 Eighth Street
Berkeley, CA 94710
(510) 524-2178
(510) 524-2221 (fax)

Find us on the World Wide Web at: http://www.peachpit.com

Peachpit Press is a division of Addison-Wesley Publishing Company

Editor: Simon Hayes
Copy Editor: Bill Cassel
Production Coordinators: Amy Changar, Lisa Brazieal
Compositor: Owen Wolfson
Indexer: Carol Burbo
Cover Design: The Visual Group

ISBN: 0-201-35349-0

0 9 8 7 6 5 4 3 2

Printed and bound in the United States of America

To the memory of Louis Lettieri,
who was always a teacher.

Acknowledgements

As always, we first need to thank the people who created QuickTime, for without them this book wouldn't exist. The QuickTime team consists of many amazing people, but we are especially grateful to Peter Hoddie, Mike Dodd, Ian Ritchie, Kathy Stevens, Mitchell Weinstock, and Charles Wiltgen, for all the information and support they've provided us while writing this book.

In addition, thanks to Darren Giles, Brian Greenstone, Brent Burgess, and Susan Kitchens, for answering miscellaneous technical questions. We also thank Marvin Stern, Lois Stern, and David Schwartz for testing steps.

Many thanks go to our editor, Simon Hayes; our copy editor, Bill Cassel; and our technical editor, Charles Wiltgen. Without the input from these three, this book would have been less useful, less clear, and less accurate. Thanks also to Victor Gavenda, Amy Changar, Owen Wolfson and others at Peachpit who've been responsible for making this project a reality.

On the personal front, thanks to Sam (who thinks all parents "go to work upstairs" at night time), and to her "village", especially those who were there to care for her while we were writing—Betsy and Garrett, Phil and Judy, Brandon, Phil and Karen, Annma, Grandma and Grandpa and the wonderful teachers at Monteverde School.

If we've missed anybody, it's because of the hour at which we're writing this. Our apologies and sincere thanks.

About the Authors

Judith Stern is an instructional multimedia specialist. Her background includes corporate training, expert systems development, educational research, and multimedia development. She works for the University of California at Berkeley, where she provides support and training to faculty and staff developing instructional multimedia software; she's also a software designer and technical writer for the Computer as Learning Partner Project and the Knowledge Integration Environment Project, both of which are NSF-funded educational research projects.

Robert Lettieri is a computer consultant, specializing in graphics and multimedia technologies. At the University of California at Berkeley, he is the multimedia courseware specialist for Synthesis, a National Engineering Education Coalition. He has been experimenting and working with digital and analog video for over 12 years. He has taught many people how to use graphics and desktop publishing software, both individually and in training workshops.

Together, Stern and Lettieri are the authors of several books and articles on multimedia. They also co-author The Little QuickTime Page (www.bmug.org/quicktime/), a weekly news Web page. In addition, they do multimedia production work and been involved in many aspects of the development of various Web, CD-ROM and kiosk projects. They can be reached at jandr@ccnet.com.

Table of Contents

Introduction xiii

Chapter 1: QuickTime Basics 1

Differences between the Pro and Standard editions 2
Checking to see if you have QuickTime 3 3
Checking to see if you have QuickTime 3 Pro 4
Hardware and software requirements 5
Getting and installing QuickTime 3 6
Upgrading to QuickTime 3 Pro 8
Getting sample movies 10

Chapter 2: MoviePlayer Basics 11

Opening QuickTime movies 12
Opening non-QuickTime files 13
Converting non-QuickTime files 15
The movie controllers 17
Changing window sizes 18
Showing copyright information 20
The Info window 21
Figuring out which tracks are in a movie 22
Choosing a language for playback 23

Chapter 3: Playing QuickTime Movies 25

Playing and pausing movies 26
Stepping through a movie frame by frame 27
Quickly moving around in a movie 28
Presenting a movie 29
Presenting a movie frame by frame (in slide-show mode) 30
Changing the audio level 31
Overriding audio 32
Looping a movie or playing it backward 33
Playing every frame 34
Playing and pausing all open movies 35
Varying the playback rate of a movie 36
Checking the frame rate 37
Using chapter lists 38

Chapter 4: **Interacting with QuickTime VR** 39
Looking around in panorama movies 40
Manipulating objects in object movies 41
Finding and using hot spots 42
Zooming in and out 44
Moving zoomed-in objects 45
Presenting QuickTime VR movies 46

Chapter 5: **Basic Movie Editing** 47
Selecting and deselecting movie data. 48
Jumping to the end or beginning of a selection. 49
Playing only what's selected 50
Getting time information about the movie and the selection 51
Copying and cutting movie data 52
Pasting movie data into a movie 54
Pasting text and graphics into a movie 56
Creating a new movie and pasting data into it 58
Combining two movies. 59
Deleting parts of a movie. 60
Replacing part of a movie with part of another. 61
Drag-and-drop editing (Mac OS only) 62
Adding and editing annotations such as copyright and artist information. 64
Setting a poster 67
Changing what's shown when you choose show copyright. 68
Setting a preview 69
Setting a preview using data from other movies (Mac OS only) 71
Saving movies 72
Checking file dependencies. 74

Chapter 6: **Working with Tracks** 75
Combining tracks with the Add and Add Scaled commands 76
Extracting tracks 78
Deleting tracks. 79
Disabling and enabling tracks 80
Scaling a track to a specific duration 81
Setting up tracks with alternate languages. 82
Specifying a language track 83
Designating a set of alternate tracks. 84
Loading tracks into memory 86

Chapter 7: Working with Visual Tracks 87
Flipping, rotating, resizing, and skewing . . . 88
Masking a visual track . . . 91
Placing visual tracks side by side . . . 92
Creating a picture-in-a-picture effect . . . 93
Relayering tracks . . . 94
Making a color in a track transparent . . . 95
Blending tracks . . . 96
Using alpha channels . . . 97
Adding visual data to QuickTime VR movies . . . 98
Adding a custom color table to a movie . . . 100
Creating a still image file from any image in a movie . . . 101

Chapter 8: Video and MPEG Tracks 103
Understanding video compression . . . 104
The Compression Settings dialog box . . . 106
Determining how a video was compressed . . . 108
Creating tracks from a sequence of still images . . . 109
Creating a video track from a single still image . . . 110
Creating video tracks from non-QuickTime animation and video files . . . 112
Adding images to an existing movie . . . 114
Creating MPEG tracks from MPEG files (Mac OS only) . . . 115

Chapter 9: Text Tracks 117
Creating a text track by importing a text file . . . 118
Specifying text track appearance when you import . . . 119
Specifying the duration and appearance of individual frames of text . . . 121
Exporting a text track with text descriptors and time stamps . . . 123
Creating a text track that's synched to other tracks . . . 125
Changing text that's already in a text track (Mac OS only) . . . 127
Adding small amounts of text . . . 129
Searching a text track . . . 130

Chapter 10: Sprite and 3D Tracks 131
Attaching a graphic or video sequence to a sprite . . . 132
Changing the background color of a sprite track . . . 133

Creating a static 3D track from a 3D file 134
Changing texture mapping for a 3D track 135
Changing the renderer for a 3D track 137

Chapter 11: **Working with Audio Tracks** **139**
Adding new audio to a movie 140
Adding a still image to an audio track 141
Having audio play when the movie isn't in front 142
Changing the default volume and balance of an audio track 143

Chapter 12: **Sound and MPEG Audio Tracks** **145**
Understanding the characteristics of digitized sound 146
The Sound Settings dialog box 147
Checking the characteristics of a sound track 148
Creating a sound track from a sound file 149
Creating a sound track from an audio CD (Mac OS only) 151
Creating an MPEG audio track from an MPEG sound file 152
Changing the characteristics of a sound track 153
Converting a music track to a sound track 155
Using MoviePlayer as a sound conversion utility 156

Chapter 13: **Music Tracks** **157**
Converting MIDI files to QuickTime 158
Converting karaoke files to QuickTime 159
Changing instruments in a music track 160
Substituting your own custom sound for an instrument in a music track (Mac OS only) 162
Playing music tracks through a MIDI synthesizer (Mac OS only) 163
Converting QuickTime music tracks back to MIDI 165

Chapter 14: **Delivery Basics** **167**
Understanding data rate and size 168
Checking data rate and data size 169
Saving movies for distribution 170
Exporting movies as QuickTime movies 171
Applying filters 174
Compressing selected tracks 176
Checking the dimensions of a movie 178

Chapter 15: Movies on Web Pages: Basics **179**

QuickTime compared to other streaming formats . . . 180
Making QuickTime movies that stream . . . 182
Compressing video for the Web . . . 183
Compressing sound for the Web . . . 187
Embedding a QuickTime movie on a Web page . . . 189
Adding parameters to your EMBED tag . . . 191
Creating a small movie to use as a poster movie . . . 194
Writing the HTML for a poster movie . . . 196
Using HREF tracks to make movies load Web pages . . . 198

Chapter 16: Movies on Web Pages: Advanced **201**

Getting important utilities . . . 202
Alternate datarate movies with MakeRefMovie . . . 203
Plug-in helper . . . 206
Creating Streaming VR movies with MoviePlayer and QTVR Flattener . . . 208
Creating panorama thumbnails with QTVR PanoToThumbnail . . . 210

Chapter 17: Movies on CD-ROM, Kiosk and Videotape **213**

Overview of issues regarding compression for CD-ROM and kiosk . . . 214
Video compression choices . . . 215
Sound compression choices . . . 217
Overview of authoring and presentation tools' support for QuickTime . . . 218
Licensing requirements for distributing QuickTime . . . 220
Outputting to analog videotape . . . 221
Exporting a video track as DV . . . 222

Appendix A: Mouse and Keyboard Tricks **225**

Appendix B: Configuring QuickTime **229**

Using the QuickTime settings conrol panel . . . 230
Using the QuickTime Plug-in Settings dialog box . . . 234

Appendix C: Resources

INTRODUCTION

Welcome to the *Visual QuickStart Guide for QuickTime and MoviePlayer Pro 3*.

In this book you'll learn how to use these remarkable yet inexpensive pieces of technology that have become standards in the multimedia industry.

We've been QuickTime and MoviePlayer users since their introduction in 1991. We wrote our first book about this technology in 1992. We wrote that book, and have continued writing and teaching about the topic, because QuickTime is such an elegant technology; it's easy for beginners to understand and use, but provides tremendous power and flexibility as you learn more about it.

With the introduction of QuickTime 3 this year, the technology is accessible to an even wider variety of users, and is even more powerful than ever.

A Visual QuickStart Guide, with its emphasis on clear, illustrated, step-by-step instructions, provides a perfect forum for us to share our enthusiasm for QuickTime and MoviePlayer.

Whether you're new to the world of QuickTime or a seasoned veteran, we think you'll find this book a good learning and reference tool.

What are QuickTime and MoviePlayer?

Unlike most other pieces of software about which you might buy a book, QuickTime isn't an application program. Rather, QuickTime is an "enabling technology": if it's installed on your system, it enables many other programs to provide important multimedia features.

QuickTime enables other software to gracefully and simply handle multimedia data, such as video, audio, and animation (actually, much more than this, but you get the idea). It allows media to be viewed, edited, combined, transformed, and manipulated in whatever way an artist, teacher, communicator, business person, video professional, or kid sees fit.

MoviePlayer is one of those many programs that get their power from QuickTime. MoviePlayer isn't just any old tool, however. It's got a pretty special place in the world of QuickTime. That's because it was written by the same people who created QuickTime in the first place. Originally it was used for internal testing; if a feature was added to QuickTime, MoviePlayer was enhanced so the QuickTime engineers could test and demonstrate that feature.

As you might imagine, over the years MoviePlayer has become a pretty powerful tool for playing, editing, and preparing movies for distribution. As you also might imagine, a lot of its functionality isn't immediately obvious; after all, the engineers knew where to find what they needed to. This book will tell you everything you need to know to gain access to all those features.

Figure i.1 A standard QuickTime movie can be viewed much like a videotape using controls at the bottom of the window.

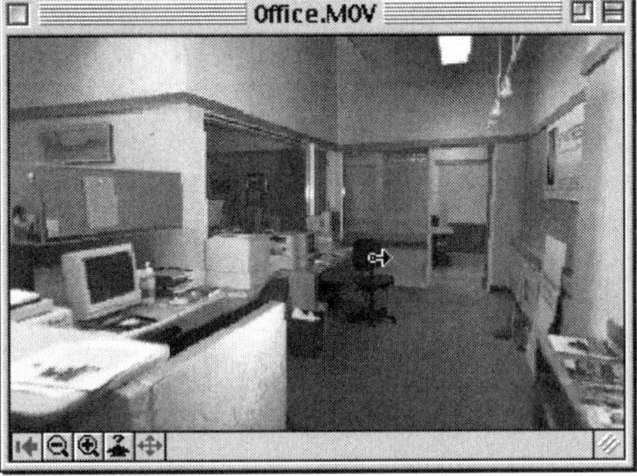

Figure i.2 A QuickTime VR movie is one in which a viewer clicks and drags in the movie window to explore a space or object.

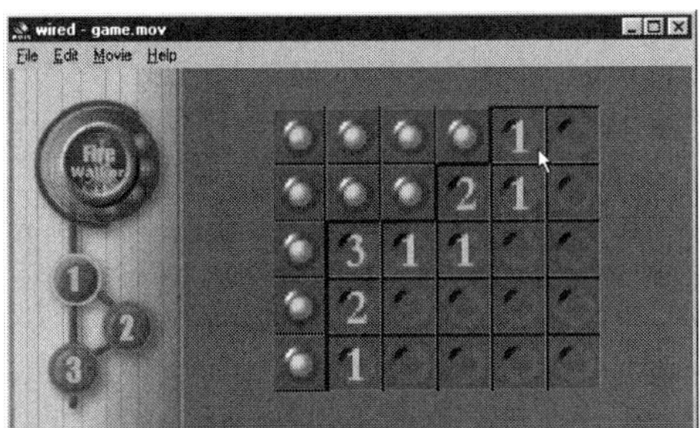

Figure i.3 An interactive movie has clickable objects (like buttons) that cause changes in the movie.

The anatomy of a QuickTime movie

A QuickTime *movie* is the container that holds multimedia data. The movie may be a standard time-based movie (**Figure i.1**), which is typically played in a linear fashion (though it can also be accessed randomly). Or it may be a QuickTime VR movie (**Figure i.2**), which provides an immersive spatial environment in which users can move around in spaces or view objects from different angles by dragging and clicking in the movie image. Or the movie may even have interactive buttons and other elements, resembling a multimedia application more than a traditional QuickTime movie (**Figure i.3**).

Regardless of whether it's linear or spatial, non-interactive or interactive, a QuickTime movie is a container that can potentially hold lots of different types of multimedia data. Most people associate QuickTime with video and audio, but there's also text, MIDI music, and animation (2D and 3D).

QuickTime stores different types of media separately in what are called *tracks*. While nobody needs to know about this underlying architecture to view QuickTime movies, if you want to understand and take advantage of the power and flexibility of QuickTime, it helps to be aware of all the different track types.

A *video track* is the standard track for holding visual data in QuickTime movies. It's composed of one image or a sequence of images, with each image usually composed of *pixels*, or individual squares of color. (However, see sidebar on the next page.)

A *sound track* is the standard track for holding digitized audio.

A *music track* contains what is essentially a musical score—information about a sequence of musical notes that QuickTime can play back. It's analogous to MIDI (Musical Instrument Digital Interface), a standard in the electronic music industry. The storage space taken up by the data in a music track is very small compared to digitized sound.

The *text track* holds only text. Since tracks in a movie are synchronized, the text track provides a way to caption a movie, index it, or even include URLs that can cause a Web page to download at a specific point in playback. Text tracks are also searchable; viewers can search for key words to find precise points in the movie.

A *3D track* holds 3D data, which includes geometric definitions of objects, as well as descriptions of the objects' surfaces (including texture and lighting). A 3D track works in conjunction with another track, the *tween track*, which defines the motion of the object. (The term "tween" comes from the animation world, where the key frames are first created and then the in-between frames are generated.)

A *sprite track* contains graphic objects (called sprites). These sprites can be pixel-based, vector-based, or even contain 3D data. Some sprites are animated; such sprites are stored only once in a movie file and the path they follow across the screen is specified separately. (Compared to most video tracks, in which changes in position of objects in a scene require storage of new sets of pixels, sprite tracks are much smaller in file size.) Some sprites are *wired*; that is, they have actions associated with them and can act as interactive buttons. Sprites can be both animated and wired.

A single QuickTime movie can have lots of different tracks, and even multiple tracks of the same type.

One of the great things about QuickTime is that it knows when to keep its tracks tightly linked together, and when to let them stand alone. That is, when someone plays a QuickTime movie, the tracks play together, at the same time, *synchronously*. When it's time to edit, however, you can edit a movie as one unified piece, or you can go in and do things to the different tracks individually. There may even be instances during playback when there's a need to turn one track off and another on, and QuickTime can handle this, too.

Of pixels and vectors

There are essentially two types of computer graphics, bitmap (or pixel-based) and vector.

The pixels in a bitmap image are a predetermined size. If you re-size a bitmap image you just stretch the pixels, causing the image to become fuzzy.

Vector images are composed of lines and curves. These lines and curves are mathematically defined. When you stretch a vector image, the computer recalculates the image so it retains its resolution. Also, representing images mathematically is much more efficient, so vector images require less disk space than do bitmap images.

Most QuickTime video tracks and sprites in sprite tracks are composed of bitmap images. However, with QuickTime 3, it's possible to have video tracks or sprites containing vector-based images (also called curve media). Shortly after QuickTime 3's release there were already a few tools to create QuickTime curve media, and we expect to see even more tools in the future.

QuickTime compared to other technologies

If you look at QuickTime and compare it to most other multimedia or video technologies, you'll find that QuickTime offers much more to many more people. None of the other technologies can boast that they handle video, audio, music, text, 3D and sprite animation. QuickTime can import files of many formats, including those of some of the competing technologies; there are currently almost 30 formats in the list (see sidebar on page xx) and this number is sure to grow. QuickTime works as well on the Internet as it does for CD-ROM and kiosks, and is an integrated solution for both Mac OS and Windows 95/98 and NT. Programmers can use QuickTime on multiple platforms without having to rewrite their code, use QuickTime's standard user interface elements for common functions, and extend QuickTime with their own features without having to worry about the basics. This in turn means that users get tools faster, and those tools are of a better and more consistent quality than would be possible without such a great foundation.

You may have seen AVI files, for example. AVI is the file type for Microsoft's Video for Windows technology. Unlike QuickTime files, AVI files can only contain video and audio. Video for Windows has always been considered an inferior technology to QuickTime—even Microsoft chose QuickTime over Video for Windows for products such as its best-selling Encarta! Video for Windows is also no longer supported by Microsoft. For several years Microsoft promised a more robust replacement technology called ActiveMovie, but it was never fully released. (Only the playback portion was ever released.) Microsoft then integrated ActiveMovie with its DirectX technology, calling the result DirectShow, but this isn't a cross-platform technology, and hasn't matured to the point where good end-user tools are being developed, as in the QuickTime world.

Another video format you may be familiar with is MPEG. This is a high-quality format that has been used by multimedia professionals for many years. Until recently, however, MPEG was difficult and expensive to create and also could only play back on computers with special MPEG decoding hardware; thus it was less useful as a technology for the masses. Now, however, MPEG encoding software has come down in price from tens of thousands of dollars to thousands or even hundreds; you can even get free tools to convert from QuickTime to MPEG. And, with today's faster computer processors, more computers are now powerful enough to play back MPEG in software without extra hardware. However, there are still many more computers in the world that can handle QuickTime. In addition, the current incarnations of MPEG (called MPEG-1 and MPEG-2) are restricted to just video and audio. MPEG-4, which should be available in a few years and will be based on QuickTime's file format, has just been approved by the International Standards Organization (ISO); see Chapter 18 for more information on this. (In case you're wondering, there is no MPEG-3.)

QuickTime also holds its own among the newer technologies, such as RealMedia, being used to stream video and audio over the Internet. While these newer technologies have certain advantages, QuickTime is still the most widely used video technology on the World Wide Web; we'll discuss how QuickTime stacks up as a Web technology in Chapter 13.

In the realm of immersive technologies, a number of developers have products similar to QuickTime VR. Companies such as IPIX and RealSpace offer their own competing versions of imersive spatial technologies, but these don't offer the full range of capabilities and smooth integration provided by the complete QuickTime architecture.

✔ Tip

- One very important point about QuickTime is that it can be used to open, play back, and edit AVI files. On the Mac (and soon on Windows) QuickTime can open and play MPEG-1 files, as well.

File formats that QuickTime can handle

- AVI
- DV
- MPEG
- OpenDML
- AIFF
- Audio CD
- DV
- MPEG Layer I & 2 audio
- Sound Designer
- AU
- WAV
- System 7 Sound
- MIDI
- KAR
- BMP
- GIF
- JPEG/JFIF
- Photoshop
- PNG
- QuickDraw GX
- QuickTime Image Format
- SGI
- Targa
- TIFF
- PICT
- Animated GIF
- FLC/FLI
- PICS
- Text

The world of QuickTime

As we've mentioned, many different products are based on QuickTime or support it in some way. We can't even begin to cover them all, but it helps to know what categories of tools are out there. We'll mention a few specific tools; these references don't necessarily mean that we endorse the product.

Tools for capturing QuickTime video and audio

A number of tools exist for capturing audio and video from a videotape, an audiotape, or even a live video signal. Generally you use these tools in conjunction with hardware inside of your computer. This hardware may come with its own software to do the QuickTime capture. Most often, however, the tool of choice for QuickTime capture is Adobe Premiere, which, though primarily an editing tool, also has a capture feature.

Tools for generating QuickTime tracks

You can also create QuickTime movies using standard media creation tools. For example, many animation tools export their data as QuickTime video tracks, and a few can also export as QuickTime sprite tracks. Macromedia Director is the most well-known tool in this category. When tools don't create QuickTime tracks, they often export in a format that a QuickTime tool like MoviePlayer can open or import.

Tools for editing QuickTime video and audio

Once you've gotten a QuickTime track, you can use MoviePlayer (or any other editor, as long as it supports the track type) to combine and edit tracks to create something completely new. The tool you are most likely to have heard of is Adobe Premiere. This is a general-purpose video editing and effects tool. It lets you do things that MoviePlayer can't, such as adding transitions between scenes and other features that video editors want. On the other hand, most video editing tools only handle a subset of the full range of QuickTime tracks, whereas MoviePlayer supports them all.

Tools for compressing and optimizing QuickTime movies

Once you have composed the movie you want, you must do some final preparation before delivering it over a network or on CD-ROM or hard disk. In particular, video and audio need to be compressed. You can use MoviePlayer, Premiere, and other editing tools for basic compression. Other tools are used exclusively for compression and optimization; one of these, Media Cleaner Pro, is generally considered to be the tool that produces the best-looking movies.

Tools for integrating QuickTime movies with other media

Macromedia Director, which we mentioned as a tool that creates animations, is also well known as a multimedia authoring tool. It lets you put together sophisticated interactive presentations that contain many types of media. For many years, QuickTime has been one of the file formats which can be included in and controlled from a Director presentation. Other authoring tools such as Apple HyperCard and Asymetrix ToolBook also support QuickTime in this way. In addition, simpler presentation tools such as Microsoft PowerPoint let you include QuickTime movies in a presentation. QuickTime movies can also be embedded in Web pages; thus most Web browsers and many Web-page creation tools offer QuickTime support. And even tools like word processors and spreadsheets often allow you to include QuickTime movies in their documents.

QuickTime on Windows and Mac OS computers

QuickTime 3 is the first release of QuickTime that is fully cross-platform. Previously you could play back QuickTime movies on Windows computers but not create or edit them.

Now, you can have virtually the same experience on either platform.

In fact, in this book we'll randomly use screen shots from both platforms, since just about all menus and dialog boxes have the same content on each platform.

When specific keys, names of screen elements, or procedures differ due to human interface requirements on the two platforms, we'll indicate this by noting both options, as in "Press the Option key (Mac OS) or the Alt and Ctrl keys (Windows) to...."

In the few cases where a feature is available on only one platform, or where the sequence of steps to follow is significantly different, we'll label the section as "Mac OS Only" or "Windows Only".

What you'll find in this book

Now that you have some general idea of what QuickTime and MoviePlayer are, you're ready to move on to Chapter 1, where we'll go over the basics of getting up and running with these pieces of software.

Starting with Chapter 1, the book is divided into three parts. The first part concentrates on using MoviePlayer to view and interact with QuickTime movies without changing them in any way.

The second part covers the vast array of techniques for editing movies, including manipulating tracks independently.

Finally, in the third part, we'll look at distributing movies, with an emphasis on Web delivery. Here you'll use some additional tools that work in conjunction with MoviePlayer to do some advanced Web publishing tasks.

If you're new to QuickTime and MoviePlayer you'll probably want to use this book as a primer: Go through it from beginning to end, making sure to work through all the step-by-step instructions. Like all Visual QuickStart Guide, we've illustrated all the instructions with lots of screen shots so you can more quickly learn how to do specific tasks.

If you've been using QuickTime or MoviePlayer for a while, you'll also find this book useful as a reference. You can look up specific tasks in the Table of Contents. (Or, if you don't find what you're looking for there, try the Index.) In some cases, the screen shots may be all you need to be on your way, successfully accomplishing what you need to do.

As you use this book, we hope you'll enjoy QuickTime and MoviePlayer as much as we do. There's a lot to learn, so let's get going.

Staying up-to-date

While everything in this book is accurate at the time of writing, QuickTime is not a technology that's staying still. If you want to be sure to stay on top of changes in QuickTime, MoviePlayer and other related technologies, we suggest you visit our Web site, Judy and Robert's Little QuickTime Page, at **http://www.bmug.org/quicktime/**

1

QuickTime Basics

Before you can learn how to use QuickTime and MoviePlayer, you need to have working versions on your computer.

Let's start by stating that MoviePlayer comes as part of the QuickTime package, so any reference to QuickTime in this chapter implicitly includes MoviePlayer.

There is a chance that you already have what you need, or part of what you need. Since QuickTime is a standard for delivering multimedia, there's always the possibility that it has already been installed on your computer as part of the installation process for another multimedia program. So, we'll show you how to check to see if you have QuickTime, and, if so, which version you have.

One key point about QuickTime is that there are a free Standard edition and a $30 Pro edition. We'll explain why you want the Pro edition.

If you don't have QuickTime 3 Pro, you need to get it. This involves being sure that you have the proper software and hardware to run QuickTime, getting the Standard edition of the QuickTime software, installing it, and then upgrading to the Pro edition by obtaining and entering a registration number. (The Pro edition only comes as an upgrade to the Standard edition.) We'll explain how to do all this in this chapter, too.

Differences between the Pro and Standard editions

There really is no difference between the Pro and Standard editions of the QuickTime system software. What is different is the MoviePlayer tool.

The name "MoviePlayer" is really appropriate only for the version that comes with the Standard edition. You use it to play movies and that's about it.

When you upgrade to QuickTime Pro, MoviePlayer gains a tremendous amount of functionality and becomes much more than just a "player." Many more items appear in the menus, providing many more features. You gain the ability to import from and export to other media formats and prepare QuickTime movies for Web playback. Editing features become available, allowing you to merge movies, add other media, alter components of the movie, and save new creations. Even some playback features, such as the ability to play movies full-screen, are added.

In addition, other software that is part of the QuickTime package becomes enhanced. An application called PictureViewer, which is used to view still images, gains the ability to save, import, and export still image files. The QuickTime plug-in, which is used to view QuickTime movies on Web pages, gains a single capability: It allows you to easily save to your hard drive most movies that you find on a Web page.

In short, you can't do most of what's in this book unless you have upgraded to the Pro version. We won't even bother to indicate which are "Pro only" features since just about everything is!

Figure 1.1 QuickTime Settings icon in the Mac Control Panels folder.

Figure 1.2 QuickTime icon in the Windows Control Panel folder.

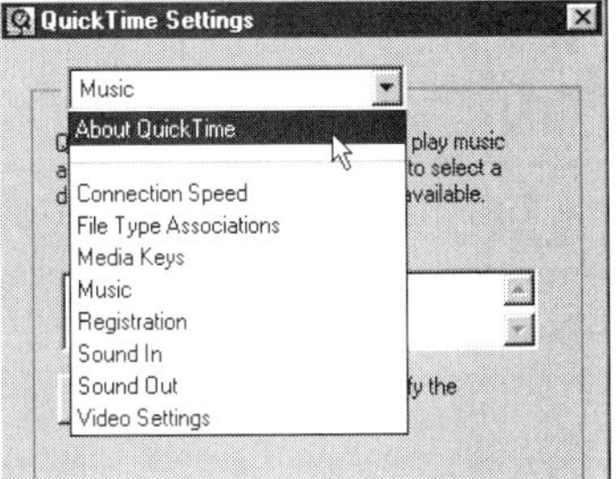

Figure 1.3 Choose About QuickTime in the QuickTime Settings (Mac OS) or QuickTime (Windows) control panel.

Figure 1.4 The About QuickTime panel shows which version of QuickTime you have if you have version 3.0 or later.

Checking to see if you have QuickTime 3

You may already have QuickTime 3.0 installed on your computer, since it is used for so many multimedia CD-ROMs. If you don't have it, you'll need to get it; we explain how later in this chapter.

To see if you already have QuickTime 3

1. Open your Control Panel(s) folder and look for a QuickTime Settings icon (Mac OS, **Figure 1.1**) or a QuickTime icon (Windows, **Figure 1.2**).

   If the icon is not there, you don't have QuickTime 3; you need to get it.

2. If there is a QuickTime Settings or QuickTime icon, double-click it to open the QuickTime Settings Control Panel.

3. If the pop-up menu at the top of the window is not already set to About QuickTime, click it and choose About QuickTime (**Figure 1.3**), if it is listed.

   You'll see text below the pop-up menu telling you what version of QuickTime is installed (**Figure 1.4**). If the version number is 3.0 or greater, you have QuickTime 3, but you may still need to upgrade to the Pro edition.

✔ Tips

- On the Mac, if About QuickTime is not one of the choices in the pop-up menu in the QuickTime Settings control panel, you probably have QuickTime 2.5. You need to get QuickTime 3.
- On a Windows computer, if you see only a QuickTime 32 or QuickTime 16 icon in the Control Panel window, you have a version of QuickTime earlier than 3. You need to get QuickTime 3.

Checking to see if you have QuickTime 3 Pro

If you know that you have QuickTime 3, you'll want to see if you have the Standard version, in which case you'll want to upgrade, or if you already have the Pro version.

To see if you have QuickTime 3 Pro

1. If it's not already open, open the QuickTime Settings control panel (Mac OS) or the QuickTime control panel (Windows).
2. Choose Registration from the pop-up menu. (**Figure 1.5**)
3. Determine which version you have:

   If the QuickTime line reads "Standard Edition" (**Figure 1.6**), then you do not have QuickTime 3 Pro.

   If the QuickTime line reads "Pro Player Edition" (**Figure 1.7**), then you do have QuickTime 3 Pro.

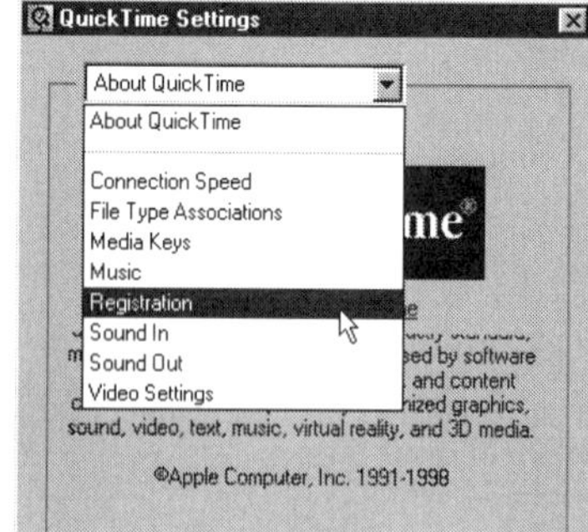

Figure 1.5 Choose Registration in the QuickTime Settings (Mac OS) or QuickTime (Windows) control panel.

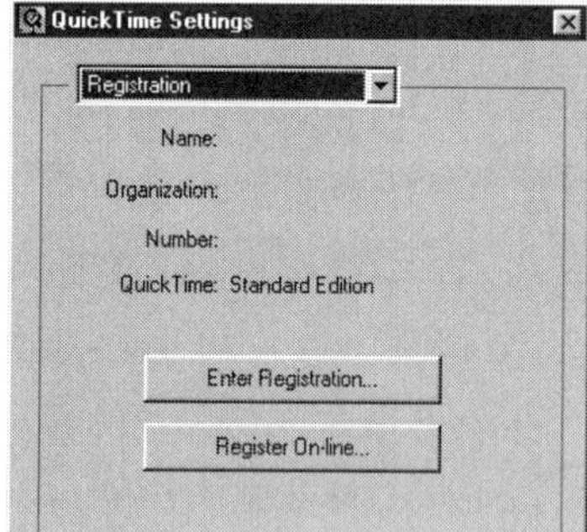

Figure 1.6 The Registration panel looks like this when you have only the Standard edition of QuickTime 3.

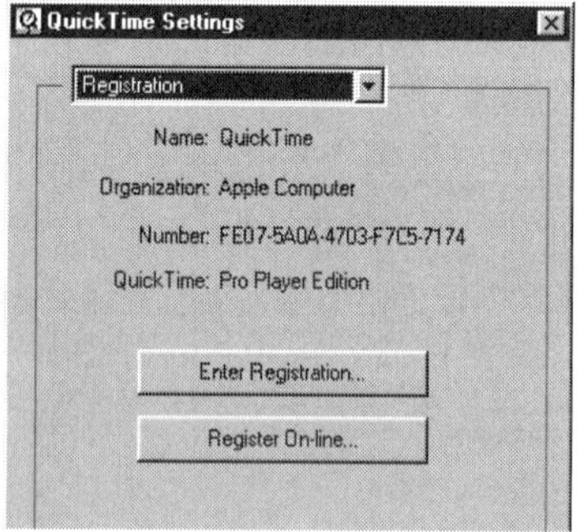

Figure 1.7 The Registration panel looks like this when you have QuickTime 3 Pro.

Hardware and software requirements

One of the reasons that QuickTime has become so popular is that it has very few software and hardware requirements.

Mac OS requirements

- Mac OS version 7.1 or higher
- 16 MB of RAM for PowerPC-based Mac OS computers or 8MB of RAM for 68K-based Macintosh computers
- 68K-based Macintosh computers must also support Color QuickDraw

Windows requirements

- Windows 95 or Windows NT 4.0 (or higher)
- Any 486DX-based computer at 66MHz or faster, any Pentium-based computer, or any MPC2 compliant PC
- 16MB RAM
- SoundBlaster-compatible sound card
- Direct X version 3.0 or higher (recommended for best performance)
- The latest DirectDraw and DirectSound drivers for your video and audio cards (recommended for best performance)

Getting and installing QuickTime 3

If you don't have QuickTime 3, you'll need to get it.

Methods of getting QuickTime 3

- Using a Web browser, go to Apple's QuickTime Web site, **http://www.apple.com/quicktime/**, (**Figure 1.8**) and follow the instructions for getting QuickTime 3 for free.
- Call Apple at 1-888-295-0648 and order a CD-ROM containing QuickTime 3. (When you call, you'll probably get a voice mail system which gives you a choice to "purchase an unlock code for QuickTime"; this is the choice you want. You'll speak with a live operator. You can either order a CD-ROM with only QuickTime 3 for either platform for $10, or a CD-ROM with QuickTime 3, along with a registration number to upgrade to the Pro version for $40.)
- Get a CD-ROM that contains QuickTime 3 from one of the various multimedia publishers, software developers or computer user groups that have a license to distribute QuickTime 3.

Figure 1.8 You can download QuickTime 3 from Apple's QuickTime Web site.

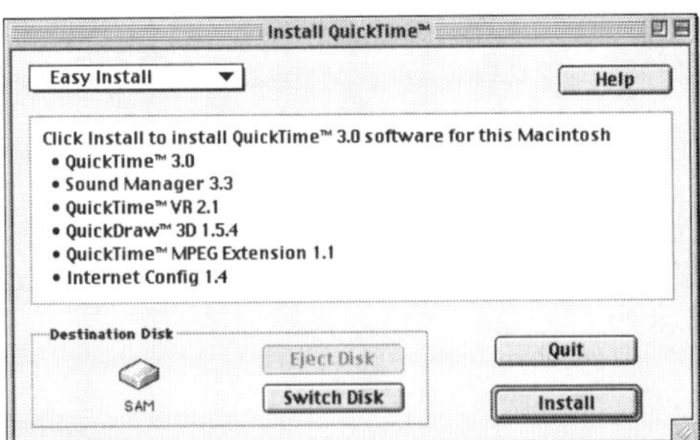

Figure 1.9 We recommend the Easy Install option on a Mac OS computer.

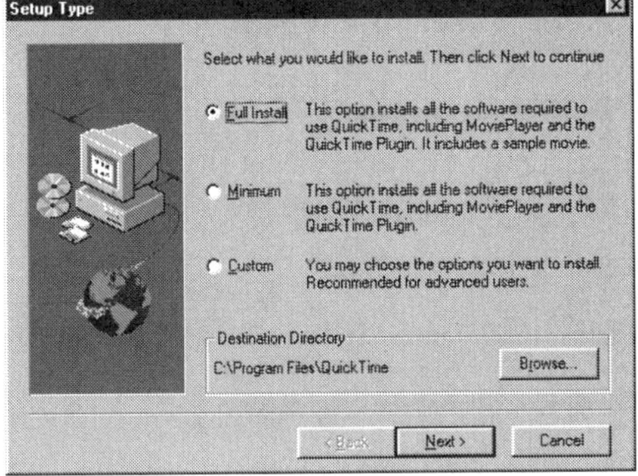

Figure 1.10 We recommend the Full Install option on a Windows computer.

QuickTime for Windows before QuickTime 3

The older, pre-3.0 versions of QuickTime for Windows (QuickTime 32 or QuickTime 16) can coexist with QuickTime 3, and may be necessary for some older applications, games, or other software. The QuickTime 3 installer will not remove older versions of QuickTime for Windows, and neither should you.

To install QuickTime 3

- Follow the instructions provided at the Installing QuickTime 3 page, http://www.apple.com/quicktime/information/install.html, or on the CD-ROM.

✔ Tips

- On a Mac OS computer, we recommend using the Easy Install option (**Figure 1.9**).
- On a Windows computer, we recommend choosing Full Install on the Setup Type screen (**Figure 1.10**) and clicking Next on each subsequent screen.

Upgrading to QuickTime 3 Pro

Unless you purchased the $40 CD-ROM from Apple, or some other CD-ROM that contains the Pro edition of QuickTime 3, you will need to upgrade to the Pro edition after installing QuickTime 3 as described on the previous page. Go to the Upgrade to QuickTime 3 Pro page at Apple's Web site (as described below) and follow the instructions. You will need to provide a credit card number to pay the $30 upgrade fee. You will receive a registration code, also called an *unlock code*, which you will need to enter to "unlock" the Pro features.

Methods of getting to the Upgrade to QuickTime 3 Pro page on the Web

- Enter the URL http://www.apple.com/quicktime/upgrade into your Web browser directly.
- Open the Get QuickTime Pro movie that appears on your desktop after installing QuickTime 3 and click the Now button (**Figure 1.11**). (The Get QuickTime Pro movie also opens automatically the first time MoviePlayer is run.)
- Open the QuickTime Settings control panel, choose Registration in the pop-up menu (**Figure 1.12**), and in the Registration panel (**Figure 1.13**) click the Register On-line button.

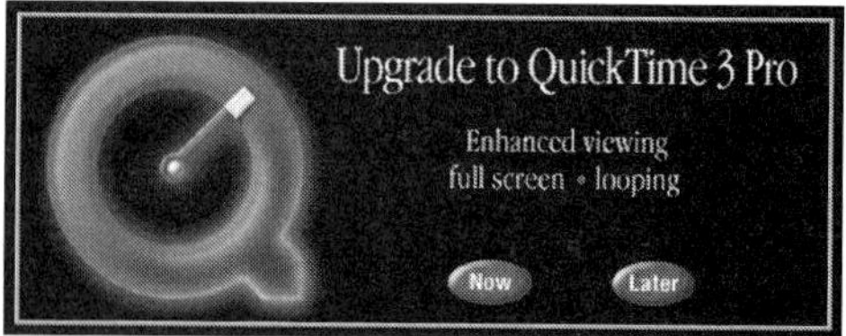

Figure 1.11 Click the Now button in the Get QuickTime Pro movie to automatically go to the Upgrade to QuickTime 3 Pro page.

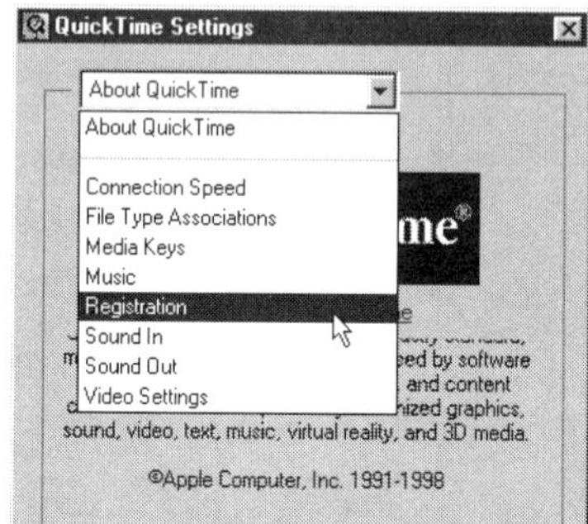

Figure 1.12 Choose Registration in the QuickTime Settings (Mac OS) or QuickTime (Windows) control panel.

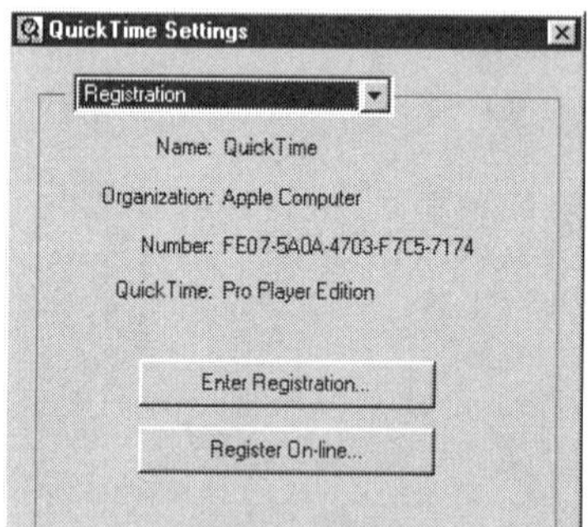

Figure 1.13 Click the Register On-line button to go to the Upgrade to QuickTime 3 Pro page; click the Enter Registration button once you have your registration information.

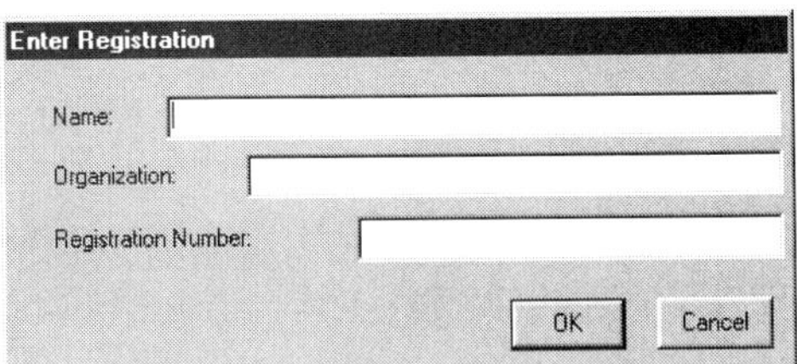

Figure 1.14 Enter the registration information provided by Apple.

To enter your registration code

1. Open the QuickTime Settings control panel (Mac OS) or the QuickTime control panel (Windows) and choose Registration from the pop-up menu (**Figure 1.12**).
2. In the Registration panel (**Figure 1.13**), click the Enter Registration button.
3. In the dialog box that appears, enter your registration information (**Figure 1.14**). Be sure to enter your Name and Organization exactly as you did on the web site, or your registration number won't match. (If you can't remember how you typed the Name, it's a good bet that it was the same as what's on your credit card.)

✔ Tip

■ If you don't have Internet access or you're uncomfortable with purchasing over the Internet, you can call 1-888-295-0648 to upgrade. (This is the same number that you call if you want to order a CD-ROM containing QuickTime 3.)

Getting sample movies

In this book we talk about a large variety of movie types and show you what you can do with some of them. If you're trying to learn everything you can about QuickTime, you may want to have some sample movies representing the various types. We recommend first going to Apple's QuickTime Web site (http://www.apple.com/quicktime), and clicking on the Samples button. You'll be taken to a page that has links to lots of categories of movies, including the hard to find ones, like movies with sprite tracks or 3D tracks.

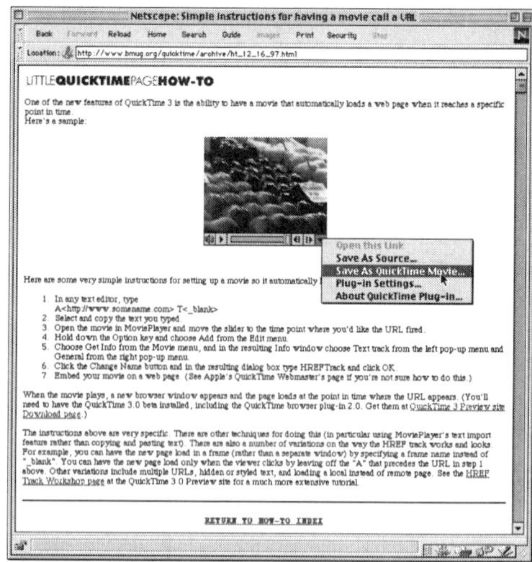

Figure 1.15 To save a movie that's on a Web page to your hard disk, click the button on the far left of the controller and select Save As QuickTime movie.

To save a QuickTime movie from a Web page

1. Wait until the movie has been completely loaded.
2. Click on the button in the lower right corner of the movie window and drag to Save As QuickTime Movie. (**Figure 1.15**)

Other good places to look are MediaCity (http://www.mediacity.com/~erweb/) which has a variety of movies, including some with music tracks, and the CNN Video Vault (http://www.cnn.com/video_vault/index.html) which mostly has just straight video and audio track movies.

You could, of course, use a search engine. For example, if you go to HotBot (http://www.hotbot.com/), you can do a Super Search for file extensions of .mov. (We got 126,000 matches when we looked for .mov)

Or, if that seems like too many to weed through, you might want to try Yahoo's Computers/Multimedia/video section (http://www.yahoo.com/Computers_and_Internet/Multimedia/Video/.)

2

MoviePlayer Basics

Once you have QuickTime installed, you're ready to become familiar with MoviePlayer.

In this chapter, we'll show you how to use MoviePlayer to open files—not only standard QuickTime movies, but also video, animation, sound, and graphics files of various other formats.

Then we'll introduce you to the controllers you see at the bottom of the window for each open file, explain how to change window sizes, and show you how to get some basic information about movie files.

Opening QuickTime movies

The steps for opening a movie are the same as those for opening a document in most any other program.

To open a QuickTime movie from within MoviePlayer

1. If MoviePlayer isn't already open, locate its icon and double-click to open it.

   (On Windows, the QuickTime installer puts MoviePlayer in a folder called "QuickTime", in the "Programs" folder. On Mac OS, the QuickTime installer puts MoviePlayer in a folder called "QuickTime Folder". If you received QuickTime 3 as part of Mac OS 8.5 or newer, you'll probably find MoviePlayer in a folder called "QuickTime", in the "Applications" folder.)

2. Choose **Open** from the File menu (**Figure 2.1**).

3. In the Open dialog box, locate and select the movie file you wish to open (**Figure 2.2**).

4. Click the **Open** button.

   A new window appears, containing the movie (**Figure 2.3**).

✔ Tip

- Windows users can also locate the MoviePlayer program via the Start menu.

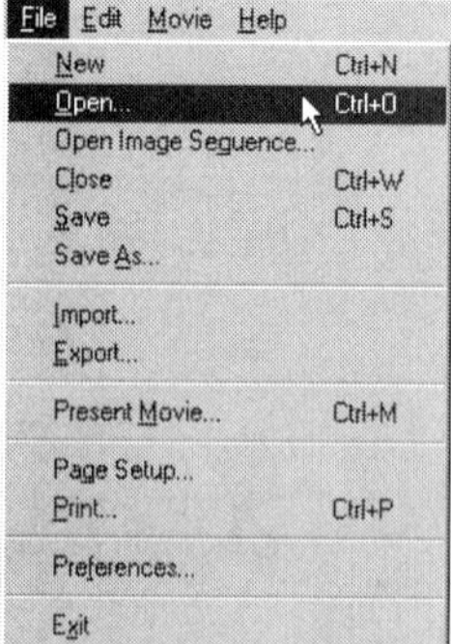

Figure 2.1 Choose Open from MoviePlayer's File menu to open a QuickTime movie.

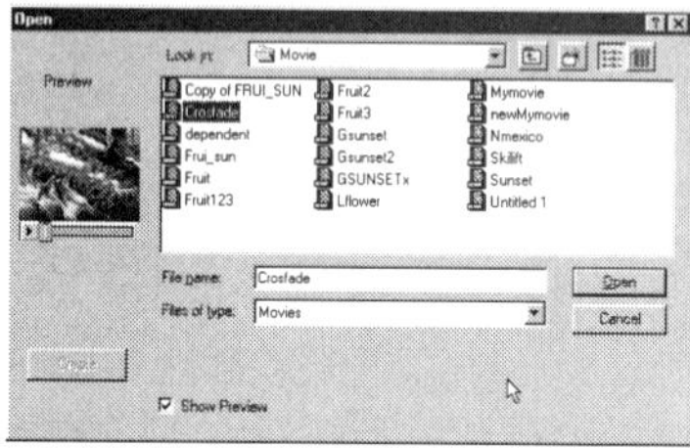

Figure 2.2 Select the QuickTime file you'd like to open, and click open.

Figure 2.3 The movie appears in a window.

Additional methods for opening a movie file

Two other methods launch MoviePlayer automatically if it's not already running:

- Drag the icon for the movie file onto the MoviePlayer application icon.
- If the movie was created using MoviePlayer, double-click the file's icon.

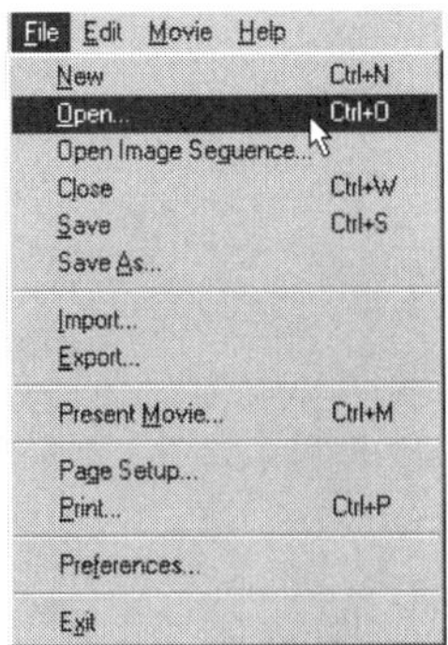

Figure 2.4 Choose Open from MoviePlayer's File menu to open many media files that aren't in the QuickTime format.

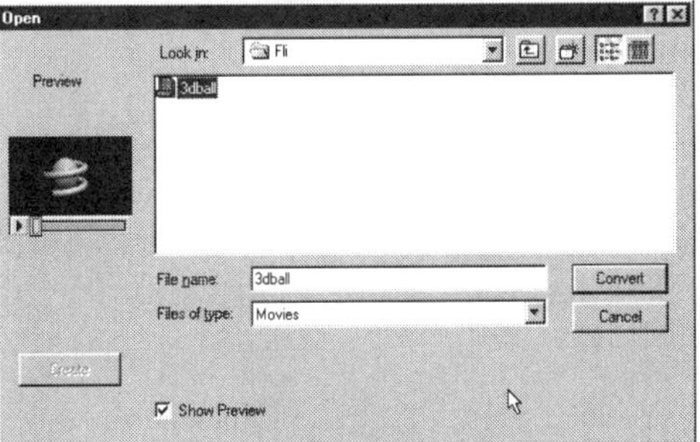

Figure 2.5 When you select a file in another format that MoviePlayer can open, the Open button changes to a Convert button.

Figure 2.6 The file opens and appears just like any QuickTime movie.

Opening non-QuickTime files

MoviePlayer, like other QuickTime-savvy applications, can open movie, animation, and sound files in many other formats as easily as it opens regular QuickTime movies. The current list of formats that QuickTime opens includes AVI, DV, MPEG, OpenDML, AIFF, Sound Designer II, Macintosh System 7, µLaw, WAV, Animated GIF, and FLI/FLC.

To open a non-QuickTime file in MoviePlayer

1. If MoviePlayer isn't already open, locate its icon in the folder called QuickTime (Windows) or QuickTime Folder (Mac) and double-click to open it.
2. Choose **Open** from the File menu (**Figure 2.4**).
3. In the Open dialog box, locate and select the movie file you wish to open.

   When you select a file in a non-QuickTime format, the Open button changes to a Convert button (**Figure 2.5**).
4. Click the **Convert** button.

   A new window appears, containing the media from the file you chose (**Figure 2.6**).

✔ Tips

- Even though you click a button called "Convert", the original file is not being altered in any way. It is simply being opened in MoviePlayer. The only time something happens to the original file is if you save from MoviePlayer using the same name as the original file.
- If, when you click on a non-QuickTime file, you see a button labeled "Convert..." rather than simply "Convert," you've selected a file type that QuickTime can't open directly. See *Converting non-QuickTime files* for information about this type of file.

File formats that MoviePlayer can open

- AIFF
- Animated GIF
- AU
- Audio CD
- AVI
- BMP
- DV
- FLC/FLI
- GIF
- JPEG/JFIF
- MPEG
- MPEG Layer 1 & 2
- OpenDML
- QuickDraw GX
- QuickTime Image Format
- QuickTime Movie
- Photoshop
- PNG
- SGI
- Sound Designer
- Targa
- TIFF

Figure 2.7
Choose Import from MoviePlayer's File menu when you have a multimedia file that QuickTime won't open directly.

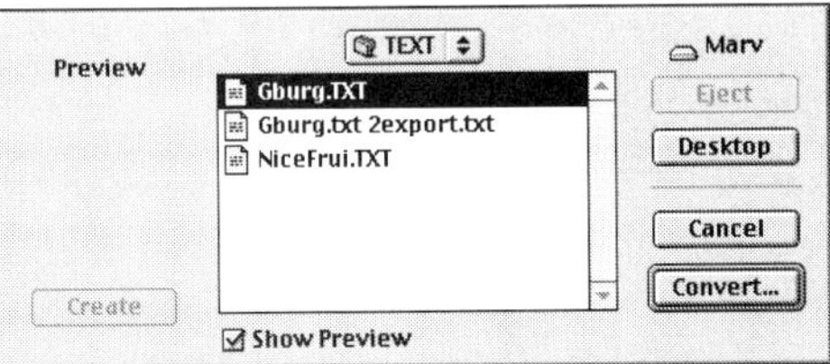

Figure 2.8 When you select a file that QuickTime can convert to a QuickTime file, the Open button changes to Convert.

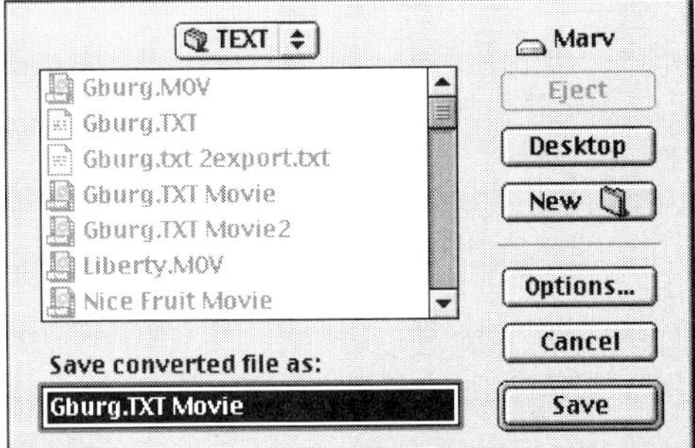

Figure 2.9 After you click the Convert button, a Save dialog box appears in which you specify the name and location of the new file that will be created by converting to QuickTime.

Converting non-QuickTime files

There are a smaller number of formats which MoviePlayer cannot open directly, but which you can convert to QuickTime movies. Once converted, these files act just like any other QuickTime file. Files which need to be converted include text, MIDI and karaoke music files, Macintosh System 7 sound files, and PICS animation files.

To import a non-QuickTime file into MoviePlayer

1. If MoviePlayer isn't already open, locate its icon in the folder called QuickTime (Windows) or QuickTime Folder (Mac) and double-click to open it.
2. Choose Import from the File menu. (**Figure 2.7**).
3. In the Open dialog box, locate and select the movie file you wish to open.
   The Open button changes to a Convert button. (**Figure 2.8**) Note that the name of this button is followed by ellipses (...) to indicate that a further step is required.
4. Click the Convert button.
   A Save dialog box appears (**Figure 2.9**), since you now need to save the file as a QuickTime movie so that MoviePlayer can open it.
5. Specify where you'd like to save the file, and change the name of the file if you wish.
6. For some files, an Options button will be active. If you click this button you will be able to change various settings particular to the type of media. We'll cover these options in later chapters.

✔ Tips

- For files other than text files, you can use the Open command rather than the Import command in step 2.
- (Mac OS only) If you have Mac OS System 7.5 or later, or have obtained Easy Open (a control panel), you can drag a non-QuickTime file onto the MoviePlayer application icon. If it's a file that QuickTime cannot open directly, the file will be translated to a QuickTime file, and will appear in an untitled movie window. You should save the file with a name and location of your choosing. Be aware that Easy Open puts the translated file in your Translated Documents folder (located in your Preferences folder in your System Folder); this folder can become quite large if you do this drag-and-drop importing frequently, so you may want to trash files from this folder.

Figure 2.10 The standard controller for interacting with time-based QuickTime movies.

Figure 2.11 The QuickTime VR controller.

The movie controllers

When you open a movie in MoviePlayer (or just about any QuickTime tool) you usually see a strip at the bottom of the window. This is called the *movie controller*.

Actually, there are two different controllers that you may see. One is the controller that appears when you open a standard time-based movie; the other is the controller for QuickTime VR movies. (Interactive movies, such as those with wired sprites, may not have any controller, since you control the movie by clicking on objects that are contained in the movie image.)

You use the standard controller (**Figure 2.10**) to play, pause, step through a movie frame by frame, and adjust volume. It's also your primary interface for editing when using the Pro edition of MoviePlayer. In other words, you interact with a movie via the controller.

When you open a QuickTime VR movie in MoviePlayer, the controller that appears (**Figure 2.11**) is useful for zooming in and out of the image, identifying clickable areas that cause other actions to occur, and doing a few specialized tasks that we'll cover in Chapter 4. However, your primary means of interacting with QuickTime VR movies involves clicking and dragging in the movie window to change your view.

These controllers are fundamental to QuickTime and its standard user interface. We'll cover the controllers and other means of interacting with both regular and VR movies more fully in the rest of the book.

Changing window sizes

It always seems that the first thing anyone new to MoviePlayer wants to do is to resize the movie window. We'll tell you now that you generally get the best performance when you don't change the window size, but we know that's not going to stop you. Besides, there are legitimate reasons for wanting to stretch out a window.

Methods for changing the window size

- Choose **Half Size**, **Double Size**, or **Fill Screen** from the Movie menu (**Figure 2.12**).
- Click in the area in the lower-right corner of the window (called the *Size box* on the Mac or the *Size grip* in Windows; see **Figure 2.13**) and drag in or out.

QuickTime is optimized to play movies at certain sizes that are multiples or fractions of the movie's normal size. Thus, a movie will perform more smoothly at exactly double size than at some size slightly smaller than double.

To drag a movie window to an optimal size

- Hold down the **Option** key (Mac OS) or **Ctrl** and **Alt** keys (Windows) while you drag the lower-right corner of the window.

Normally when you drag, the movie retains its original proportions. However, you can change its proportions if you want to, making the window wider or taller.

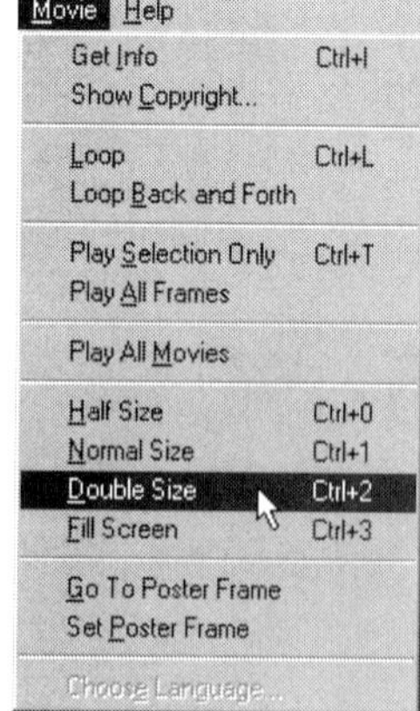

Figure 2.12 The Movie menu contains options for changing the window size.

Figure 2.13 You can also change the window size by dragging from the lower-right corner of the window.

CHANGING WINDOW SIZES

Figure 2.14 On Windows computers, you can drag the window border in or out. The movie is not resized proportionately.

Methods of changing the proportions of a movie window

- (Windows only) Place your pointer over the window border until it changes to a double-headed arrow, then drag in or out (**Figure 2.14**).
- Hold down the **Shift** key as you drag the lower-right corner of the window.

Showing copyright information

If you've been given a movie and you're looking for information about who owns it, where it came from, who created it, or other copyright information, follow these steps.

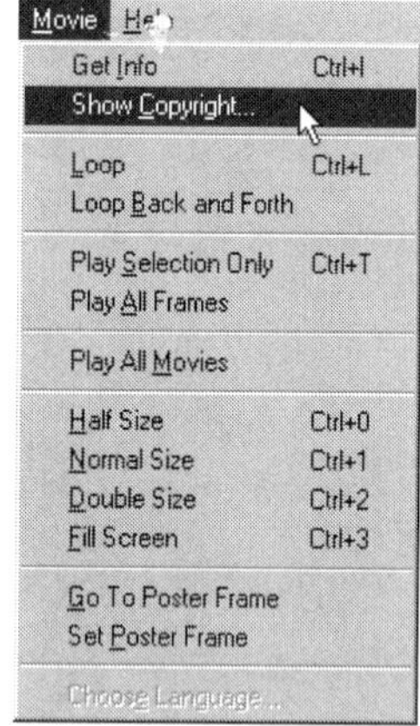

Figure 2.15 Choose Show Copyright from the Movie menu to display copyright information.

To show copyright information

1. Choose Show Copyright from the Movie menu (**Figure 2.15**).

   The Movie Information dialog box appears (**Figure 2.16**). It may or may not show information.

2. When you're done reading, click OK to close the dialog box.

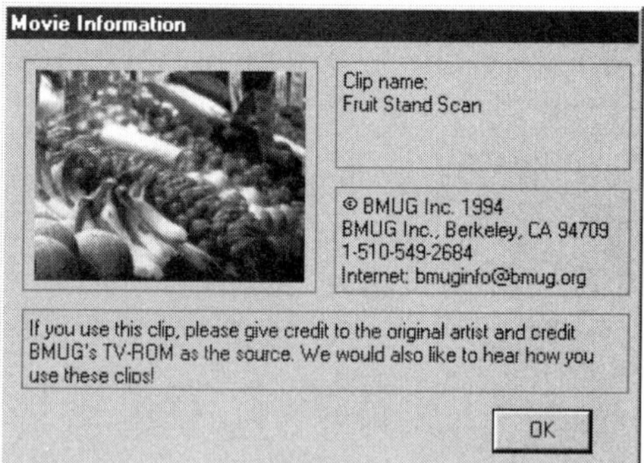

Figure 2.16 The Movie Information dialog box provides basic information about the ownership of the movie.

The text shown here is a subset of the annotation information that is added to a movie. The image is the movie's poster frame. (We'll cover annotations and posters in Chapter 5.)

Note that not everybody who creates a movie adds this information, so don't assume that the movie isn't copyrighted just because there is no copyright information.

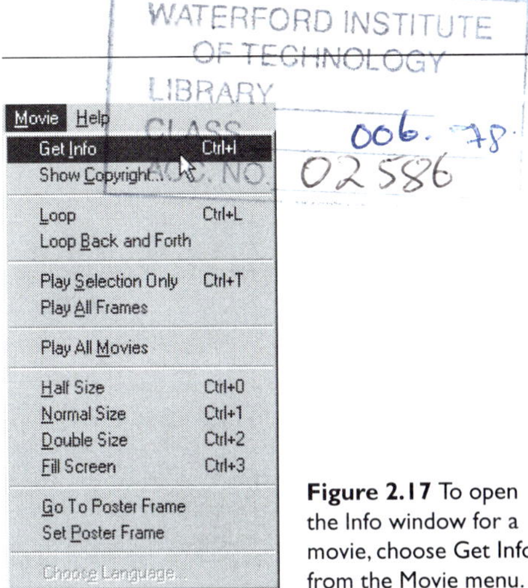

Figure 2.17 To open the Info window for a movie, choose Get Info from the Movie menu.

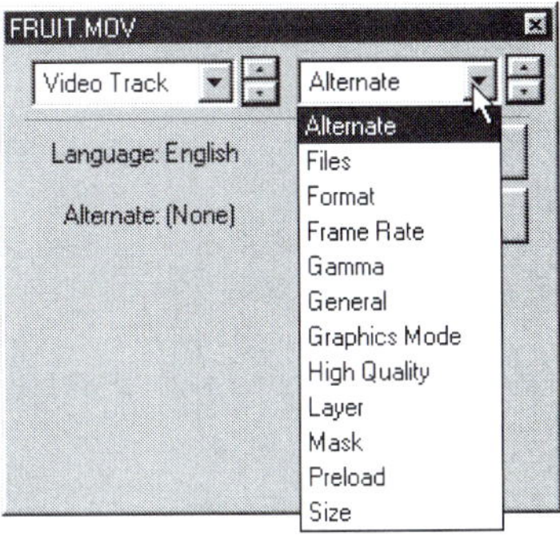

Figure 2.18 The choices in the pop-up menu on the right depend on what's been chosen in the pop-up menu on the left. Here you see what's available for a video track.

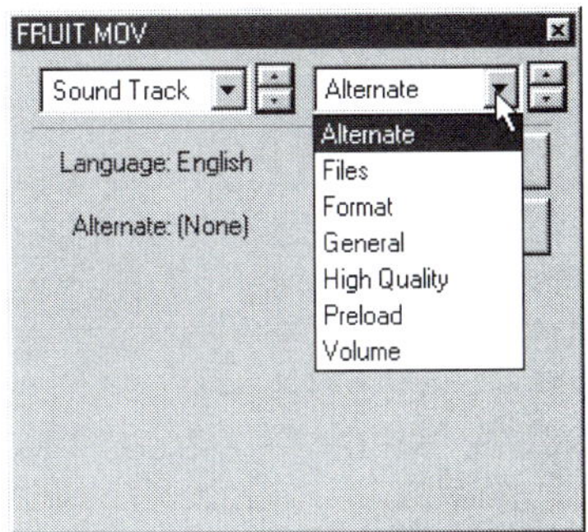

Figure 2.19 Here you see what's available for a sound track.

The Info window

MoviePlayer's Info window is extremely extensive. It enables you to get detailed information about the structure of your movie and the individual tracks in your movie. It also enables you to make various changes to tracks in your movie.

To open the Info window for a movie

1. Choose **Get Info** from the Movie window (**Figure 2.17**).
2. The Info window for the movie appears. There are two pop-up menus at the top of this window. In the left pop-up you can choose the movie itself or any of the tracks in the movie. For each choice you make in the left pop-up you'll find a different set of choices in the right pop-up menu (**Figures 2.18 and 2.19**). Altogether, there are almost 80 total panels that may appear, including 30 unique panels. We'll be covering these throughout the book, but we thought it would be good for you to just be aware of the Info window. We'll often refer to what you see in the window by the choice made in the right pop-up menu, e.g. "the Size panel."

✔ Tip

- Don't confuse the Info window, which we describe here, with the Movie Information dialog box that appears when you choose Show Copyright from the Movie menu.

Figuring out which tracks are in a movie

You don't have to do very much to find out how many tracks a movie has or what types of tracks they are.

To see which tracks are contained in a movie

1. If the Info window isn't already open, choose **Get Info** from the Movie menu to open it (**Figure 2.20**).
2. In the Info window for the movie, pull down the left pop-up menu (**Figure 2.21**).
3. The items in the menu below the word "Movie" are the names of the tracks.

In most cases the names of the tracks correspond to the track types. For example, a video track will be listed as "Video Track." However, since it's possible to edit the name of a track, you may occasionally have to dig a little bit deeper to determine the type of track.

To determine the track type if the track name doesn't correspond to a track type

1. Choose the track in which you're interested from the left pop-up menu in the Info window.
2. Choose General from the right pop-up menu.
3. In the middle of the window you'll find a listing for track type (**Figure 2.22**).

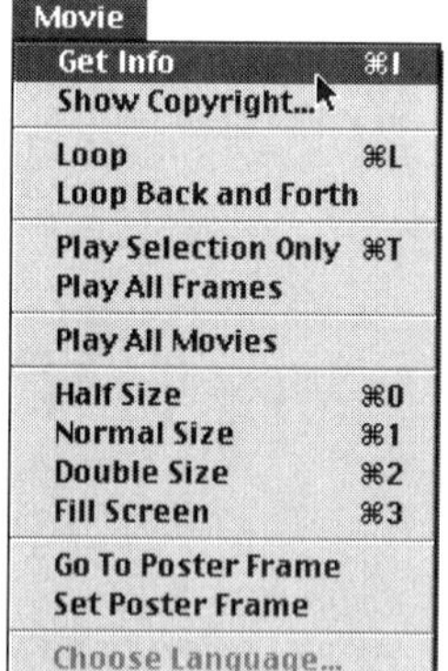

Figure 2.20 Choose Get Info from the Movie menu to access information about the movie and its tracks.

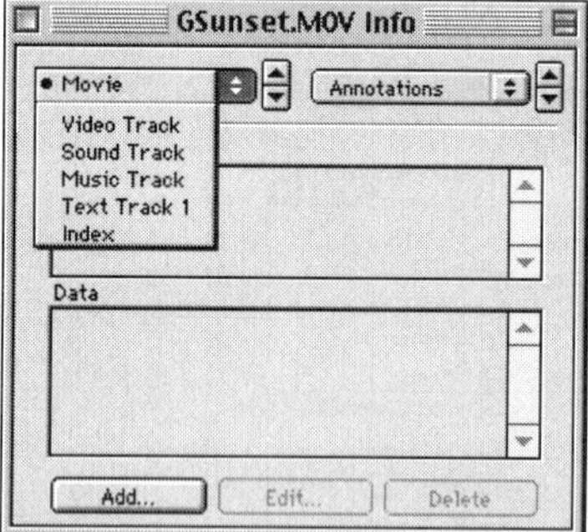

Figure 2.21 The left pop-up menu in the Info window lists the tracks in the movie.

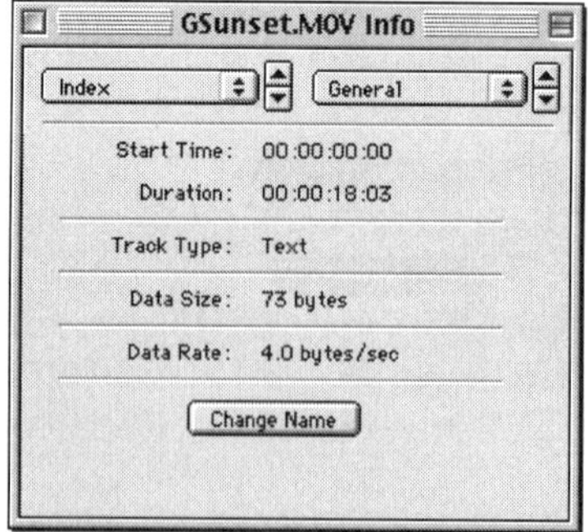

Figure 2.22 If you choose a track, then choose General in the right pop-up menu, the track type is listed in the middle of the window. (This is useful when a track's name isn't the same as its type.)

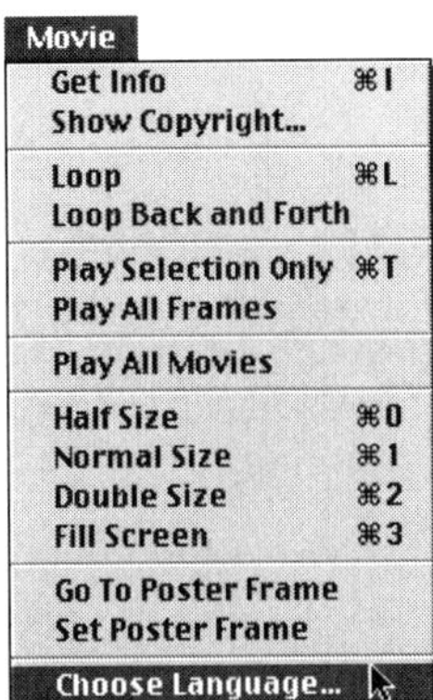

Figure 2.23 Select Choose Language from the Movie menu.

Figure 2.24 Select the language of your choice in the Choose Movie Language dialog box.

Running a non-English version of your operating system?

When a movie is first opened, it will automatically enable tracks that match the current system language and disable any other tracks that have been designated as alternates for those tracks. For example, if you are running the Japanese version of your operating system, and one track in a set of tracks has been designated as a Japanese track, the Japanese track will be enabled when the movie is first opened.

Choosing a language for playback

Some movies may have tracks, usually sound or text, in multiple languages. If you have such a movie you can switch from one language to another. (We'll cover how to create such movies in Chapter 6.)

To choose a language for playback

1. Select Choose Language from the Movie menu (**Figure 3.35**).
2. In the Choose Movie Language dialog box, select the language of your choice and click OK (**Figure 3.36**).

   When you play the movie, the tracks that are in your chosen language are enabled. (That is, they appear and/or are audible.) Tracks designated as alternates to those tracks are automatically disabled.

3 Playing QuickTime Movies

If all MoviePlayer did was play movies it would still be quite useful. You have a great many options to choose from when you play back a movie. You can access different points of a movie quickly and efficiently. You can increase or decrease its playback rate, image size, or audio volume. You can play it backward or have it loop. You can even control more than one movie at a time.

In this chapter we'll show you how to use all the buttons on the movie controller, the commands in the menus, and various hidden tricks that help you play back movies in a variety of ways.

This chapter covers only linear QuickTime movies. Make sure to read the next chapter to learn methods of interacting with QuickTime VR movies. (The way you interact with other interactive movies, such as those containing wired sprites, will be dependent on the way the movie's creator intended it to be played, so we can't teach you anything about that.)

Playing and pausing movies

The most common thing you'll do with movies is play them. When you've heard and/or seen enough, you'll want a way to stop the movie from playing, that is, to pause it. There are many ways to both play a movie and pause it.

Methods of playing a movie

- Click the Play button, the button on the left side of the controller marked with a triangle (**Figure 3.1**).
- Press the Return key (Mac OS) or Enter key (Windows).
- Press the Spacebar.
- Double-click the movie image.

When the movie is playing, the Play button is replaced by the Pause button, which is marked with two vertical bars.

Methods of pausing a movie

- Click the Pause button, the button on the left side of the controller marked with two vertical bars (**Figure 3.2**).
- Press the Return key (Mac OS) or Enter key (Windows).
- Press the Spacebar.
- Click the movie image.

Figure 3.1 Click the Play button to start playing a paused movie.

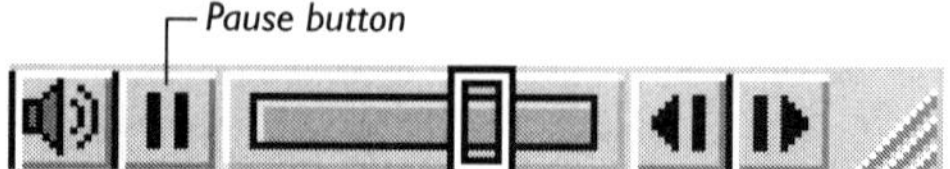

Figure 3.2 When a movie starts playing, the Play button is replaced by a Pause button. Click the Pause button to pause a playing movie.

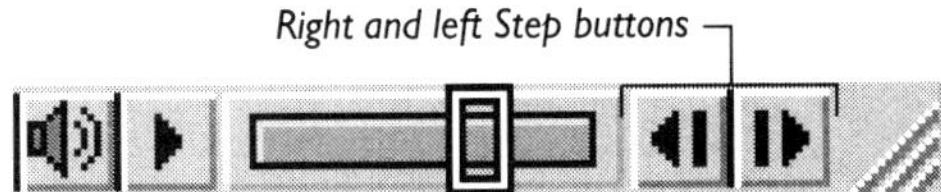

Figure 3.3 The right Step button moves you one frame forward and the left Step button moves you one frame backward.

Stepping through a movie frame by frame

Most QuickTime movies are composed of a sequence of individual images, or *frames*. You can step through a QuickTime movie frame by frame if you'd like to see each image by itself.

Methods of stepping through a movie frame by frame

- Click the right **Step** button to move forward a frame and the left **Step** button to move backward a frame. (The Step buttons are the buttons on the right side of the controller that look like a triangle and vertical bar pointing right and a vertical bar and triangle pointing left; see **Figure 3.3.**)
- Press the **Right** or **Left Arrow** keys on your keyboard.

✔ Tip

- Some QuickTime movies, such as those containing only audio or 3D data, are not comprised of frames so the Step buttons do not work as described above. In 3D movies, the Step buttons send you to the end or beginning of the movie. In audio-only movies, the step buttons move you in quarter second increments.

Quickly moving around in a movie

You can quickly move to any point in a movie without having to play it or step through it frame by frame. (Unlike a videotape you have random access to a QuickTime movie!)

As a movie plays, a rectangle moves in the area to the right of the Play/Pause button. That little rectangle is called the *slider* and the area in which it moves is called the *play bar* (**Figure 3.4**). The play bar represents the entire length of the movie; the slider marks your current location in the movie.

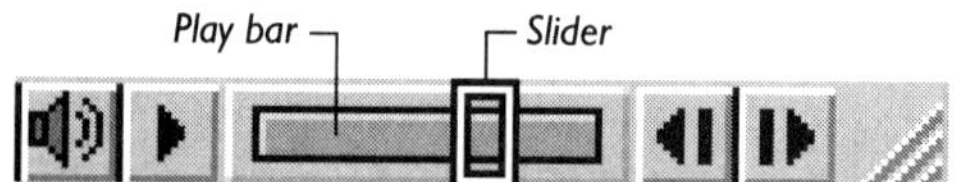

Figure 3.4 The slider marks your current location in the movie; the play bar represents the entire duration of the movie.

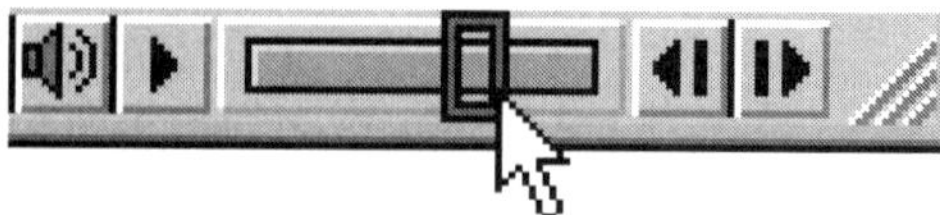

Figure 3.5 Moving the slider in the play bar changes where you are in the movie. For example, if you move the slider halfway across the play bar, you'll go to a point halfway through the movie.

To quickly move to any point in a movie

- Drag the **slider** to the right or left.

  You'll see the movie image change as you are dragging. When you release the mouse button, the movie remains at the place in time represented by the location of the slider (**Figure 3.5**).

To jump to the beginning of a movie

- Hold down the **Option** key (Mac OS) or **Ctrl** and **Alt** keys (Windows) while you click the left **Step** button.

  The slider jumps to the beginning of the play bar.

To jump to the end of a movie

- Hold down the **Option** key (Mac OS) or **Ctrl** and **Alt** keys (Windows) while you click the right **Step** button.

  The slider jumps to the end of the play bar.

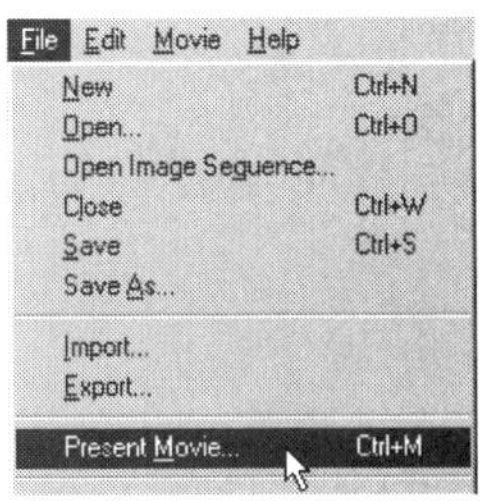

Figure 3.6 To present a movie so it plays from the current frame to the end, first choose Present Movie from the File menu.

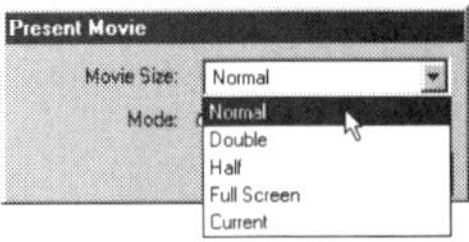

Figure 3.7 In the Present Movie dialog box, choose a window size.

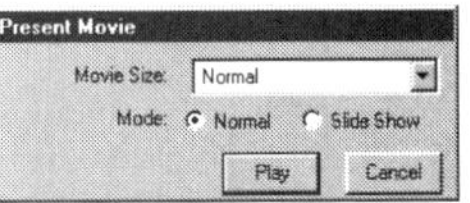

Figure 3.8 Select the Normal radio button and then click Play.

Figure 3.9 The movie appears on a black background and plays from the current image to the end. To stop play before the end, click anywhere.

Choosing movie size when presenting movies

If you choose Normal, Double, or Half from the Movie Size pop-up menu and your monitor and system software support switching resolutions, QuickTime automatically switches your screen resolution to the size that is closest to the movie's size without being smaller. Thus, the movie may appear larger than expected. If you choose Current, the movie will always appear the same size that it is normally.

Presenting a movie

There's an option in MoviePlayer that puts your movie on your monitor with nothing else around it but black. No controller is visible and the movie plays all the way to the end. This is called *presenting* a movie and it's an effective way to show your movie on the screen, particularly when you want a dramatic effect.

To present a movie so it plays automatically

1. Position the slider at the point in the movie where you'd like playback to begin.
2. Choose **Present Movie** from the File menu (**Figure 3.6**).

   The Present Movie dialog box appears.
3. Use the Movie Size pop-up menu to choose your desired movie window size (**Figure 3.7**).
4. For Mode, make sure that the **Normal** radio button is selected (**Figure 3.8**).
5. Click the **Play** button at the bottom of the Present Movie dialog box.

   The movie appears on a black background with no controller (**Figure 3.9**) and plays from its current location to the end to end.

Methods of stopping movie presentation before the movie reaches the end

- Press the **Esc** key.
- Click anywhere on the screen.
- Press **Command-period** (Mac OS only).

✔ Note

- Present Movie is not available for audio-only movies.

Presenting a movie frame by frame (in slide-show mode)

Sometimes you may have a movie that you'd like to present one frame at time. It may actually be a movie that's composed of a sequence of still images that would make no sense if shown rapidly in succession. Or perhaps you want to analyze a clip very closely.

To present a movie one frame at a time

1. Position the slider at the frame in the movie that you'd like to show first.
2. Choose Present Movie from the File menu (**Figure 3.10**).
3. In the Present Movie dialog box, use the Movie Size pop-up menu to choose your desired movie window size (**Figure 3.11**).
4. Click the Slide Show radio button to select it as the Mode (**Figure 3.12**).
5. Click Play.

   The current frame of the movie appears on a black background (**Figure 3.13**).
6. Press your mouse button to show each subsequent frame. (You can also use the Right and Left Arrow keys to move forward and backward one frame at a time.)

Methods for exiting slide-show mode

- Press the Esc key.
- Press Command-period (Mac OS only).

✔ Tip

- If you try to play a movie that's not composed of frames (e.g. a movie with only a 3D track) in slide-show mode, only the current image shows. The movie doesn't advance even when you click.

Figure 3.10 To present a movie frame by frame, first choose Present Movie from the File menu.

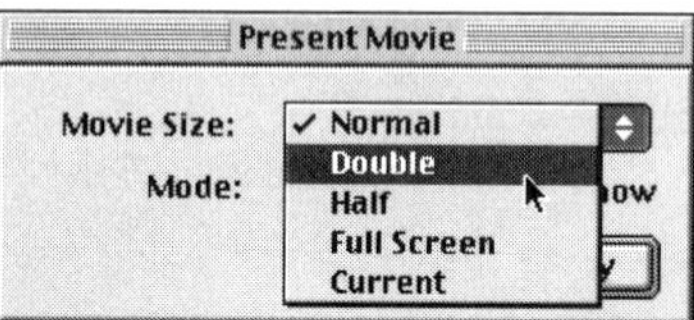

Figure 3.11 In the Present Movie dialog box, choose a window size.

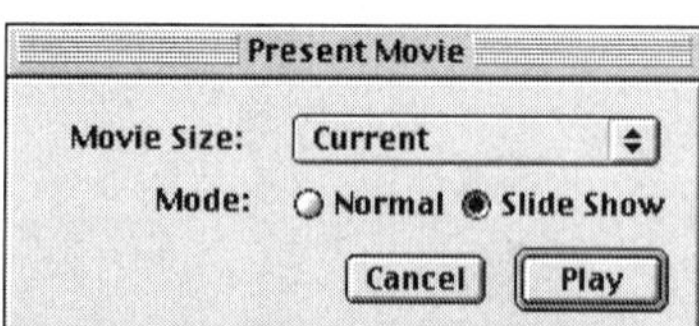

Figure 3.12 Select the Slide Show radio button, and then click Play.

Figure 3.13 The current frame of the movie appears on a black background. Click anywhere to show the next frame, or use the Right and Left Arrow keys to move forward and backward one frame at a time. To exit the slide show, press the Esc key.

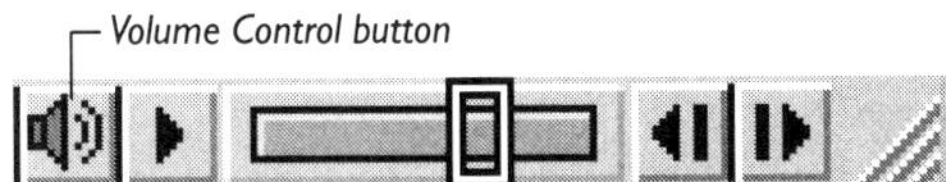

Figure 3.14 Use the Volume Control button to change the audio volume of a movie.

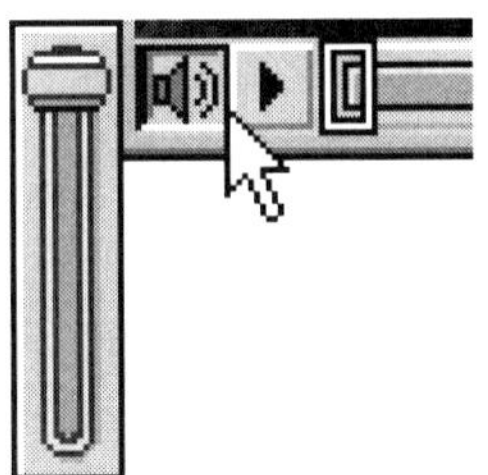

Figure 3.15 Click and hold the Volume Control button until the thermometer-looking image appears; then slide the cursor up to increase the volume or down to decrease the volume.

Figure 3.16 If there's no Volume Control button, the movie has no audio (i.e. neither a sound nor a music track).

Changing the audio level

You may want to make the volume of the audio in your movie louder or quieter.

To change the audio level

1. Click and hold on the button with the speaker icon that's at the far left of the controller. This is the Volume Control button (**Figure 3.14**).

   A thermometer-looking image pops up to the left of the button (**Figure 3.15**).

2. Continuing to hold down your mouse button, slide the pointer up or down to move the slider up or down.

   As you slide up or down, the number of lines emanating from the speaker changes.

   Moving the slider up increases the volume, and moving it down decreases the volume.

   When you play the movie, the volume of the audio will be accordingly louder or quieter.

To mute the audio

- Hold down the Ctrl and Alt keys (Windows) or the Option key (Mac) and click the Volume Control button.

To return the audio to the volume at which it was set before muting

- Hold down the Ctrl and Alt keys (Windows) or the Option key (Mac) and click the Volume Control button again.

✔ Tip

- If you don't see a Volume Control button in the movie controller (**Figure 3.16**), it means that this is a movie with no audio.

Overdriving audio

If you've set the volume of a movie as high as it can go, but it's still not loud enough, never fear! You can overdrive the audio in a QuickTime movie, increasing the actual sound above the normal maximum sound level.

To overdrive the audio in a movie

1. Hold the **Shift** key down when you click on the **Volume Control** button.

   The area in which you can move the slider now has two black horizontal lines through it (**Figure 3.17**).

2. Drag the slider up to anywhere above the lower black line.

   When you play the movie, the audio level will be higher than it had been previously. The lower of the two black lines represents the normal maximum volume. The higher line represents double the normal maximum volume. The top of the area in which you can move the slider represents three times the normal maximum volume (**Figure 3.18**).

✔ Warning

- Overdriving the audio will likely reduce the acoustical quality of the sound, and will generally create some distortion.

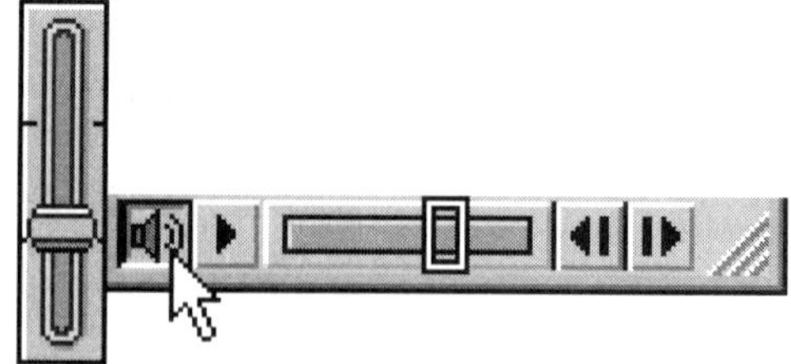

Figure 3.17 When you hold the Shift key down while clicking on the Volume Control button, you see two black horizontal lines.

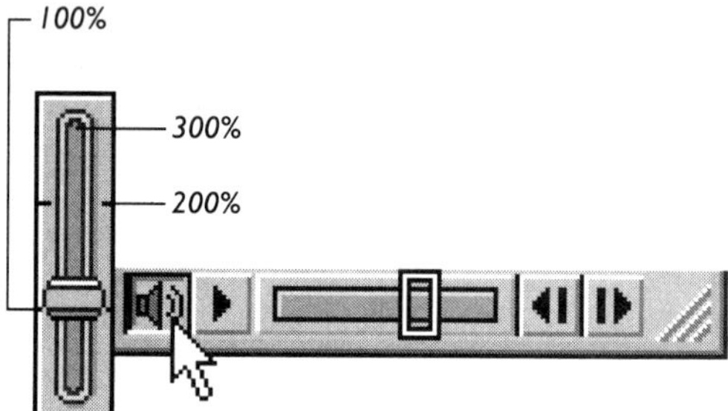

Figure 3.18 You can then set the volume to up to 300% of the normal maximum volume.

Looping a movie or playing it backward

Normally, when you play a movie, it will stop when it gets to the end. Sometimes, however, you may want a movie to play continuously, not stopping until you choose to pause it. Or you may want to play it backward.

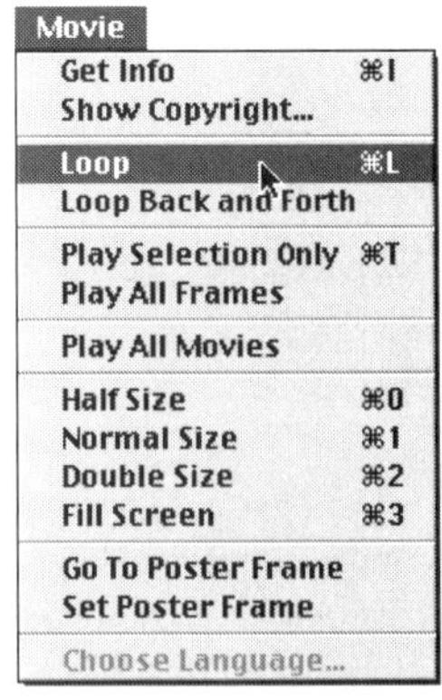

Figure 3.19 To have a movie loop, choose Loop from the Movie menu and then play the movie.

To have a movie play over and over again

1. Choose Loop from the Movie menu (**Figure 3.19**).
2. Play the movie.

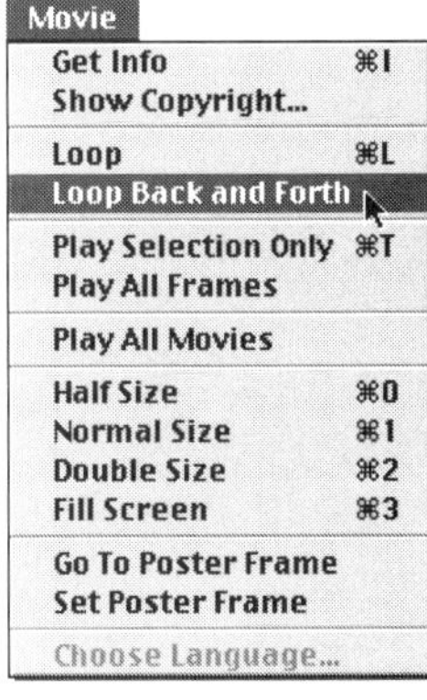

Figure 3.20 To have a movie play continuously forward then backward, choose Loop Back and Forth from the Movie menu and then play the movie.

To have a movie play continuously forward then backward

1. Choose Loop Back and Forth from the Movie menu (**Figure 3.20**).
2. Play the movie.

   It plays forward from beginning to end, then backward from end to beginning, then forward again, and so on.

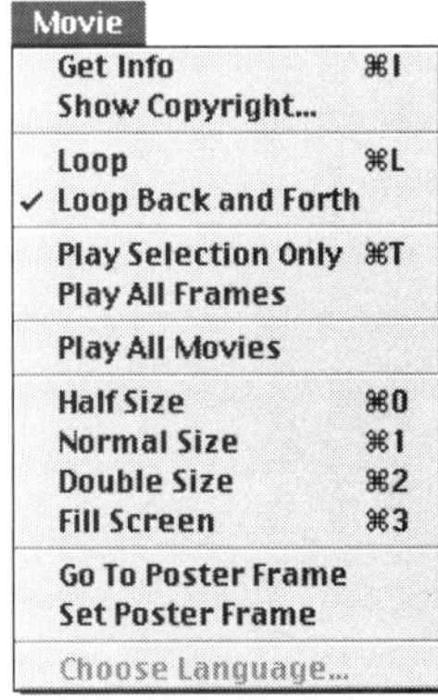

Figure 3.21 To return a movie to normal (non-looping) play, select whichever option (Loop or Loop Back and Forth) has a checkmark in front of it.

To set a movie to play normally

1. Pull down the Movie menu.

   If you have previously chosen Loop or Loop Back and Forth, the command has a checkmark in front of it (**Figure 3.21**).
2. Choose the command that is checked.

   The next time you play the movie it stops when it gets to the end.

Methods for playing a movie backward

- Hold down the Command key (Mac) or the Ctrl key (Windows) and click the left Step button or press the Left Arrow key.
- Hold down the Shift key and double-click the movie image.

Playing every frame

Are you playing movies on a computer that's maybe not quite as powerful as you'd like? If that's the case, you should know that QuickTime normally skips (or *drops*) frames if the computer doesn't have the power to show all the frames as quickly as they are supposed to be shown. You can, however, tell MoviePlayer to show each and every frame, no matter how long it takes.

To play all the frames in a movie

1. Choose Play All Frames from the Movie menu (**Figure 3.22**).
2. Play the movie.

   Since QuickTime wouldn't necessarily be able to keep the audio synchronized with the video, no audio plays.

   Movies designed for very fast machines take longer than normal to play on slow machines in order to show all the frames.

✔ Tip

- You can check to see if the computer on which you're playing a movie is capable of playing all frames in real time. See *Checking the frame rate*, later in this chapter.

Figure 3.22 To play all the frames in a movie, no matter how long it takes, choose Play All Frames from the Movie menu.

Figure 3.23 To start all open movies playing at the same time, choose Play All Movies from the Movie menu.

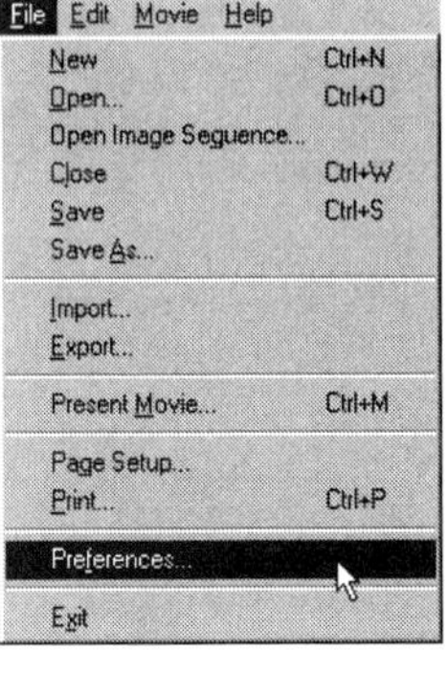

Figure 3.24 If you want to hear the audio from multiple playing movies, you'll need to open the Preference dialog box by choosing Preferences from the File menu.

Figure 3.25 In the Preferences dialog box, make sure that "Only front movie plays sound" is not checked.

Figure 3.26 To stop all open movies at the same time, choose Stop All Movies from the Movie menu.

Playing and pausing all open movies

MoviePlayer lets you have many movies open at one time. You can start and stop playing them all at the same time, if you're so inclined.

To play all open movies

◆ Choose Play All Movies from the Movie menu (**Figure 3.23**).

To play sound from all playing movies

1. Choose Preferences from the File menu (**Figure 3.24**).
2. Make sure that the option labeled Only front movie plays sound is not checked (**Figure 3.25**).

To pause all open and playing movies

◆ Choose Stop All Movies from the Movie menu (**Figure 3.26**).

✔ Tip

■ If the first checkbox in the Preferences dialog box, the one labeled "Play sound in background," is checked, you'll be able to hear the audio from any playing movies even when MoviePlayer is in the background and you are using a different application.

Varying the playback rate of a movie

You can play a QuickTime movie in fast or slow motion, forward or backward, using a hidden interface element.

Figure 3.27 If you hold down the Control key (Mac OS) or Alt key (Windows) while clicking on either Step button, a tiny slider and sliding area appear. Move the slider all the way to the right to play the movie at two and a half times normal playback speed.

To vary the playback rate of a movie

1. Hold down the **Control** key (Mac OS) or **Alt** key (Windows) while you click either **Step** button.

   The Step buttons will disappear and you'll find your pointer on top of a tiny white slider that sits on a gray horizontal bar (**Figure 3.27**).

2. Move your pointer to the right or left.

   The slider moves and the movie plays at different rates:

- When the slider is all the way to the right, the movie plays at two and a half times normal playback speed.
- When the slider is three-quarters of the way to the right, the movie plays at normal speed.
- When the slider is just slightly to the right of center, the movie plays in slow motion (**Figure 3.28**).
- When the slider is in the middle the movie is paused.
- When the slider is just slightly to the left of center, the movie plays backward in slow motion.
- When the slider is all the way to the left, the movie plays backward at two and a half times normal speed (**Figure 3.29**).

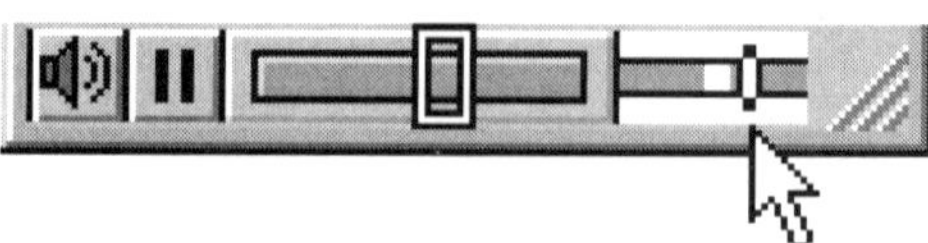

Figure 3.28 Move the slider just slightly to the right of center for slow-motion playback.

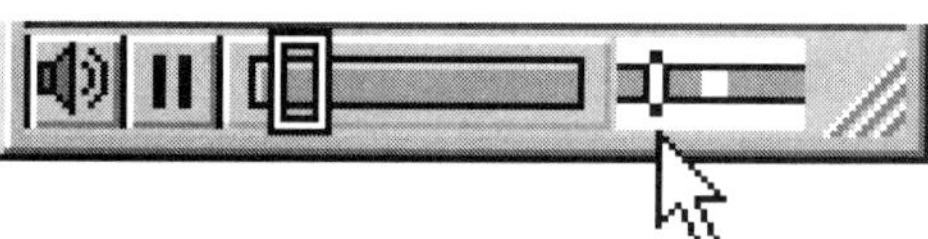

Figure 3.29 Move the slider to the left of center for backward play.

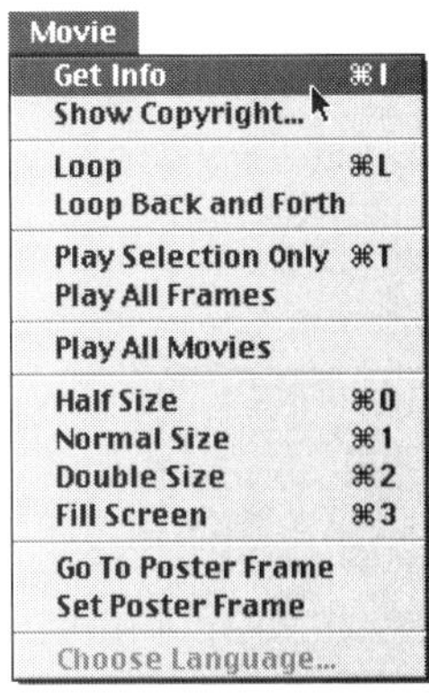

Figure 3.30 To check the frame rate, start by choosing Get Info from the Movie menu to open the Info window.

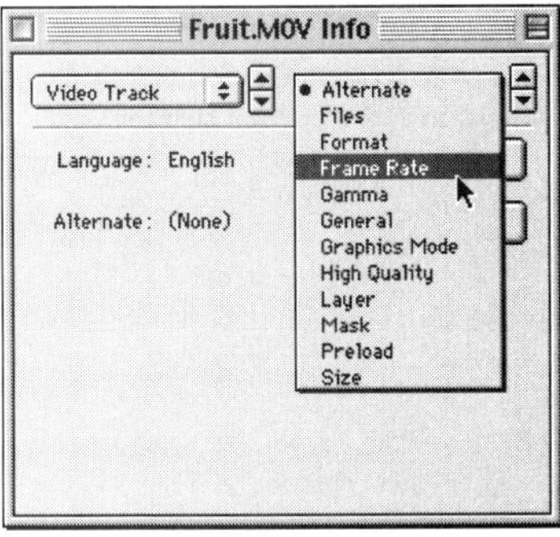

Figure 3.31 In the Info window, choose Video Track from the left pop-up menu and Frame Rate from the right pop-up menu.

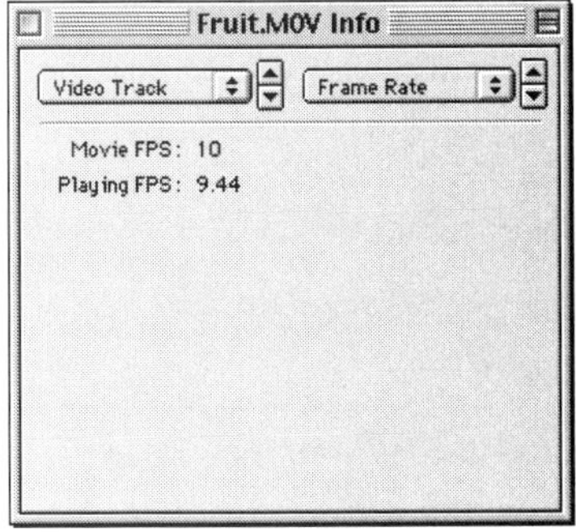

Figure 3.32 The Movie FPS shows the average number of frames per second contained in the movie and the Playing FPS shows the number of frames per second actually being played.

Checking the frame rate

Whether you're playing a movie at normal speed, playing all frames, or using the fast- or slow-motion techniques described on the previous page, as long as you have a movie with a video track, you can check to see how many frames per second are playing and how many frames per second are contained in the movie.

To check the frame rate

1. Choose **Get Info** from the Movie menu (**Figure 3.30**).
2. Choose **Video Track** from the left pop-up menu. (If you have more than one video track, you'll need to pick one to check at a time.)
3. Choose **Frame Rate** from the right pop-up menu (**Figure 3.31**).
4. Play the movie.

   The average number of frames per second (FPS) contained in the track is listed on the top line. The second line shows the number of frames actually being played per second (**Figure 3.32**).

   (The Playing FPS is a rough estimate, and if a movie has a changing frame rate, it sometimes takes a bit for the display to catch up with what's really going on.)

Using chapter lists

When you open some movies, you'll see an extra element in the movie controller: an area between the play bar and the Step buttons that has text in it (**Figure 3.33**). This is called the *Chapter List button*, and it provides a way to jump quickly to designated points in the movie, called *chapters*.

To jump to a chapter

1. Click and hold on the Chapter List button (**Figure 3.34**).
2. Select the chapter to which you'd like to jump.
3. The slider jumps to the beginning of the portion of the movie represented by the chapter you selected.

Figure 3.33 The Chapter List button only appears for some movies.

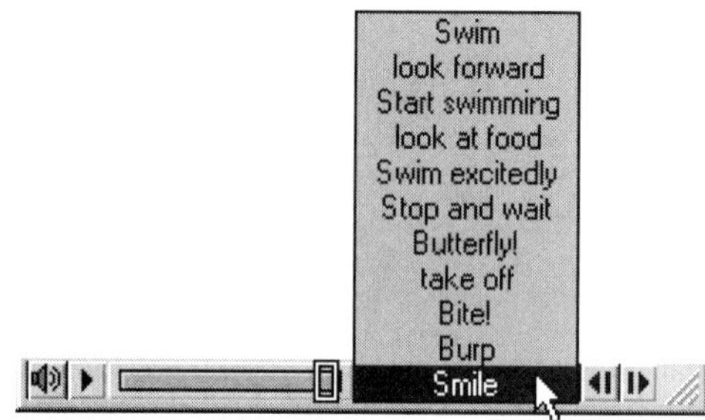

Figure 3.34 To jump to a chapter, click and hold on the Chapter List button and select the chapter.

4

INTERACTING WITH QUICKTIME VR

QuickTime VR is one of the newer additions to the QuickTime architecture. The "VR" is short for virtual reality, but this isn't virtual reality with special gloves and headsets. This is what's often called *desktop virtual reality*. Computer users can experience QuickTime VR using just a keyboard and a mouse.

The file format of QuickTime VR files is the same as standard QuickTime files, so QuickTime VR movies can be played in MoviePlayer, as well as in most other applications that can handle QuickTime. (With a few exceptions, however, MoviePlayer can not be used to create or edit QuickTime VR movies.)

There are fundamentally two types of VR movies—*panoramas* and *objects*. The basic distinction between the two is that panoramas give you the experience of being in the center of a space and looking around, usually a full 360 degrees, whereas object movies give you the experience of looking at and rotating an object. Individual VR movies of either type are sometimes combined into one large file to provide the experience of exploring an extensive space.

In this chapter we'll look at how you interact with all types of QuickTime VR movies.

Looking around in panorama movies

Panorama movies are those in which you, the viewer, are placed in the center of a space, and can look around that space.

To look around in a panorama movie

1. Press the **mouse** button and drag across the image in the direction you want to look.

   The pointer changes to an arrow pointing in the direction you are dragging (**Figure 4.1**). The view changes as if you had moved your head in that direction.

2. Continue holding the mouse button down to continue changing the view in the direction the arrow is pointing.

   The further you drag from the initial location where you clicked, the faster the view changes. (You can drag beyond the borders of the window to get the image spinning extremely rapidly. People have been known to feel nauseous spinning around a room at high speed, however!)

   When you have changed the view as far as possible in any one direction, the pointer changes to include a bar indicating that you have gone as far in that direction as possible (**Figure 4.2**). Usually you will only reach a limit when looking up or down, since most QuickTime VR panorama movies provide a 360-degree view and you will just continuously loop around. (Some movies may provide a less-than-360-degree view, however, in which case you will bump up against a right or left edge.)

Figure 4.1 Drag in a QuickTime VR panorama in the direction you want to look. The pointer shows the direction in which you're dragging.

Figure 4.2 The pointer changes to show a bar when you have dragged as far as possible in a certain direction.

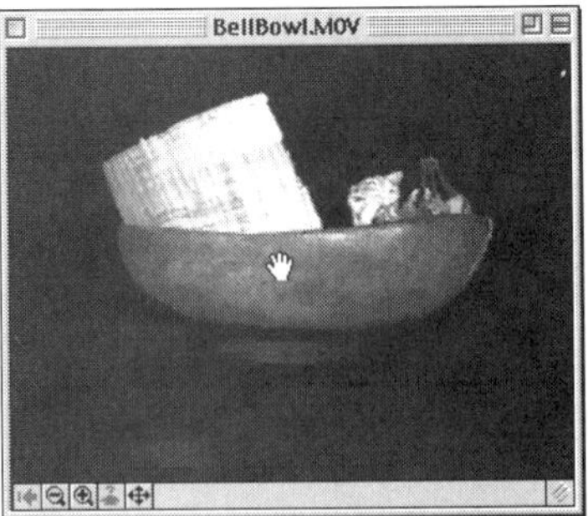

Figure 4.3 The normal object movie pointer.

Figure 4.4 The object movie pointer as it appears when you click.

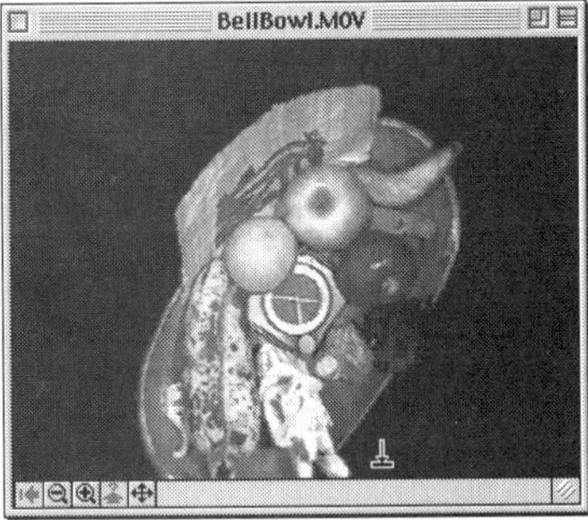

Figure 4.5 When an object has been rotated as far as it can go in a particular direction, the pointer changes to an arrow with a bar.

Manipulating objects in object movies

Object movies are those which are composed of a sequence of different views. Usually these are views of a single object in different rotational positions.

To manipulate an object in an object movie

1. Click in the movie window.

   Your pointer changes from an open hand (**Figure 4.3**) to a clenched fist (**Figure 4.4**). This is to indicate that you have grabbed the object.

2. Continuing to hold down the mouse button, drag in the direction you wish to rotate the object.

   You can drag beyond the movie window's border to continue rotating the object. However, it's often easier to repeatedly release the mouse and click and drag again in the movie window.

   If the object has already been rotated as far as it can go in a particular direction, the pointer, when near the window border, changes to an arrow with a bar (**Figure 4.5**).

   Some object movies provide views of an object only in a single vertical position, so your view doesn't change if you drag up or down.

Finding and using hot spots

Hot spots are predefined areas in QuickTime VR movies that cause some action to occur when you click them. In MoviePlayer, you click on hot spots to move from one panorama or object to another when they are combined in a single file. (Each individual panorama or object is referred to as a *node*; a file with multiple nodes is referred to as a *multi-node movie*.) In MoviePlayer, you can also click on hot spots to send a predefined URL to a Web browser, causing the Web browser to open if it's not already open, and the page to load. (When used in certain multimedia applications that support QuickTime VR or on Web pages, hot spots can also be assigned additional tasks that the environment allows; this is accomplished with a program or script external to the VR movie, but which references the hot spot by number.)

Methods of locating hot spots

- Click the Show Hot Spots button in the controller (This is the button with the question mark and squished upwards pointing arrow; see **Figure 4.6**).

  As long as you continue holding the mouse button, hot spots are highlighted with translucent blue shapes.

  If you double-click the Show Hot Spots button it will remain depressed, so you can drag in the movie window and still have the hot spots highlighted.

- Move your pointer in the movie window. When it's over a hot spot, the pointer changes.

  Typically, a squished upward-pointing arrow (**Figure 4.7**) indicates a hot spot that opens another node. A pointing finger over a globe (**Figure 4.8**) usually indicates that the hot spot opens a Web

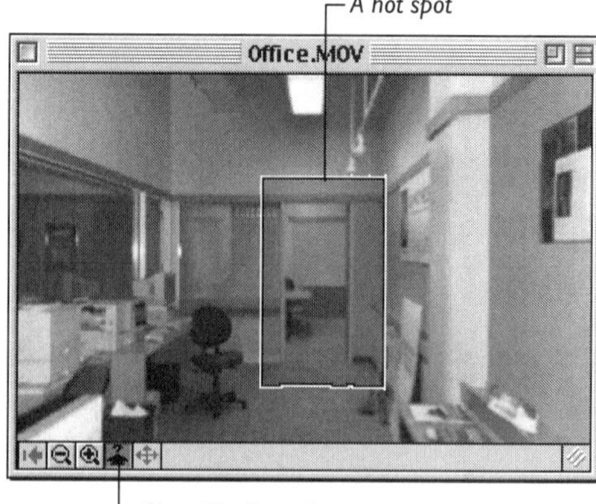

Figure 4.6 When you click the Show Hot Spots button, hot spots in a movie are highlighted with translucent blue shapes.

Figure 4.7 How the pointer appears when it's over a hot spot that takes you to another panorama or object contained in the movie file.

Figure 4.8 The pointer looks like this when it's over a hot spot that opens a Web page.

Figure 4.9 Here the pointer is over a hot spot that doesn't necessarily do anything in MoviePlayer, but might do something in some other environment.

Back button

Figure 4.10 Click the Back button to open the node you were in when you clicked a hot spot to get you to the current node. This button is not active unless the open movie is a multi-node movie; it becomes active once you have used a hot spot to jump from one node to another.

page. The pointer appears as a hand over a bulls-eye (**Figure 4.9**) when a hot spot has been defined but no action has been assigned to it; such hot spots can be assigned an action on a Web page or in a multimedia authoring tool, but not currently in MoviePlayer.

To use a hot spot

- Click in the area of the translucent blue rectangle or where the cursor has changed.

To return to a node after using a hot spot to jump to another node

- Click the **Back** button (This is the button with the left-pointing arrow; see **Figure 4.10**).

✔ Tip

- As you move your pointer over the buttons in the QuickTime VR controller, their names appear in the area to the right of the buttons. Also, text may appear in that same area when you move your cursor over some hot spots.

QuickTime VR pointers

While the pointers we describe here are the default pointers for QuickTime VR, developers can specify alternative pointers for their QuickTime VR movies. Thus, you may encounter pointers different than those shown here.

Zooming in and out

Zooming into a QuickTime VR movie is like using a zoom lens on a camera. It allows you to get a closer look at the image. Zooming out is just the opposite; it allows you to see a wider view.

Methods of zooming in

- Click the Zoom In button. (This is the button with the plus sign in the middle of the magnifying glass; see **Figure 4.11**).
- With the pointer in the movie window, press the Shift key.

If you continue to hold down your mouse button or press the Shift key, you continue to zoom in until the image has been magnified as much as possible or as much as the movie's creator specified (**Figure 4.12**).

Methods of zooming out

- Click the Zoom Out button. (This is the button with the minus sign in the middle of the magnifying glass; see **Figure 4.11**).
- With the pointer in the movie window, press the Control key or the Ctrl key .

If you continue to hold down your mouse button or press the Control or Ctrl key, you continue to zoom out until the image is zoomed out as much as possible (**Figure 4.13**).

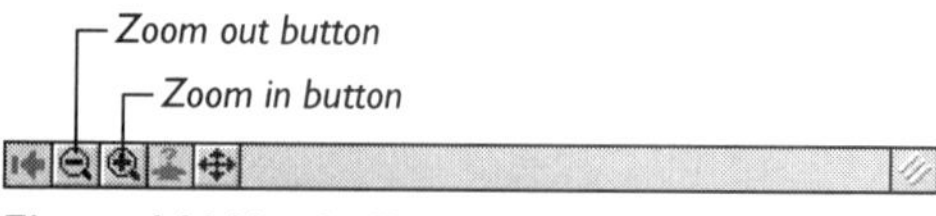

Figure 4.11 Use the Zoom buttons to change the magnification of the image in the movie window.

Figure 4.12 A movie when it has been zoomed in as much as possible

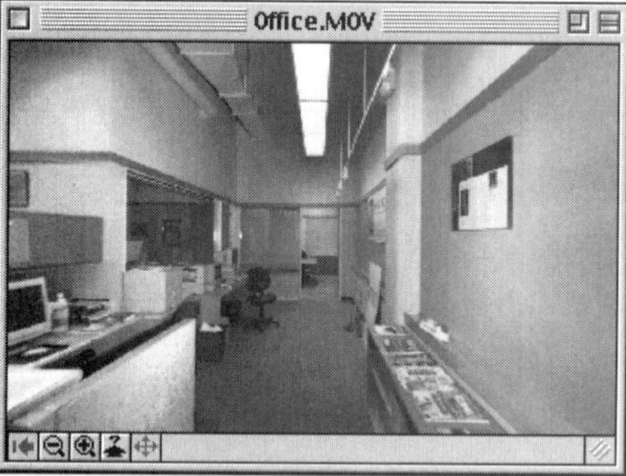

Figure 4.13 A movie when it has been zoomed out as much as possible

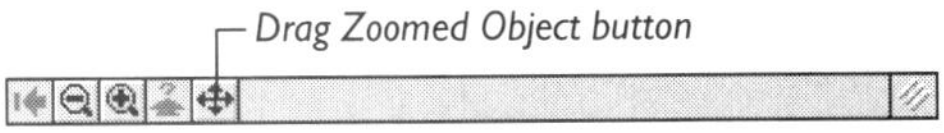

Drag Zoomed Object button

Figure 4.14 Use the Drag Zoomed Object button or hold down the Option key (Mac OS) or the Ctrl and Alt keys (Windows) when you want to move a zoomed-in object.

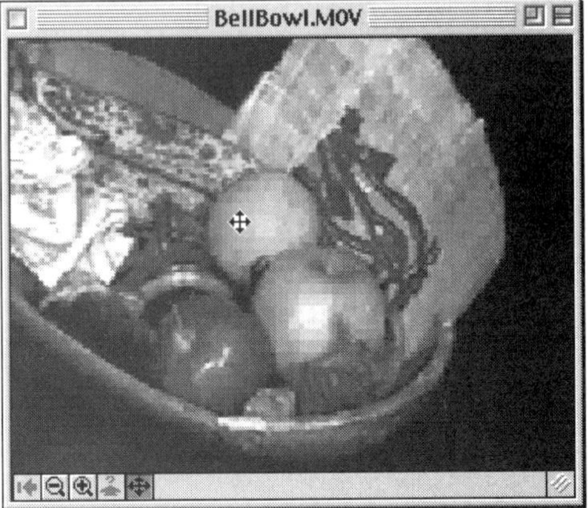

Figure 4.15 The cursor changes to show that you are in object-moving rather than object-rotating mode.

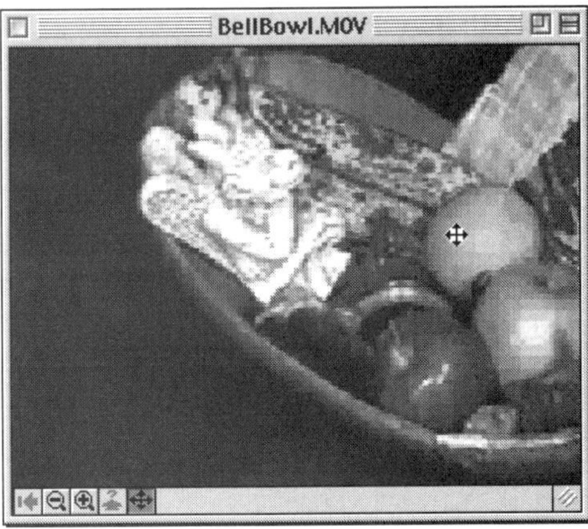

Figure 4.16 Notice that the object has not changed its rotational position.

Moving zoomed-in objects

Normally when you drag in an object movie you change the rotational position of the object. However, when an object movie is zoomed in, you sometimes want to view part of the image that is off-screen. You can do this by moving the object so that the part you want to see is visible on the screen.

Methods of moving zoomed-in objects

1. Click the Drag Zoomed Object button (the one with the arrows pointing in four directions; see **Figure 4.14**) or hold down the Option key (Mac OS) or the Ctrl and Alt keys (Windows).

   The pointer changes (**Figure 4.15**) to look like the icon on the Drag Zoomed Object button.

2. Click and drag in the direction you want to move the object.

   The object remains in the same rotational position as you drag (**Figure 4.16**).

Presenting QuickTime VR movies

You can show a QuickTime VR movie on a black background, as you can a linear QuickTime movie. This is how we recommend showing VR movies to large groups of people.

To present a QuickTime VR movie

1. Drag to put your movie in the rotational position you'd like it to appear in when the presentation begins.
2. Choose **Present Movie** from the File menu (**Figure 4.17**).

   The Present Movie dialog box appears.
3. Use the Movie Size pop-up menu to choose your desired movie window size (**Figure 4.18**).
4. Click **Play**.

   Your screen goes black and the movie appears in the center of the screen, with a QuickTime VR controller below it (**Figure 4.19**). You can control the movie as you would normally.

Methods for stopping QuickTime VR presentation

- Press the **Esc** key.
- Type **Command-period** (Mac OS only).

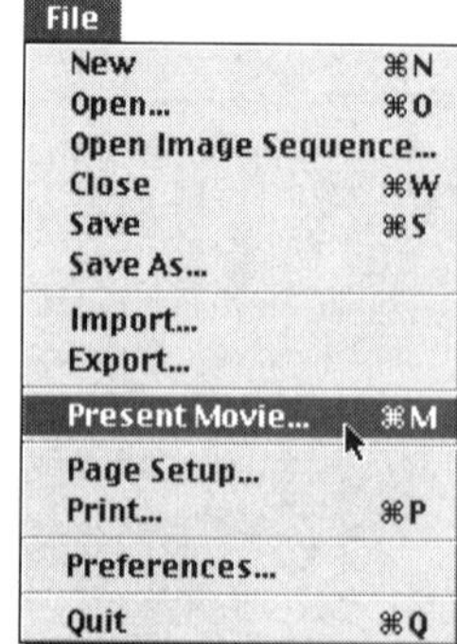

Figure 4.17 Choose Present Movie from the File menu.

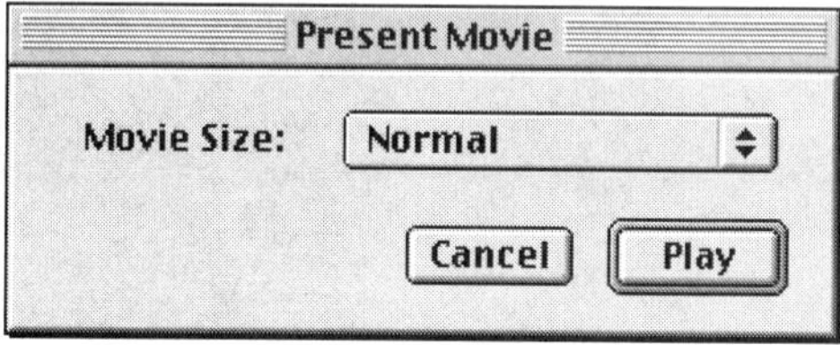

Figure 4.18 Change the window size if you'd like. Then click Play.

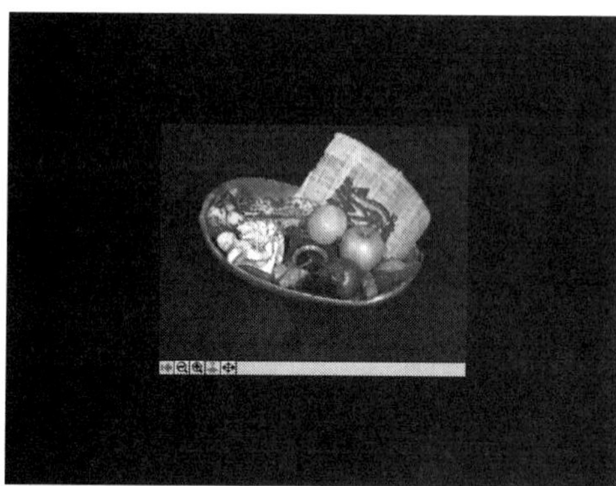

Figure 4.19 The VR movie is shown on a black background, and can be controlled in the usual fashion. Press Esc to get out of Presentation mode.

5

Basic Movie Editing

We call this chapter "Basic Movie Editing," but you'll still be impressed with some of the things you'll be able to do when we're done. If you're a Windows user and have played with Media Player or ActiveMovie Control, you'll be blown away by MoviePlayer's editing features. Even many Mac users aren't aware of MoviePlayer's longtime editing features.

And while MoviePlayer doesn't have all the fancy features that a professional QuickTime editing program like Adobe Premiere does, for certain jobs MoviePlayer is the best tool. As a matter of fact, we use Adobe Premiere for many functions, but find that for a lot of our simple cut, copy, and paste editing, we get our work done more efficiently with MoviePlayer.

In this chapter, we'll start by covering one of the very first skills you need to develop if you're going to edit QuickTime movies in MoviePlayer: selecting portions of a movie. Once you've selected data, you can copy that data and paste it elsewhere, remove it, or use it in various other ways.

We'll also cover some basic techniques for editing portions of the movie that you don't see or hear when it's played, like annotations, the poster, and the preview. And finally, we'll cover what you need to know when it's time to save your edited movie.

Selecting and deselecting movie data

To select data in a word processor, you drag across the text you wish to select and it becomes highlighted. In a QuickTime movie, since you can't see all the data at once, you select portions of the play bar, using it to represent the movie.

Figure 5.1 Hold down the Shift key while you move the slider to select movie data. The area that is black in the play bar represents the selected portion of the movie.

To select a portion of a movie

1. Move the slider to the point in the movie where you want to begin selecting data.
2. Hold down the Shift key and move the slider to the point in the movie where you want the selection to end.

   The play bar turns black to represent your selection (**Figure 5.1**). The image you see when you are done selecting is actually not part of the selection, unless you are at the very end of the movie.

✔ Tip

- Remember that you have a large number of ways to move the slider: You can drag it directly, you can move it a single frame at a time using the Step buttons or arrow keys, and you can even play the movie and then pause it when it gets to the point where you want the selection to end. (Just remember to hold the Shift key down when you're doing any of these.)

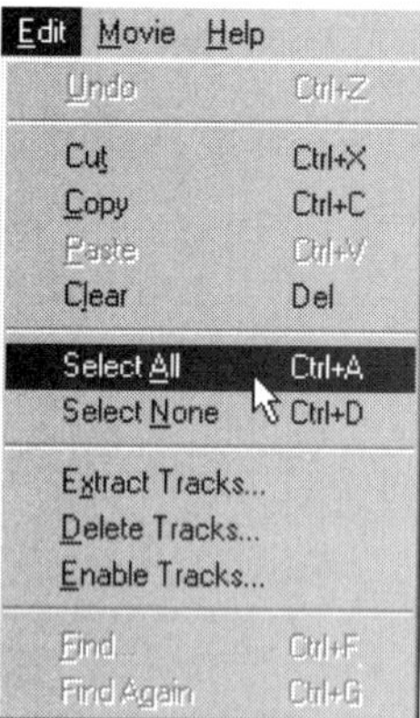

Figure 5.2 Choose Select All to select all the data in the movie.

To select all the data in a movie

1. Choose Select All from the Edit menu (**Figure 5.2**).

   The entire play bar turns black (meaning the movie is now selected).

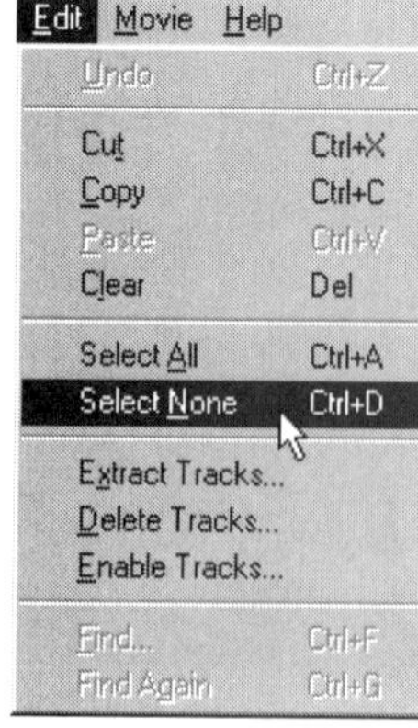

Figure 5.3 Choose Select None to remove any selection in the movie.

Methods of canceling a selection

- Choose Select None from the Edit menu (**Figure 5.3**).
- Click anywhere in the play bar.

Figure 5.4 Hold down the Option key (Mac OS) or Ctrl and Alt keys (Windows) while you click the right Step button to jump to the end of the selection.

Figure 5.5 Hold down the Option key (Mac OS) or Ctrl and Alt keys (Windows) while you click the left Step button to jump to the beginning of the selection.

Jumping to the end or beginning of a selection

When you're trying to determine if you've selected exactly the right data it's helpful to have a way to jump to the beginning and/or end of the selection.

To jump to the end of the selection

1. Hold down the **Option** key (Mac OS) or **Ctrl** and **Alt** keys (Windows) and click the right **Step** button (**Figure 5.4**).

To jump to the beginning of the selection

1. Hold down the **Option** key (Mac OS) or **Ctrl** and **Alt** keys (Windows) and click the left **Step** button (**Figure 5.5**).

After you have jumped to the beginning or end of the selection, it may help to step forward or backward a frame or two using the Step buttons or arrow keys to verify that you have selected the proper portion of the movie.

Playing only what's selected

Another way to verify that you've selected what you intended is to play only the selection.

To play only the selection

1. Choose Play Selection Only from the Movie menu (**Figure 5.6**).
2. Play the movie.

   Only the portion of the movie that you've selected plays (**Figure 5.7**).
3. Return the movie to normal playback by again choosing Play Selection Only (which is now checked) from the Movie menu.

✔ Tip

■ If you are going to play only the selection, you may find it helpful to turn looping on, as well. (Choose Loop from the Movie menu.)

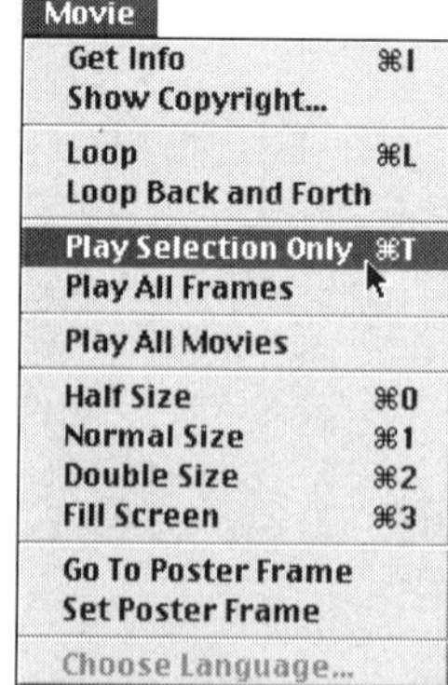

Figure 5.6 Choose Play Selection Only from the Movie menu.

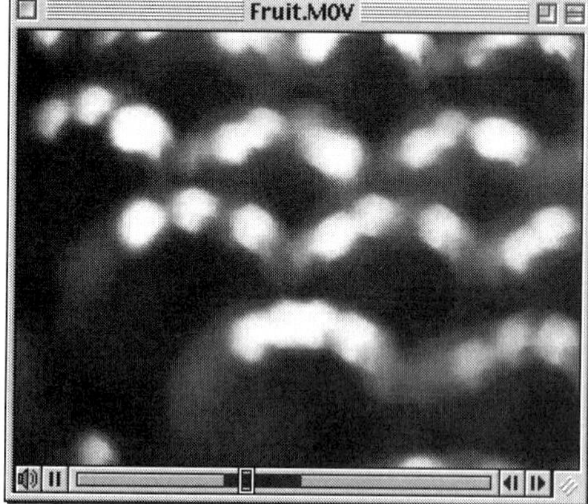

Figure 5.7 When you play the movie, the slider moves only in the area that's selected.

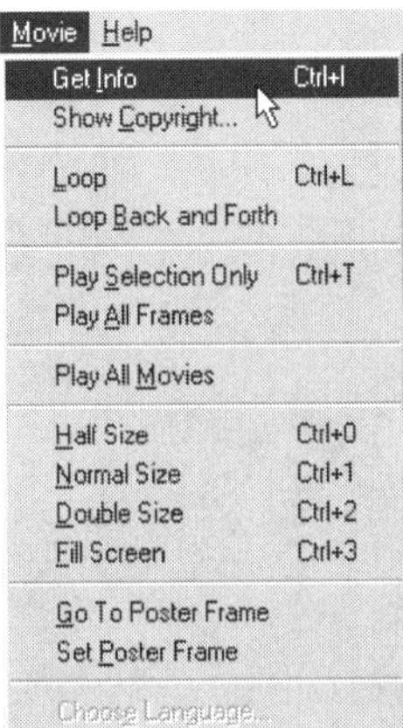

Figure 5.8 Choose Get Info from the Movie menu to open the Info window.

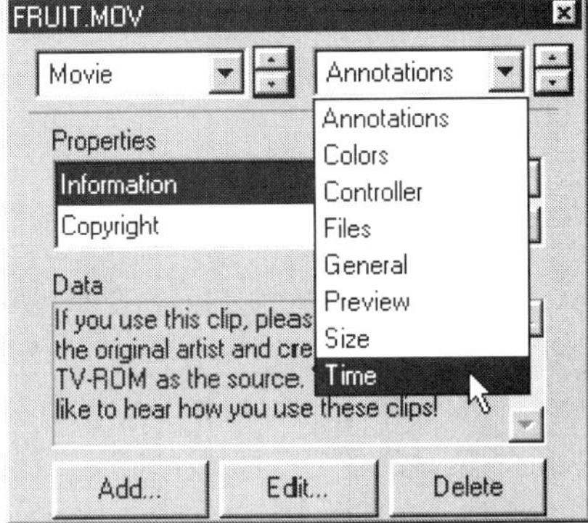

Figure 5.9 Choose Time from the right pop-up menu.

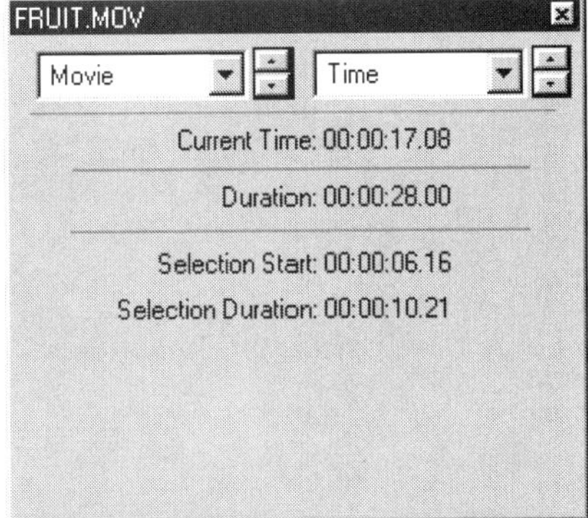

Figure 5.10 The Time panel provides time-related information.

Getting time information about the movie and the selection

Sometimes when you're editing it's useful to have precise information about the duration of the movie and the selection.

To get time information

1. Choose **Get Info** from the Movie menu to open the Info window for the movie (**Figure 5.8**).
2. In the movie's Info window, make sure **Movie** is chosen in the left pop-up menu, and choose **Time** from the right pop-up menu (**Figure 5.9**).

   The Time panel provides four pieces of information concerning time (**Figure 5.10**). The first line ("Current Time") shows the point in time relative to the start of the movie at which the slider is currently positioned. The second line shows the duration of the movie. The bottom two lines show the point in time relative to the start of the movie at which the selection starts and how long the selection lasts.

   Time values in the Time panel are represented as hours:minutes:seconds:thirtieths of a second. Thus, 00:12:45:15 represents zero hours, 12 minutes, 45 seconds, and fifteen thirtieths (or half) of a second.

Copying and cutting movie data

Of course, MoviePlayer provides the standard Copy and Cut commands that you find in just about all Mac OS and Windows applications. Since you can't see all the data you're working with, however, things are a little different than they are in most programs.

To copy movie data

1. Select the movie data you wish to copy (**Figure 5.11**).
2. Choose **Copy** from the Edit menu (**Figure 5.12**).

   As usual when you copy any kind of data, it appears that nothing has happened. Nonetheless, the data had been copied and is ready to be pasted elsewhere.

Figure 5.11 Before copying or cutting, make a selection in the movie window.

Figure 5.12 Choose Copy from the File menu when you want to copy the data without removing it.

Figure 5.13 Choose Cut from the File menu when you want to copy the data and remove it at the same time.

Figure 5.14 Once you've cut data, the selection disappears.

To cut movie data

1. Select the movie data you wish to cut.
2. Choose **Cut** from the Edit menu (**Figure 5.13**).

   The selection disappears from the play bar (**Figure 5.14**). Unless you had moved the slider into the area of the selection, nothing appears to happen to the movie image.

   If you play the movie, however, you'll see that the portion of the movie that was selected isn't played at all. That portion is ready to be pasted elsewhere.

✔ Tips

- Remember that when you are making a selection, the current image is never part of the selection, unless you are at the end of the movie.
- Use the Undo command in the Edit menu to return the movie to its state before your last action.

Pasting movie data into a movie

Pasting is not a terribly complicated operation, but it too has its idiosyncrasies. One of the slightly confusing aspects of pasting is that things happen one way if you place the new data at the very end of the movie, and another way if you place it anywhere else. Consequently, we'll explain these two things separately here.

To paste previously copied or cut data at the end of a movie

1. Move the slider as far to the right in the play bar as possible (**Figure 5.15**).
2. Choose **Paste** from the Edit menu (**Figure 5.16**).

   The slider remains at the end of the play bar. The last frame of what you had previously copied or cut appears in the movie window. A portion of the play bar is selected, representing the pasted data.

   The data has been pasted after the data that was there originally.

Figure 5.15 When you want to paste data at the end of the movie, put the slider as far to the right as it will go.

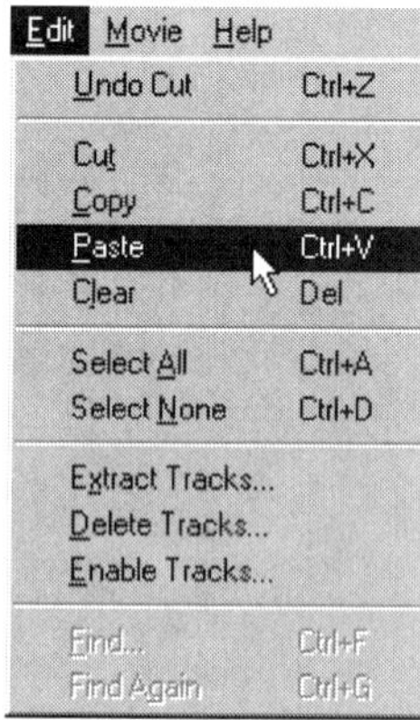

Figure 5.16 Choose Paste from the Edit menu to paste previously copied or cut movie data.

Pasting data into other applications

Data that you've copied or cut from a movie can often be pasted into other applications that can handle that type of data. For example, if you copy data from a video track, you can paste into a graphics program like Adobe Photoshop. Text-track data can be pasted into some text or word processors. Typically, only the first frame of the selection is pasted.

Figure 5.17 When you want to paste data anywhere but the end, put the slider at the frame before which you want the data pasted. The current image will be the one immediately after the pasted data.

To paste previously copied or cut data anywhere but the end of a movie

1. Move your slider to the point in the movie just after where you want the data pasted (**Figure 5.17**).
2. Choose **Paste** from the Edit menu.

   You will then see a selected area to the left of the slider representing your pasted data. If you play the movie or step through it, you'll see that the data has been inserted just before the point in the movie where you had the slider when you pasted.

✔ Note

- In MoviePlayer, when you paste into a movie with a selection, the selection is not replaced with the pasted data, as occurs in many other applications. MoviePlayer does have a Replace command, however, that does this; see *Replacing part of a movie with part of another* later in this chapter.

Transitional edits

When you combine movies as described here, you do what's called a *straight cut edit*: one clip ends and another begins. A *transitional edit*, on the other hand, is one in which one clip begins before the other ends, with some kind of visual effect happening during the overlap. (A common effect used in video editing is a dissolve.) QuickTime 3 has built-in effects which can be used by editing software to provide transitional editing capabilities; unfortunately MoviePlayer isn't one of these tools. Apple does have a free utility, however, called MakeEffectMovie that will allow you to experiment with these effects; you can get it at **http://www.apple.com/quicktime/developers/tools.html#effects**.

Pasting text and graphics into a movie

As long as you are not pasting into an empty movie, you can paste data copied from applications that handle text or images. The steps you follow are the same as those for pasting movie data. The rules for where the data gets pasted are also the same as those for pasting movie data: unless the slider is at the end of the movie, the data is pasted immediately *before* the current image.

When you paste graphics from a graphics application

If the movie into which you are pasting already has a visual component, any image pasted is resized and reproportioned to fit into the movie window's current dimensions (**Figure 5.18**); thus, it's best to make sure that the graphic is the same size as the existing window before pasting. If the movie is an audio-only movie, the image retains its original dimensions.

A new frame is added to the movie when you paste graphics. If there was a video track in the movie before the paste, the new frame becomes part of the existing video track. If no video track was in the movie before the paste, a video track is added.

If the movie contained a video track before the paste, the duration of the new frame is usually the same as the duration of the frame visible when you paste. If the movie contained no video track, the new frame has a duration of two seconds.

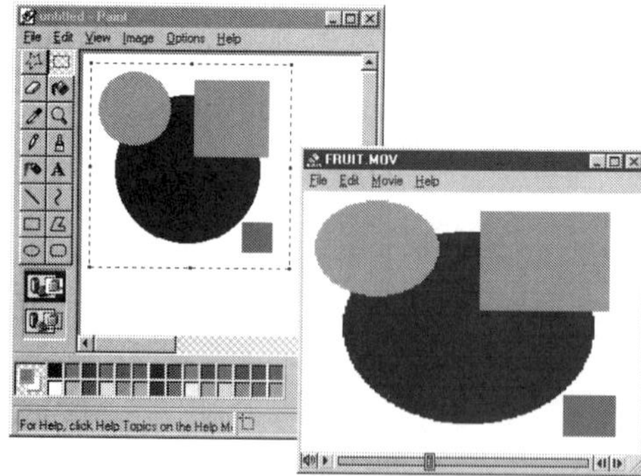

Figure 5.18 When you paste a graphic copied from a graphic application into a movie, the image is resized and reproportioned to fit in the existing movie window. It's given a duration of two seconds.

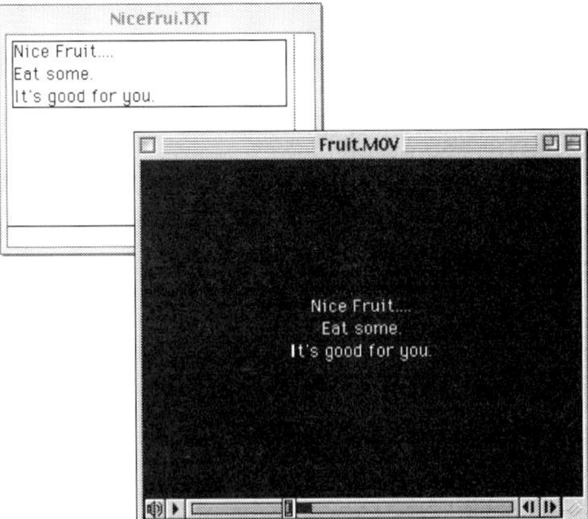

Figure 5.19 When you copy text from a word processor and paste it into a movie, the text is white on a black background and is centered. It may retain other formatting characteristics.

When you paste text from a word processor

Pasted text appears centered in a new frame, and is white on a black background (**Figure 5.19**). Depending on the word processor from which the data was copied, the text may retain other formatting, such as font, size, and style. (Some word processors don't copy styled text in a way that other applications, such as MoviePlayer, understand.)

The width of the window does not change. If the amount of text pasted is very large, the movie window's height is extended enough to fit the text; white is added to the bottom of the window in the rest of the movie. (The height is only extended as much as is possible on your current screen; only the text that will fit in that height appears.)

The duration of the frame containing the text is two seconds.

✔ Tips

- There is a technique that will allow you to change these default durations. This is covered in Chapter 6, *Scaling a track to a specific duration.*
- If you have a lot of graphics or text to paste, you may be better off importing the data, creating a new movie with a video or text track, as we'll discuss in Chapters 8 and 9. These chapters also discuss techniques for doing such things as adding a graphic that can be used as a logo or changing the way text looks.
- In some situations, MoviePlayer may not interpret data copied from other applications as you might expect. For example, when you copy multiple cells from an Excel spreadsheet, MoviePlayer treats it as a graphic.

Creating a new movie and pasting movie data into it

There's nothing terribly complicated about creating a new movie and putting copied movie data into it. We'll assume that you have already copied data from another movie. (Note that you can only paste data copied from a QuickTime movie into an empty movie; you cannot paste text or graphics copied from another application.)

To create a new movie and paste something into it

1. Choose **New** from the File menu (**Figure 5.20**).

   A new movie window appears, consisting of only a title bar and a movie controller (**Figure 5.21**).

2. Choose **Paste** from the Edit menu (**Figure 5.22**).

   Assuming the pasted data has a visual component, the movie window expands to the dimensions of that data. The entire play bar is selected (**Figure 5.23**).

   When you play the movie you'll see that it now contains the pasted data.

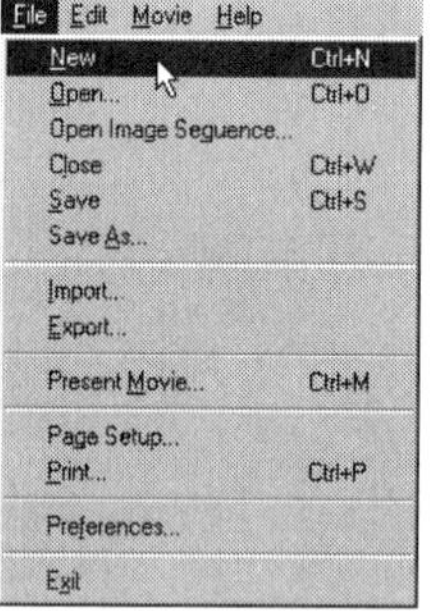

Figure 5.20 Choose New from the File menu.

Figure 5.21 A new, untitled movie window appears.

Figure 5.22 Choose Paste to paste previously copied movie data.

Figure 5.23 The movie window expands to the dimensions of the pasted data.

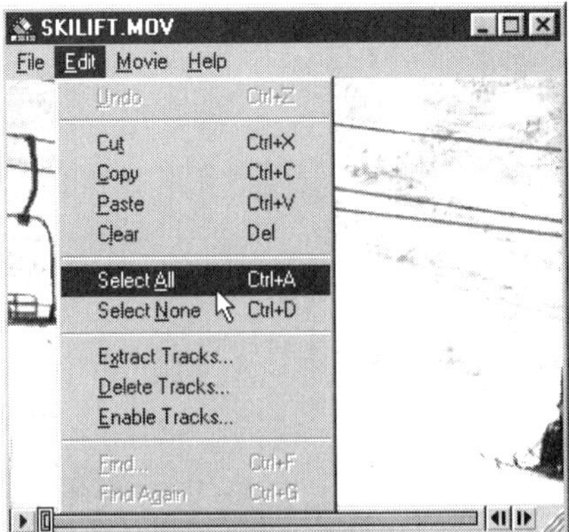

Figure 5.24 Choose Select All from the Edit menu in one movie.

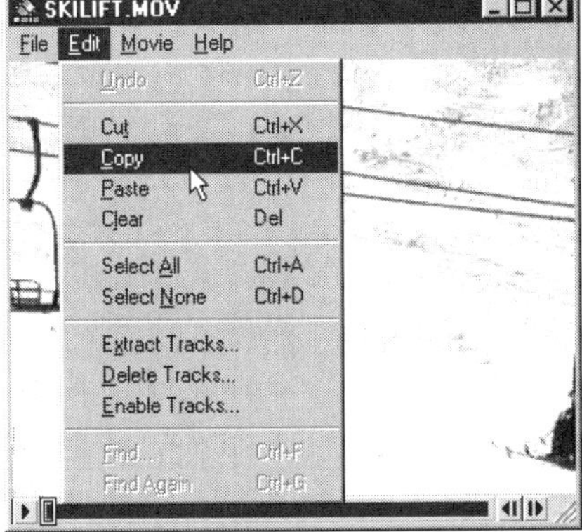

Figure 5.25 Choose Copy from the Edit menu.

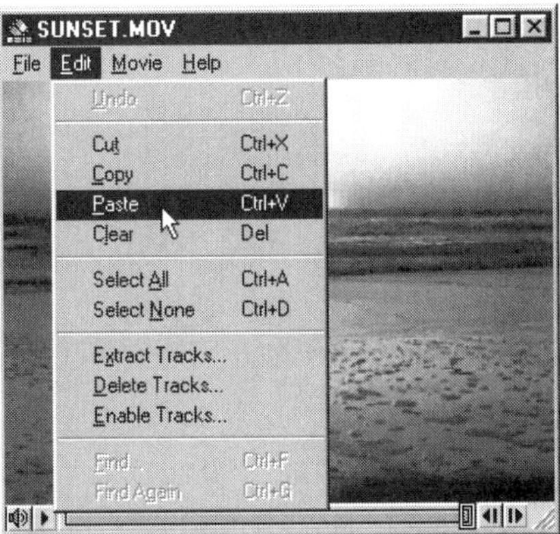

Figure 5.26 Click in the other movie, move the slider, and choose Paste form the Edit menu.

Combining two movies

Once you know how to copy and paste movie data, you know how to combine movies, so one plays after the other but we'll review the steps here anyway.

To combine two movies

1. In the movie window containing the movie data that you want to play second, choose **Select All** from the Edit menu (**Figure 5.24**).
2. Choose **Copy** from the Edit menu (**Figure 5.25**).
3. Click in the other movie window.
4. Move the slider to the far right of the play bar.
5. Choose **Paste** from the Edit menu (**Figure 5.26**).

You can, of course, select less than the whole movie in step 1. You can also put the slider somewhere other than the far right of the play bar in step 4 in order to paste data someplace other than the end of the movie.

✔ Tip

- You can use the tab key to switch between MoviePlayer windows.

Deleting parts of a movie

When you want to get rid of movie data, you have two ways to go. You can delete the selected data or you can delete everything but the selection.

To delete a section of a movie:

1. Select the portion of the movie you wish to delete.
2. Choose Clear from the Edit menu (**Figure 5.27**) or press the Delete key on your keyboard.

Figure 5.27 Choose Clear from the Edit menu to delete the selection.

To keep a portion of a movie, deleting everything around it

1. Select the portion of the movie you wish to keep.
2. Hold down the Option key (Mac OS) or Ctrl and Alt keys (Windows) and choose Trim from the Edit menu (**Figure 5.28**).
   (Holding down the modifier keys causes Trim to replace Clear in the Edit menu.)

Figure 5.28 Trim appears in the Edit menu when you hold down the Option key (Mac OS) or Ctrl and Alt keys (Windows). Use this command to delete everything but the selection.

✔ Warning

■ If you have no data selected when you clear or trim in a movie with a track consisting of frames (such as video, sprite, and text tracks), MoviePlayer treats the current frame as the selection, so clearing removes the current frame and trimming gets rid of everything but the current frame. With 3D movies all the data is deleted when you choose Clear and nothing happens when you choose Trim. You can't clear or trim in audio-only movies without a selection.

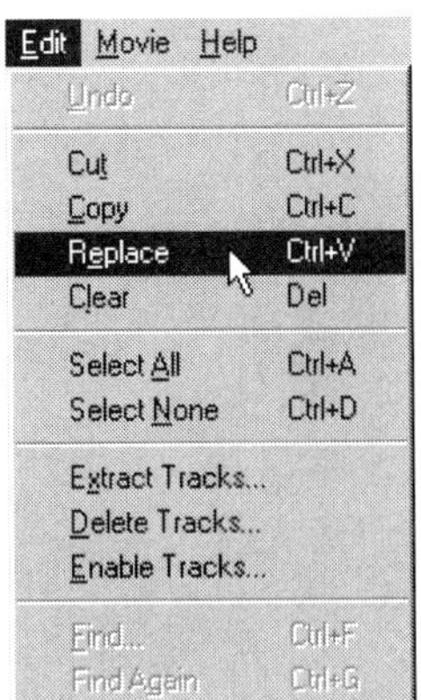

Figure 5.29 Hold down the Shift key while pulling down the Edit menu to choose Replace.

Replacing part of a movie with part of another

You can easily replace a portion of a movie with a portion copied from another movie.

To replace a section of a movie with data from another movie

1. Select the data you want to use as replacement data.
2. Choose **Copy** from the Edit menu.
3. Click in the movie window that has data you want to be replaced.
4. Select the data you want replaced.
5. Holding down the **Shift** key, choose **Replace** from the Edit menu (**Figure 5.29**).

   (When you hold down the Shift key, Replace appears instead of Paste in the Edit menu.)

   The movie may have a longer or shorter duration than it did originally, depending on whether the replacement data is shorter or longer than what it replaced.

Drag-and-drop editing (Mac OS only)

Drag-and-drop editing (a feature of the Mac OS) allows you to easily drag data from one window to another within and between any applications that support drag-and-drop. It provides the same functionality as copying and pasting, but is usually faster. MoviePlayer is one of the applications that supports drag-and-drop on the Mac.

To perform a simple drag-and-drop edit in MoviePlayer

1. Arrange your desktop so you have at least part of two movie windows visible. Select a portion of one of the movies. (If you don't make any selection, it's assumed that the selection is the current frame.)
2. Click in the image and, continuing to hold down the mouse button, drag toward the other window.

   You'll see a ghosted frame the size of the movie window with a small translucent image of the movie in it (**Figure 5.30**).

   As you drag over the other movie window, a moving border (somewhat like a barber pole) appears in that window, indicating that it can receive the data (**Figure 5.31**).
3. Release the mouse button while over the other movie window. ("Drop" the data, in other words.)

   The data is pasted into the movie prior to the location of the slider, or at the end of the movie if the slider was at the end.

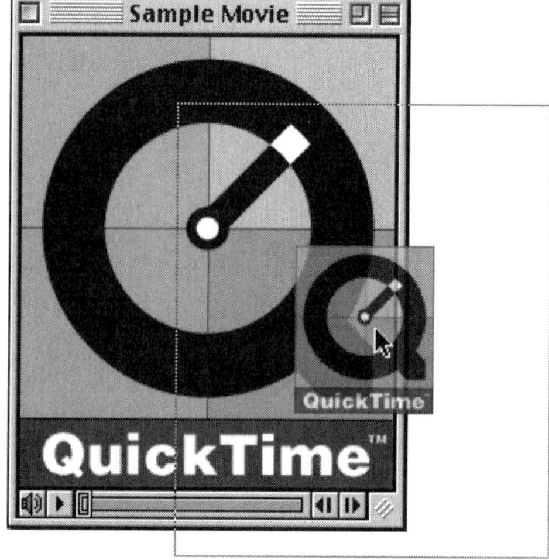

Figure 5.30 When you click in the movie window and drag, a ghosted image appears.

Figure 5.31 When you drag over another movie window, an animated border appears to show that you can drop the data there.

✔ Tips

- You can drag movie data in this way to any application that supports drag and drop, as long as it is capable of handling the type of data that's in the movie window in which you made the selection. (For example, you can drag an image from the movie window to Adobe Photoshop, or text to a word processor.) You can even drag movie data to the Mac Desktop; a movie file called "Movie Clipping 1" is created the first time you do this, "Movie Clipping 2" the second time, etc. (These clipping files are dependent on the movie from which you dragged; see *Saving movies* at the end of this chapter.)
- You can also drag from drag-and-drop aware applications to a movie window. You can even drag files of formats that QuickTime understands from the Finder (which itself is drag-and-drop aware) to a movie window; data will be pasted as if you had selected and copied all the data in the file.

Adding and editing annotations such as copyright and artist information

QuickTime movies can contain textual information describing various important properties of the movie's creation and ownership. There are over 20 of these properties (see sidebar for a complete list); they're referred to collectively as *annotations*. Several annotations—Copyright, Full Name, and Information—appear in the Movie Information window accessed by choosing Show Copyright from the Movie menu.

When you are working on a movie (or at least before you give it to anyone else), it's a good idea to add some of this information.

Annotations a movie can contain

- Artist
- Author
- Comment
- Copyright
- Creation Date
- Description
- Director
- Disclaimer
- Full Name
- Host Computer
- Information
- Make
- Model
- Original Format
- Original Source
- Performers
- Producer
- Product
- Software
- Special Playback Requirements
- Warning
- Writer
- Edit Date 1
- Edit Date 2
- Edit Date 3
- Edit Date 4
- Edit Date 5
- Edit Date 6
- Edit Date 7
- Edit Date 8
- Edit Date 9

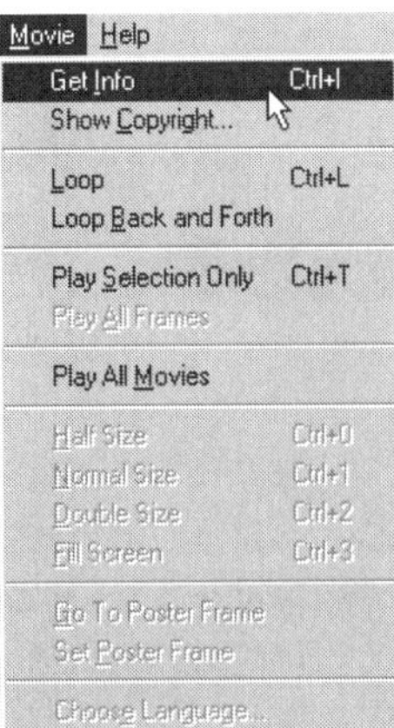

Figure 5.32 Choose Get Info to open the movie's Info window.

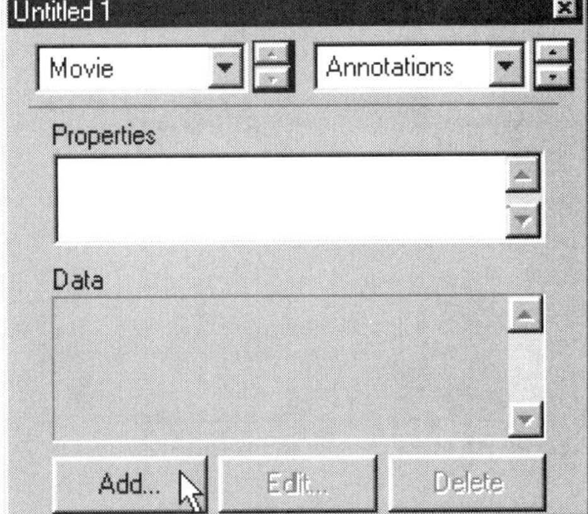

Figure 5.33 In the Annotations panel, click Add.

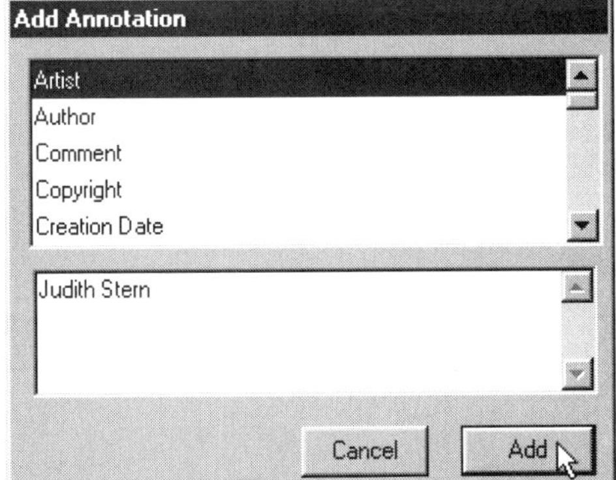

Figure 5.34 Select the property you want to add, type the text for that property, then click the Add button.

To add annotation data

1. Choose **Get Info** from the Movie menu (**Figure 5.32**).
2. If the Annotations panel isn't already visible, choose **Movie** from the left pop-up menu and choose **Annotations** from the right pop-up menu.
3. Click the **Add** button in the Annotations panel (**Figure 5.33**).
4. In the Add Annotation dialog box, select the property you'd like to add (**Figure 5.34**).
5. In the field at the bottom of the window, type the appropriate text for the property (or paste it if you've previously copied it from elsewhere).
6. Click the **Add** button at the bottom of the Add Annotation dialog box.

   When you click the name of the property you chose in step 4 in the movie's Info window, you'll see the text you typed in step 5, in the bottom field labeled Data.

To change annotation data

1. In the Annotations panel, select the property for which you wish to change data and click **Edit** (**Figure 5.35**).
2. In the Edit Annotation dialog box, edit the text and click **OK** (**Figure 5.36**).

To delete annotation data:

1. In the Annotations panel, select the property for which you want to delete data and click **Delete** (**Figure 5.37**).
2. An alert dialog box appears asking if you really want to delete the property.
3. Click **Delete**.

✔ Note

- The names of the annotations represent properties that were anticipated by the QuickTime team to be most useful to multimedia developers. It makes the most sense for you to provide data that is appropriate for any particular annotation name, but there is nothing preventing you from adding whatever alphanumeric information you want for any annotation. Also, feel free to use as few or as many of these annotations as you wish.

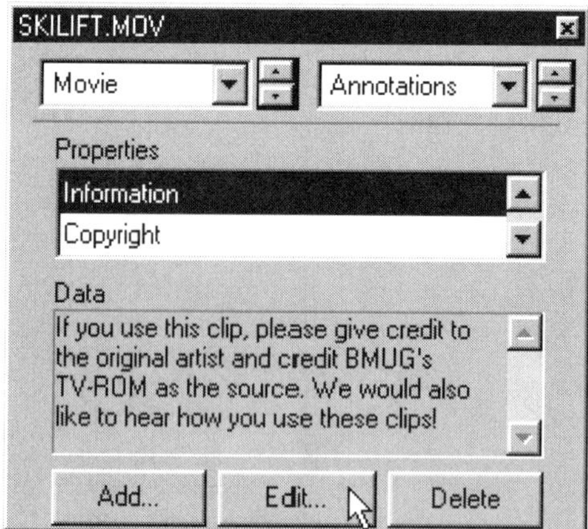

Figure 5.35 To make changes to existing annotation data, select the property you want to change and click Edit.

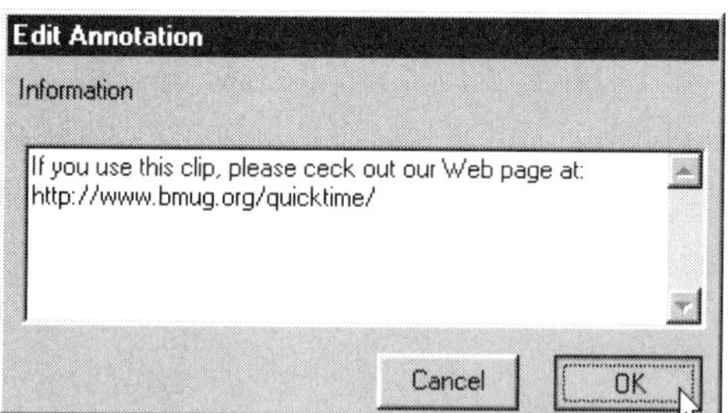

Figure 5.36 Make changes to the text and click OK.

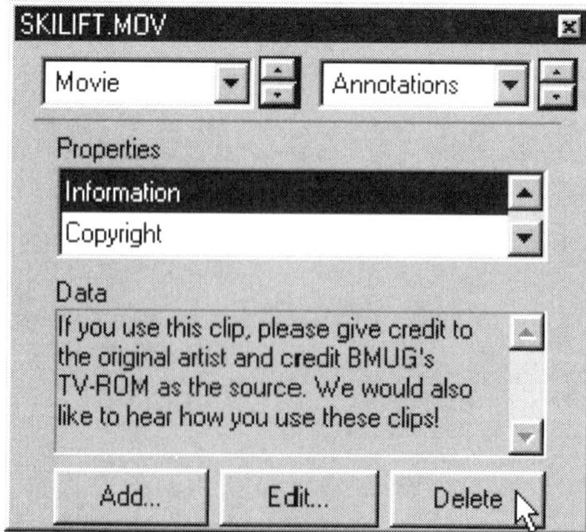

Figure 5.37 To completely get rid of annotation data, select the property you want to delete and click Delete.

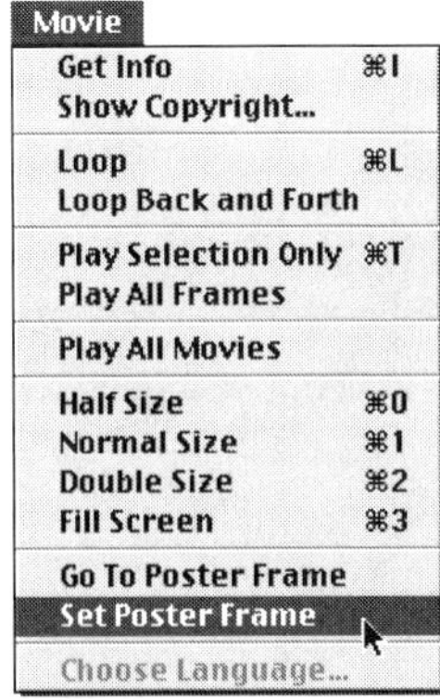

Figure 5.38 Choose Set Poster Frame from the Movie menu to use the current image as the poster.

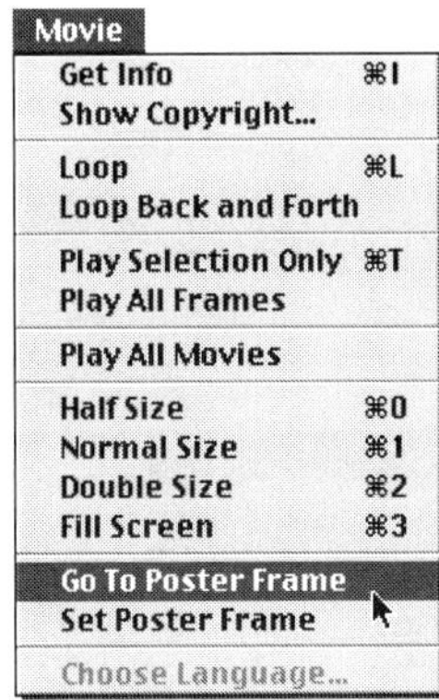

Figure 5.39 Choose Go To Poster Frame to jump to the poster image.

Setting a poster

The *poster* is the image that shows in the Movie Information window that you access by choosing Show Copyright from the Movie menu. It also is sometimes shown in the Open dialog box, and it can be printed when you print a movie.

The poster is a single image from the movie. By default, it is the first frame or first image of the movie. (That is, even movies that aren't composed of frames, like 3D movies, have a poster.)

To set a poster

1. Use the slider (or any other method) to move to where the image that you want to be the poster is located.
2. Choose Set Poster Frame from the Movie menu (**Figure 5.38**).

To check to make sure the correct image is the poster

1. Move the slider to a random point on the play bar.
2. Choose Go To Poster Frame from the Movie menu (**Figure 5.39**).

   The slider moves to the location that you set as the poster.

Changing what's shown when you choose Show Copyright

When a viewer chooses Show Copyright from the Movie menu, a Movie Information dialog box appears. For your own movies, you control what gets shown here by entering certain annotations and choosing a poster frame (**Figure 5.40**). We've covered both of these previously, but will review them here for convenience.

To add the text

1. Choose **Get Info** from the Movie menu.
2. In the Info window, choose **Movie** in the left pop-up menu and **Annotations** in the right pop-up menu, if they're not already chosen.
3. Click **Add**. In the Add Annotation dialog box, choose **Full Name**, type the text you want to appear at the upper right of the Movie Information dialog box (**Figure 5.41**), then click Add.
4. Click **Add**, choose **Copyright**, type the text you want to appear at the middle right of the dialog box, then click **Add**.
5. Click **Add**, choose **Information**, type the text you want to appear at the bottom, then click **Add**.

To change the text

1. In the Annotations panel, choose **Full Name**, **Copyright**, or **Information**, and click **Edit**.
2. Change the text and click **OK**.

To change the image

1. Move the slider to the point in the movie that has the image you want.
2. Choose **Set Poster Frame** from the Movie menu (**Figure 5.42**).

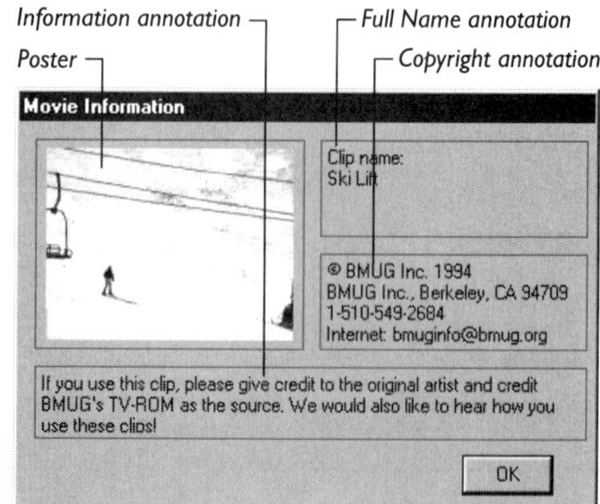

Figure 5.40 The text shown in the Movie Information dialog box is dependent on what you enter for Full Name, Copyright, and Information annotations. The image shown is the movie's poster frame.

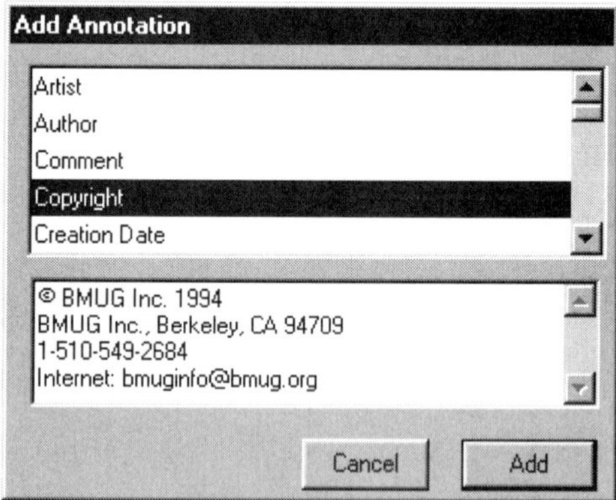

Figure 5.41 Use the Annotations panel to add the annotations.

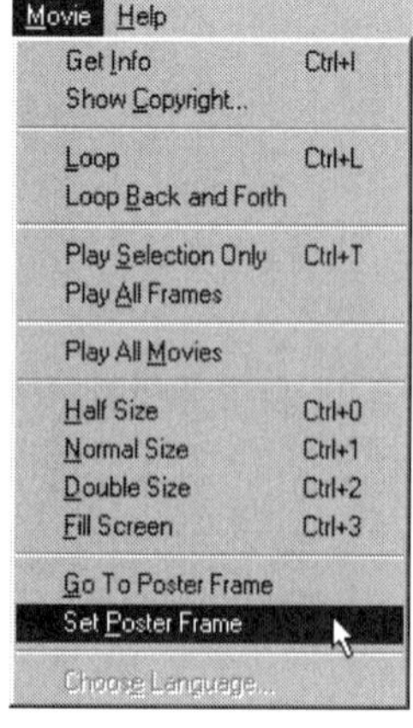

Figure 5.42 Go to the point in the movie that shows the image you'd like to appear in the Movie Information dialog box and choose Set Poster Frame.

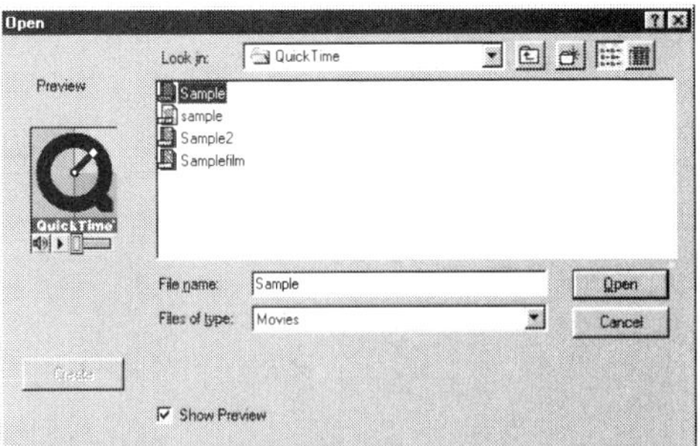

Figure 5.43 A dynamic preview often appears on the left side of the Open dialog box for applications that can open QuickTime movies.

Figure 5.44 To set the preview for your movie, select the portion of the movie you want.

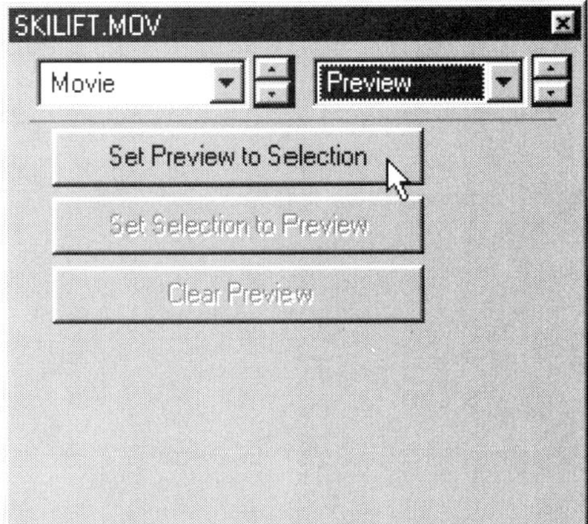

Figure 5.45 Then, in the Preview panel of the Info window, click Set Preview to Selection.

Setting a preview

In the Open dialog box for QuickTime applications, there is usually a preview area on the left (**Figure 5.43**). This is sometimes a static image and sometimes a portion of the movie that can be played. (For movies created on Mac OS computers, it's the poster by default. For movies created on Windows computers, it's the first ten seconds of the movie by default.) You can specify exactly what you want to appear here for your movies by setting a preview.

To set a preview

1. Select the portion of the movie that you want to use for a preview (**Figure 5.44**).
2. Choose Get Info from the Movie menu.
3. In the Info window, choose Movie from the left pop-up menu if it is not already chosen, and choose Preview from the right pop-up menu.
4. In the Preview panel, click the button labeled Set Preview to Selection (**Figure 5.45**).

To view the current preview

1. Click Set Selection to Preview in the Preview panel.
2. Choose Play Selection Only from the Movie menu (**Figure 5.46**).
3. Play the movie.

To remove a preview

1. Click Clear Preview in the Preview panel.

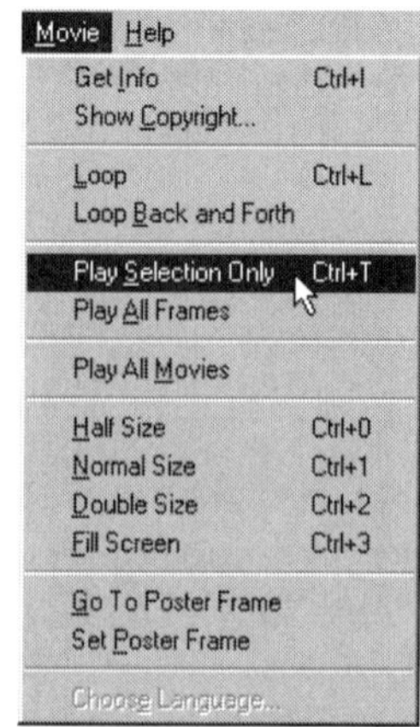

Figure 5.46 If you want to check the current preview while the movie is still open, click Set Selection to Preview, then choose Play Selection Only from the Movie menu.

Figure 5.47 You can make a selection in a completely different movie to be used as a preview. Simply drag from the other movie window and drop in the Preview panel of the movie for which you're setting a preview.

Setting a preview using data from other movies (Mac OS only)

Just as "coming attractions" for a film aren't always composed of exact scenes from the film, you may want the preview for your QuickTime movie to show segments from some other movie. (The other movie might be composed of highlights edited together expressly for this purpose.)

To set a preview that's composed of data from another movie

1. Open the other movie and make a selection in that movie.
2. Click on the image and drag to the preview panel of the Info window for the movie for which you're setting a preview.
3. Release the mouse button when a blue frame appears around the words "Drop Preview Movie Here" (**Figure 5.47**).

Saving movies

Once you're done editing, you'll want to save your work. When saving it's important to understand the concept of *file dependencies*. After you've pasted data into a movie, the movie actually contains *references* (pointers) to the file(s) from which you copied the data. The file is said to have *dependencies*. You can leave it this way (which saves disk space), but the movie won't play unless the other files are available. Or, you can specify when you save that all the data be moved into the file, making it larger but *self-contained*.

To save a movie file, allowing dependencies

1. Choose **Save As** from the File menu. (**Figure 5.48**).

   MoviePlayer displays a standard Save dialog box with a pair of radio buttons at the bottom of the window.

2. Make sure the **Save normally (allowing dependencies)** radio button is selected (**Figure 5.49**).

3. Name the file, navigate to the location where you want to save it, and click the **Save** button.

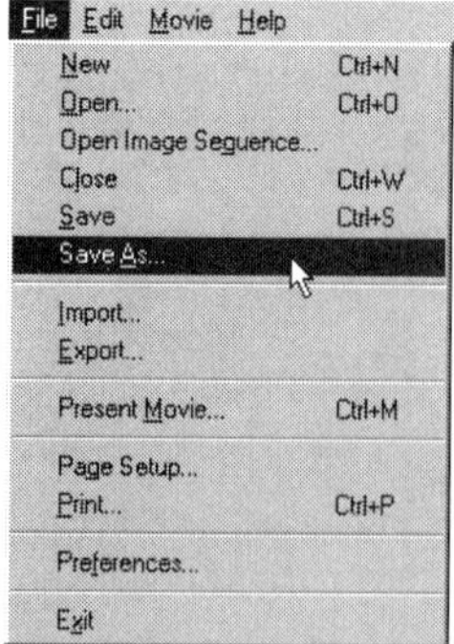

Figure 5.48 Choose Save As from the File menu when you want to save a file.

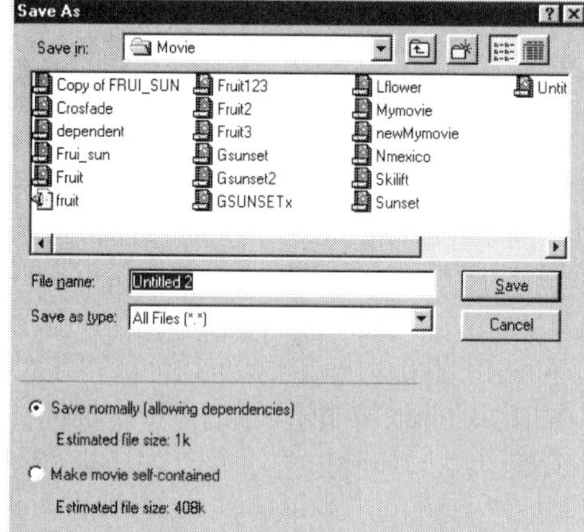

Figure 5.49 If you want the file to be saved with dependencies, choose the "Save normally (allowing dependencies)" radio button.

SAVING MOVIES

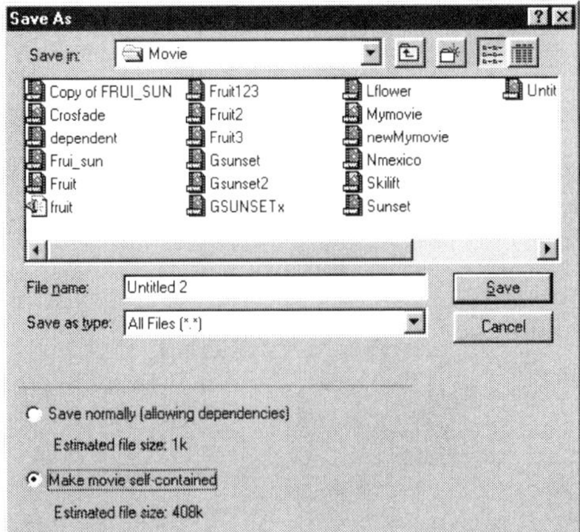

Figure 5.50 If you want to make sure that the file doesn't depend on other files to play, choose the "Make movie self-contained" radio button.

To save a movie file so it is self-contained

1. Choose Save As from the File menu.
2. In the Save dialog box, select the Make movie self-contained radio button (**Figure 5.50**).
3. Name the file, navigate to the desired location, and click the Save button.

✔ Tip (or Warning, depending on your needs)

- If you choose Save rather than Save As for a movie that's had new data pasted into it but has previously been saved, it will automatically be saved with dependencies.

✔ Note

- If you've changed the audio volume, resized the window, or have selected Loop, Loop Back and Forth, Play All Frames, or Play Selection Only, these settings will remain when the movie is saved.

Checking file dependencies

MoviePlayer's Info window provides a way for you to see which files a movie is dependent on, if any.

To check file dependencies

1. Choose **Get Info** from the File menu (**Figure 5.51**).
2. Make sure **Movie** is selected in the left pop-up menu and select **Files** from the right pop-up menu.
3. The Files panel lists the files upon which this movie depends.

   If only one file is listed, it is usually the file currently open and active. This means that the movie is dependent only on itself (**Figure 5.52**).

   If the listed file doesn't match the name of the file that's open, or if more than one file is listed, the movie depends on other files to play (**Figure 5.53**).

   You can also determine which specific tracks are dependent on other files by looking at the Files panel for each track. This lists the files upon which the track depends.

   You can double-click the file name to open any of these reference files.

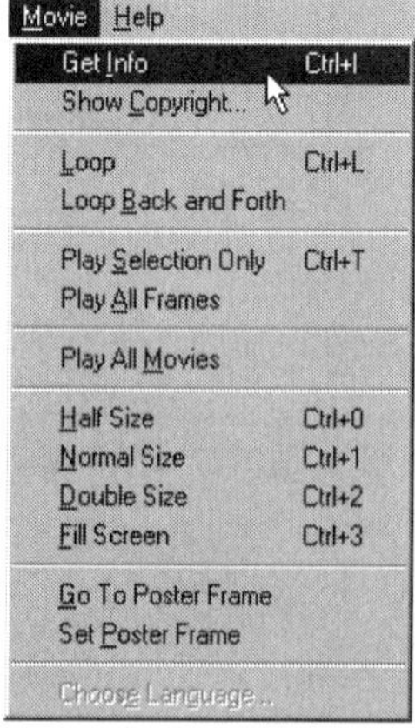

Figure 5.51 Choose Get Info from the File menu to open the Info window.

Figure 5.52 If the Files panel shows only the current file, the movie has no dependencies other than itself. That is, it's self-contained.

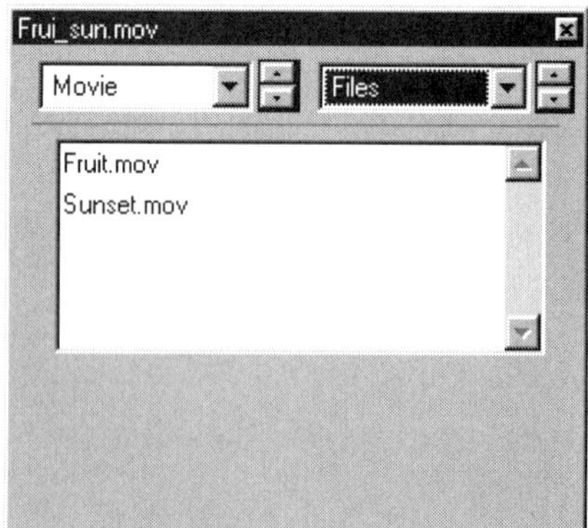

Figure 5.53 When more than one file is listed the movie needs all the files listed to be present in order to play.

WORKING WITH TRACKS

In the previous chapter you learned editing techniques that operate on the movie as if it were a single entity, without regard to the fact that a movie is actually composed of separate tracks.

In this chapter we'll show you how you can "decompose" a movie into its component media tracks, put separate tracks together to make a new movie, get rid of tracks, and hide tracks.

We also show you how to get slightly better performance by specifying how certain tracks should be loaded into memory.

And, finally, we'll explain the process of assigning alternate languages to tracks.

Combining tracks with the Add and Add Scaled commands

When you use the Paste command, as covered in the previous chapter, any data you paste gets placed before and/or after existing data. Sometimes, however, you want to add data so it plays at the same time as the existing data. The most common reason for this is to add a new audio track to a movie, but other examples include adding text to use as subtitles or new graphics to enhance the image already there.

You can add the data so it lasts as long as it did originally—a good idea for audio, unless you want to intentionally speed up or slow down the audio. Or you can add it so its duration is scaled to a certain length—as you'll often want to do when adding text or graphics.

To add new data to a movie so it lasts for its original duration

1. Select and copy the data you want to add.
2. In the movie to which you want to add the data, move the slider to the point at which you want the added data to begin playing.
3. Hold down the Option key (Mac OS) or Ctrl and Alt keys (Windows), and choose Add from the Edit menu (**Figure 6.1**).

   (Add replaces Paste in the Edit menu when you hold down the Option or Ctrl and Alt keys.)

   When you play the movie, upon reaching the point at which you added the new data, you'll find that it begins playing along with whatever data was already there.

Figure 6.1 To add data so it plays concurrently with existing data, hold down the Option key (Mac OS) or Ctrl and Alt keys (Windows) while pulling down the Edit menu. Choose Add.

Track names

If you already have a track of the type you add, the tracks names are automatically changed to include sequential numbers (e.g. Video Track 1, Video Track 2, etc.) To make later editing easier, it may help to rename tracks with more meaningful names. In the Info window, choose the track for which you want to provide a new name in the left pop-up menu and choose General in the right pop-up menu. Then click the Change Name button, type a new name, and click OK.

Figure 6.2 When you want added data to last for a certain length of time, make a selection of that length in the movie to which you're adding the data.

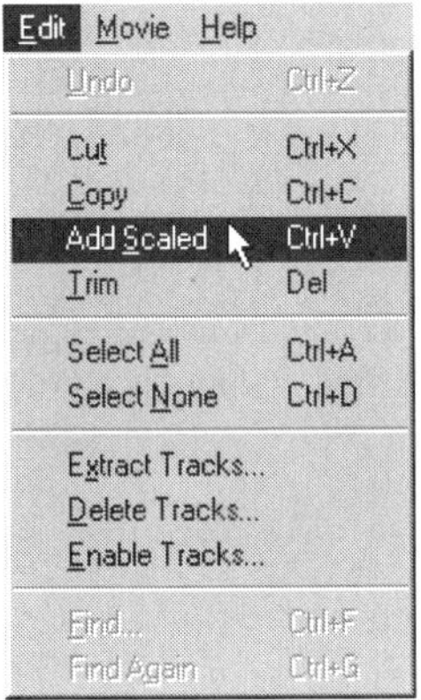

Figure 6.3 Then hold down the Option and Shift keys (Mac) or the Ctrl, Alt, and Shift keys (Windows) and choose Add Scaled from the Edit menu.

To add new data to a movie so it lasts for a duration of your choosing

1. Select and copy the data you want to add.
2. In the movie to which you want to add data, select the portion of the movie during which you want the added data to play (**Figure 6.2**).
3. Hold down the Option and Shift keys (Mac OS) or the Ctrl, Alt, and Shift keys (Windows) and choose Add Scaled from the Edit menu (**Figure 6.3**).

   (Add Scaled is located in the Edit menu in the same location as Paste and Add.)

   When you play the movie, you'll see or hear that the added data lasts for the duration of the selection. For data that originally had a time component (i.e. changed over time), this gives you a fast- or slow-motion effect, depending on whether the length of the selection was shorter or longer than the original duration of the added data.

✔ Tips

- Don't get confused by the term "scaled." You're scaling the data in time, not space.
- When you use the Add Scaled command to add to a movie with no selection, the added data is actually scaled to the entire movie, as if you had selected it all in step 2, above.

Extracting tracks

While you can create single-track movies by importing various media files, it's also useful to know how to take an existing movie and pull out a single track.

To extract a track from a movie

1. With the movie open, choose **Extract Tracks** from the Edit menu (**Figure 6.4**).
2. In the Extract Tracks dialog box, select the track you want to extract and click the **Extract** button (**Figure 6.5**).

   A new movie window appears. When you play this new movie, you'll see or hear that it contains only the data from the track you extracted.

   If you save this movie, or another movie into which you paste data from this movie, make sure to save it as a self-contained file, or the movie will depend on the original file from which you extracted the track.

✔ Tip

- You can select more than one track in the Extract Tracks dialog box. If you hold down the Shift key, you can make a contiguous selection. If you hold down the Command key (Mac OS) or Ctrl key (Windows), you can make a discontiguous selection.

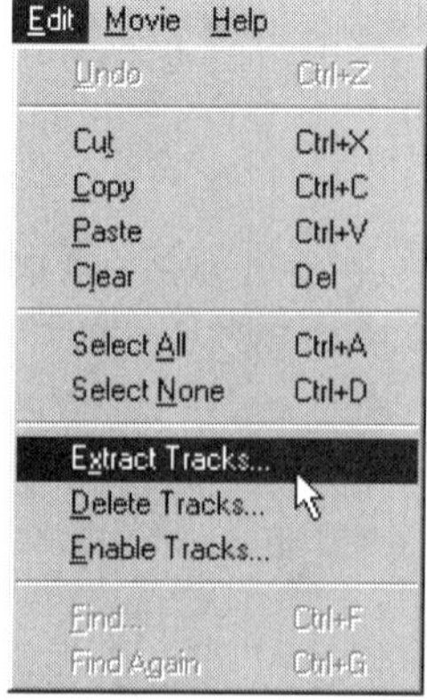

Figure 6.4 Choose Extract Tracks from the Edit menu.

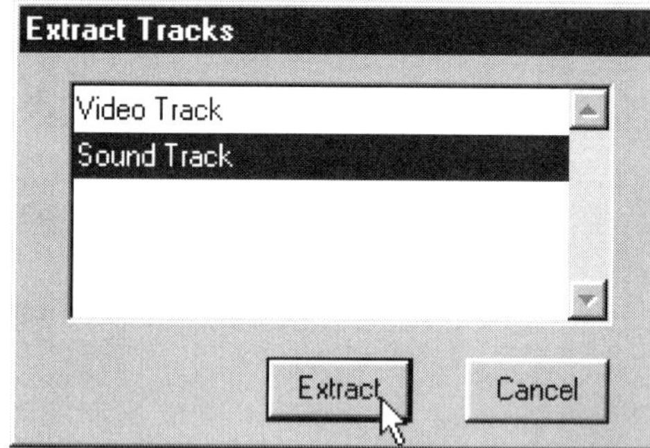

Figure 6.5 Select the track(s) you wish to extract and click Extract.

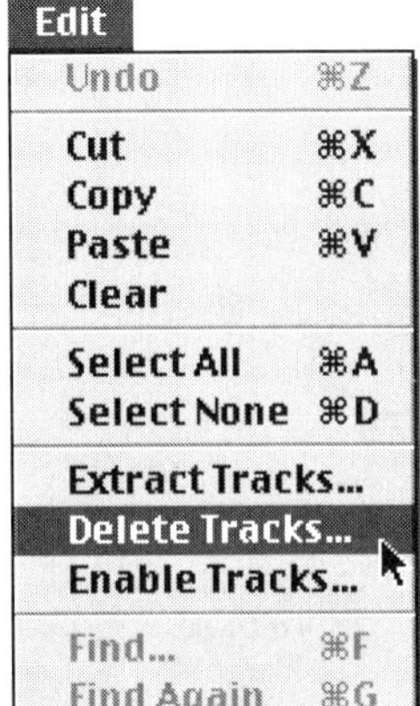

Figure 6.6 Choose Delete Tracks from the Edit menu.

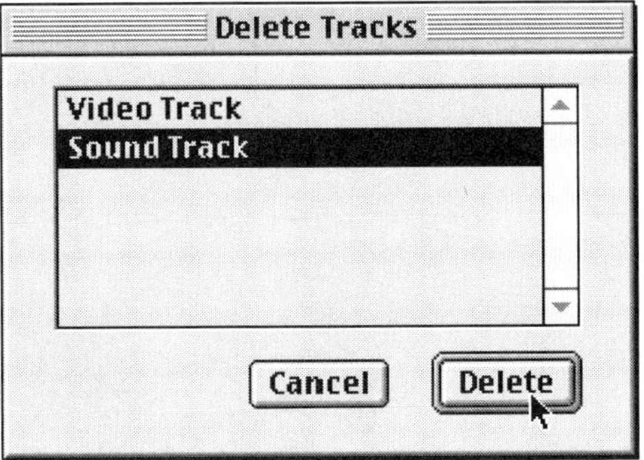

Figure 6.7 Select the track(s) you wish to remove and click Delete.

Deleting tracks

At times you may want to get rid of a single track in a movie, leaving the remaining tracks.

To delete a track

1. With the movie open, choose Delete Tracks from the Edit menu (**Figure 6.6**).
2. In the Delete Tracks dialog box, select the track you want to delete and click the Delete button (**Figure 6.7**).

   If the track you selected was a visual track and was visible in the movie window, you will notice that it disappears. If the track was the sole audio track in the movie, the Volume Control button in the controller disappears.

   When you play the movie, you'll see or hear that the deleted track no longer plays.

   The deleted data, however, remains in the movie until you save it as a self-contained file, though that data is not accessible to you and there's no way to get it back.

✔ Tip

- You can select more than one track in the Delete Tracks dialog box. If you hold down the Shift key, you can make a contiguous selection. If you hold down the Command key (Mac OS) or Ctrl key (Windows), you can make a discontiguous selection.

Disabling and enabling tracks

You can selectively disable and enable tracks in a movie. For visual tracks this provides a means of hiding and showing tracks. This may be useful during editing, when you want to focus on individual tracks without being distracted by others, or it may be something that you want to do for a final movie. (For example, you can make a text track invisible, yet still searchable.) Unlike a deleted track, a disabled track can always be enabled, even after the movie is saved.

To disable a track

1. Choose **Enable Tracks** from the Edit menu (**Figure 6.8**).
2. In the Enable Tracks dialog box (**Figure 6.9**), click on the line in the list that contains the name of the track you want to disable.

   The text in the box to the left of the track name changes from a green "ON" to a red "OFF."
3. Click **OK**.

To enable a disabled track

1. Choose **Enable Tracks** from the Edit menu.
2. In the Enable Tracks dialog box, click on the line containing the name of a disabled track (one with a red "OFF") you wish to turn back on.

   The text in the box to the left of the track name changes from a red "OFF" to a green "ON."
3. Click **OK**.

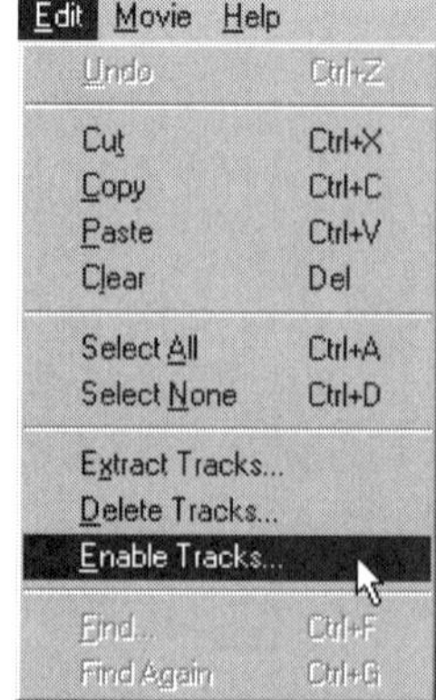

Figure 6.8 Whether you want to enable or disable a track, choose Enable Tracks from the Edit menu.

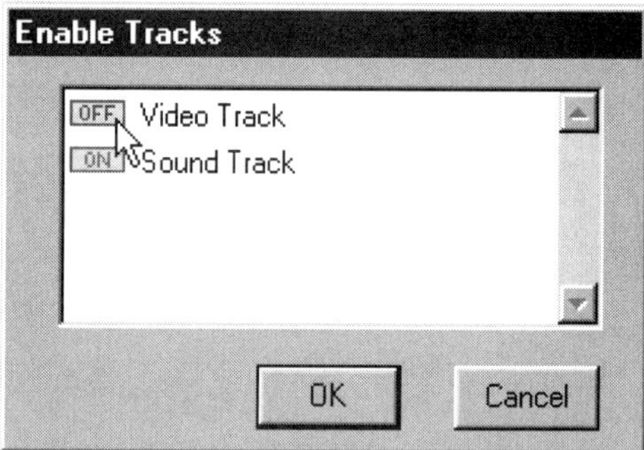

Figure 6.9 Click on any line to toggle between "ON" (enabled) and "OFF" (disabled).

DISABLING AND ENABLING TRACKS

Scaling a track to a specific duration

Using the MoviePlayer features covered in this and the previous chapter, it's possible to take an existing QuickTime track and change its duration to whatever you'd like. The technique isn't as simple as you might like, however.

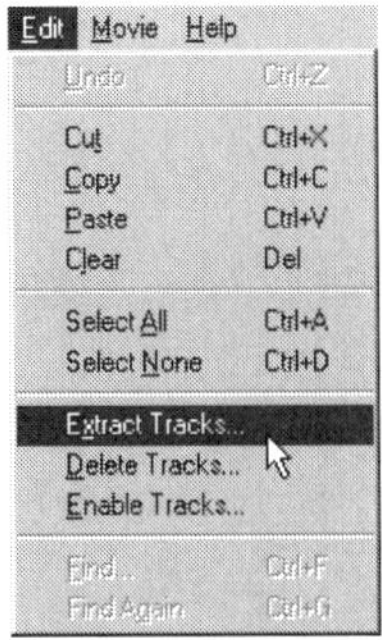

Figure 6.10 Use the Extract command to extract the track you want to scale.

To change the duration of a track

1. If the track in question is combined with other tracks, use the **Extract** command in the Edit menu to create a movie containing only that track.
2. Click in the window which contains the track for which you want to change duration, choose **Select All** in the Edit menu and then choose **Copy** in the Edit menu.
3. Locate and open another movie that has a duration that is equal to or greater than the duration you desire for your track. (It doesn't matter at all what's in this movie; you're only interested in its duration.)
4. If the movie's duration is greater than the desired duration, select a portion of the movie that is equal to the desired duration (**Figure 6.11**). (Use the Time panel of the Info window to help you do this; see *Getting time information about the movie and the selection* in the previous chapter.)
5. Hold down the **Shift** and **Option** keys (Mac OS) or the **Shift**, **Ctrl**, and **Alt** keys (Windows) and choose **Add Scaled** in the Edit menu (**Figure 6.12**).
6. Using the **Extract** command in the Edit menu, separate the track you just added from the other tracks (**Figure 6.13**).

   The track now has the desired duration.

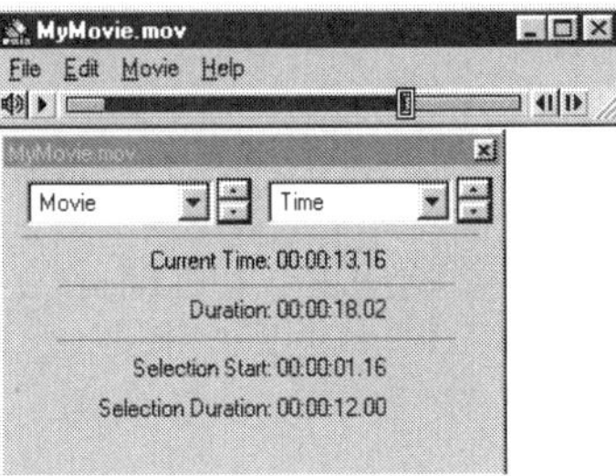

Figure 6.11 Find another movie and select a portion of it equal to your desired duration.

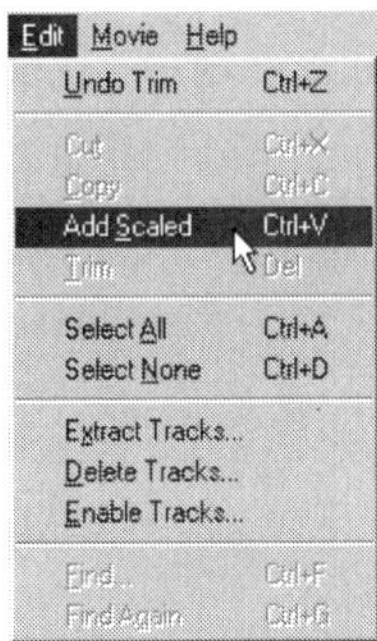

Figure 6.12 When you use the Add Scaled command, accessed by holding down the Shift and Option keys (Mac OS) or Shift, Ctrl, and Alt keys (Windows) the added track scales to the duration of the movie.

Figure 6.13 Use the Extract command so you're left with only your scaled track.

Setting up tracks with alternate languages

In Chapter 3, you saw how movie viewers switch between languages in movies containing alternate versions of certain tracks. Now we'll show you how to set up your movies to make this work.

You can use any set of tracks as alternate language tracks, though this is typically done for sound and text tracks.

To set up alternate language tracks

1. Specify the language for each track (see *Specifying a language for a track*, on the next page).
2. Designate the tracks as alternates for each other (see *Designating a set of alternate tracks*, page 84).

After you've taken these steps you'll see that the Choose Language command is available in the Movie menu.

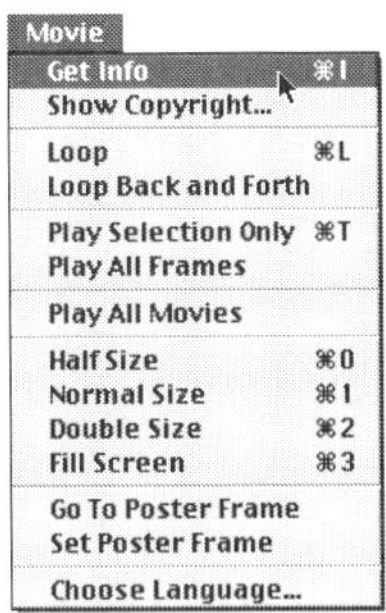

Figure 6.14 Choose Get Info from the Movie menu to open the Info window.

Click this button to designate a language

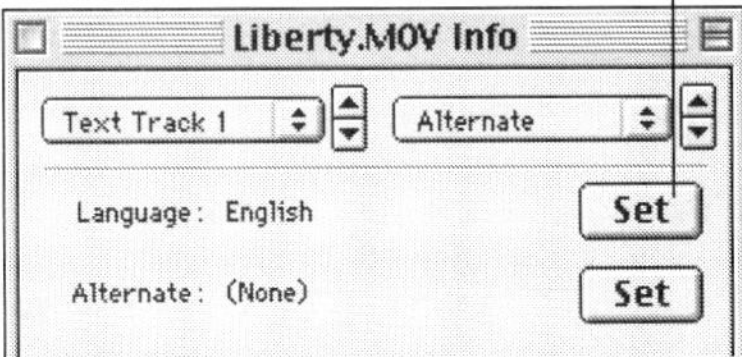

Figure 6.15 Select a track in the left pop-up menu and Alternate in the right pop-up menu. Then click the upper Set button.

Figure 6.16 Pick a language from the list and click OK.

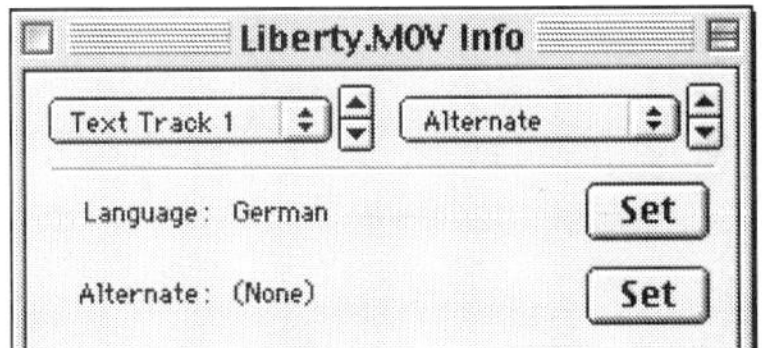

Figure 6.17 The selected language is listed as the language for the track.

Specifying a language for a track

You generally want a track to be designated as being in a specific language when you are setting up alternate language tracks, as described on the previous page. However, you may also want to have tracks designated as a specific language for use in a multimedia project when you are using an authoring tool that can refer to tracks by language.

To specify the language of a track

1. Choose Get Info from the Movie menu (**Figure 6.14**).

   The Info window for the movie appears.

2. In the left pop-up menu, choose the track to which you'd like to assign a language, and in the right pop-up menu, choose Alternate.

3. In the Alternate panel (**Figure 6.15**), click the upper Set button.

4. In the Set Track Language dialog box, select the appropriate language for your track and click OK (**Figure 6.16**).

   The selected language appears in the Info window (**Figure 6.17**).

Designating a set of alternate tracks

When you have a set of tracks, only one of which you want to play at a time, you can specify them as being in what's called an *alternate track group*. For movies being played back in MoviePlayer, this is currently only useful if the tracks in the group are also assigned languages (as described on the previous page), but you may have other ideas for how to make use of this feature if the movie will be played back in a multimedia project created using a tool that provides a way to access alternate tracks.

To designate tracks as alternates for each other

1. Open the Alternate panel in the Info window for one of the tracks you wish to designate as belonging to a group of tracks that will be alternates for each other.
2. Click the lower **Set** button (**Figure 6.18**).
3. In the Set Track Alternate dialog box, select the track you want to designate as an alternate for the track selected in the info window and click OK (**Figure 6.19**).
   The track you selected is listed as the alternate in the Info window (**Figure 6.20**).
   If you use the left pop-up menu in the Info window to switch to the track you selected, you'll see that it already has the other track designated as its alternate (**Figure 6.21**).The two tracks are now an alternate group.
4. If you wish to include more than two tracks in the alternate group, select the additional track(s) in the left pop-up menu and repeat step 3, assigning any track already in the alternate group as an alternate for the new track(s). Note that in the Alternate panel of the Info window, only

Click this button to designate an alternate

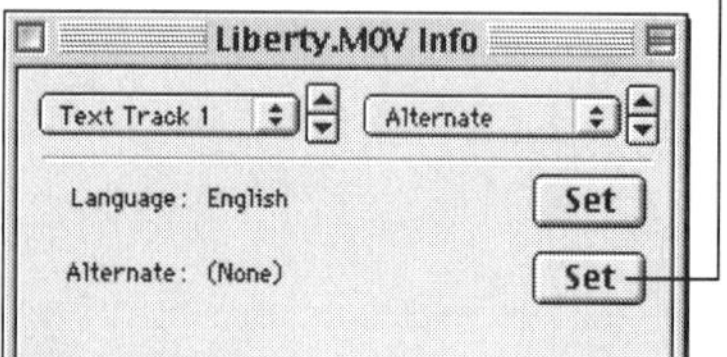

Figure 6.18 Click the lower Set button in the Alternate panel of the Info window.

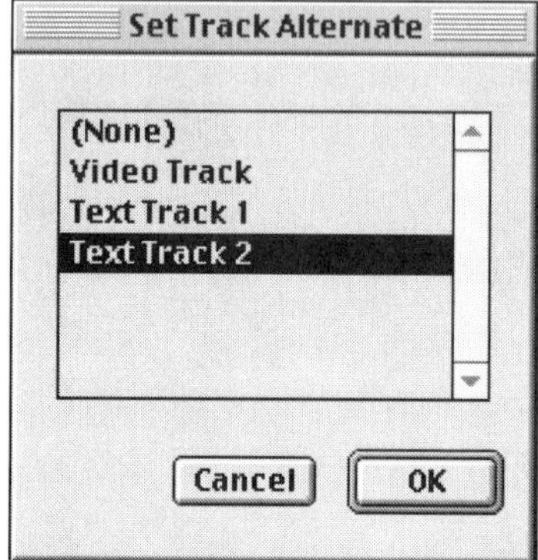

Figure 6.19 Select the track you want to be an alternate.

Figure 6.20 The track you selected is listed as an alternate...

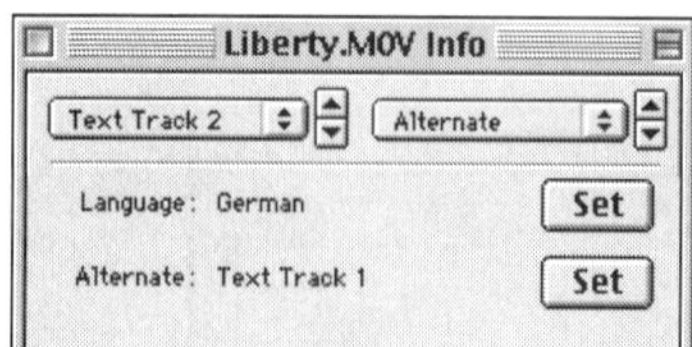

Figure 6.21 ...and if you switch to the track listed as alternate, it automatically has been assigned the first track as its alternate.

one of the alternates is listed even though a track may have multiple alternates.

✔ Note

- QuickTime 3 also lets you create *alternate movies* to be used on the Web; we'll cover this in Chapter 16. Be aware that alternate movies are not the same as *alternate tracks*.

Loading tracks into memory

Normally, when QuickTime movies play, only small amounts of data are loaded into memory (RAM) at a time. For very small tracks, you can achieve slightly better performance by specifying that all the data from the track be put into memory or kept in memory.

To specify that a track be loaded into memory

1. Choose **Get Info** from the Movie menu to open the Info window for the movie (**Figure 6.22**).
2. Choose the track you want loaded into memory from the left pop-up menu, and choose **Preload** from the right pop-up menu (**Figure 6.23**).

   The Preload panel has two checkboxes (**Figure 6.24**).
3. If you want the track to be loaded into memory before being played, select **Preload**.

   This option is ideal for tracks containing small amounts of data, such as text and music tracks. It allows the movie to play smoothly while the system is doing other things, such as loading another movie from a CD-ROM.
4. If you want the track to stay in memory for as long as possible after it has been played, select **Cache hint**.

   This option is useful for small files you wish to loop. If the track is too large to remain in memory, however, it will perform poorly.

✔ Warning

- Use these preloading options with caution. They should only be used to preload tracks containing small amounts of data.

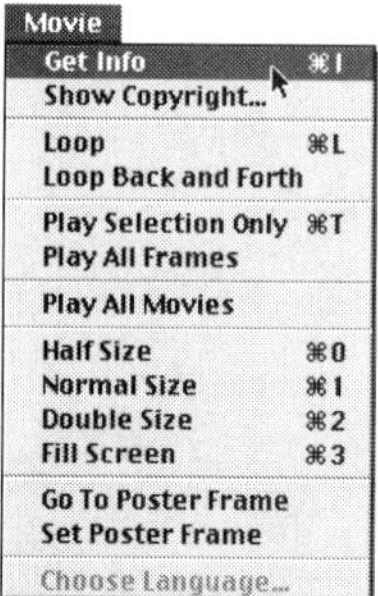

Figure 6.22 Choose Get Info to open the Info window.

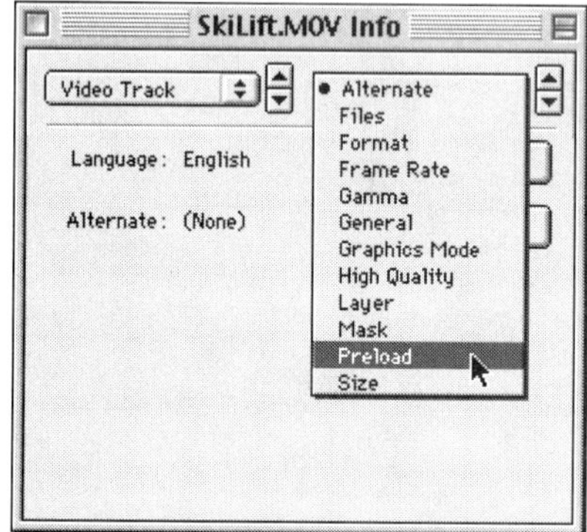

Figure 6.23 Select a track in the left pop-up menu and Preload in the right pop-up menu.

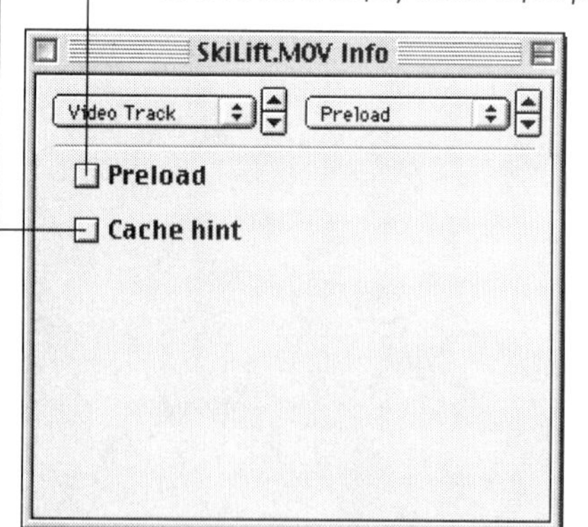

Figure 6.24 Choose options for loading track data into memory.

7 Working with Visual Tracks

There are a number of QuickTime track types that have a visual component: video, sprite, 3D, and text. For Mac OS users, there's also the MPEG track.

In this chapter we'll show you how to use MoviePlayer functions that apply to all these visual tracks—to change their size, shape, and location in the window; to make portions transparent or translucent so you can see other tracks layered below; and to change the colors used to display them. You'll find many of these techniques to be most useful when you have put two or more tracks together (using the Add or Add Scaled commands covered in Chapter 6), but some may be of interest even if your movie has only a single visual track.

For more information about what you can do with visual tracks, make sure to read the chapters concerning each individual track type that follow this one. Also, in Chapter 14, *Delivery Basics,* we'll cover how you can add visual effects to movies when you do your final export.

Flipping, rotating, resizing, and skewing

Flipping, rotating, resizing, and skewing tracks are functions typically performed in still image processing software. With MoviePlayer, you perform these operations on entire visual tracks at one time. We'll cover all these tasks at the same time because they're all accessed from the same panel of the Info window, the Size panel (**Figure 7.1**).

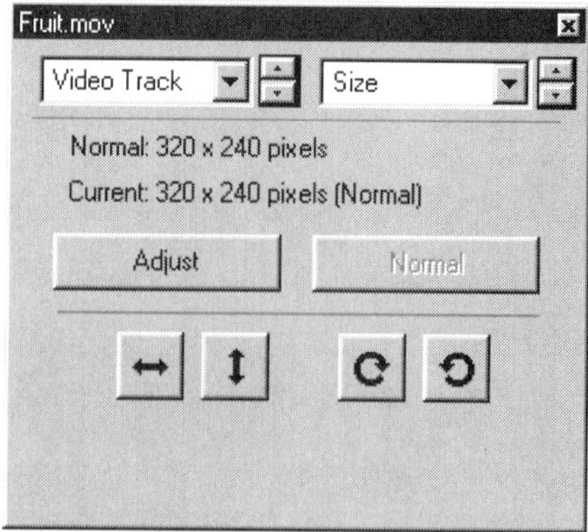

Figure 7.1 The Size panel is available in the Info window for all visual tracks.

To open the Size panel

1. Choose **Get Info** from the Movie menu.
2. Choose the visual track from the left pop-up menu and **Size** from the right pop-up menu.

To rotate a track's image 90 degrees

- Click the button with the looping arrow pointing clockwise to rotate the image 90 degrees clockwise (**Figure 7.2**).
- Click the button with the looping arrow pointing counterclockwise to rotate the image 90 degrees counterclockwise.

Figure 7.2 A track can be rotated 90 degrees

Figure 7.3 If you start with a track that looks like this...

Figure 7.4 ...you can flip it horizontally to look like this...

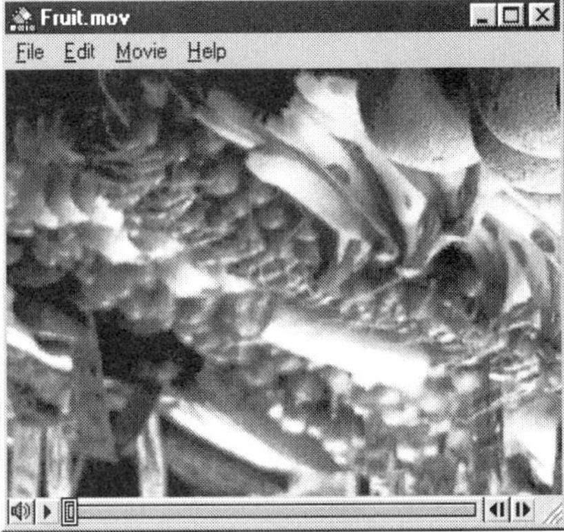

Figure 7.5 ...or vertically to look like this.

To flip a track's image

- Click the horizontal arrow to flip the track horizontally. The result is a mirror image of the original (**Figures 7.3** and **Figure 7.4**).
- Click the vertical arrow to flip the track vertically, to get an upside-down image (**Figure 7.5**).

To change the dimensions of a track, reposition it, skew it, or rotate it other than 90 degrees

1. In the Size panel, click the Adjust button (**Figure 7.6**).

   In the movie window, red markings appear on the selected track. The name of the button you clicked changes from Adjust to Done.

2. Click in the movie window.

3. Make your changes:

   To resize: Click on any of the red corners and drag in any direction to stretch or shrink the image size (**Figure 7.7**). (If you hold down the Option key on a Mac OS computer or the Ctrl and Alt keys on a Windows computer, the size of the image will jump to half-size when you drag in or double-size when you drag out.)

   To skew: Click on a circular mark located at the center of an edge of the image (**Figure 7.8**) and drag. (Drag right or left if using the marks on the bottom or top to slant the vertical edges; drag up or down if using the marks on the left or right to slant the horizontal edges.)

   To rotate: Click on the circle in the center of the image and drag in any direction (**Figure 7.9**).

   To reposition: Click anywhere in the movie image except on a red marking, and drag the image to the desired location. Or, press the arrow keys on your keyboard to move the image a pixel at a time.

4. Click in the Info window.

5. Click the Done button.

To return a track to the size and orientation it had before you clicked any buttons on the Size panel

◆ Click the Normal button.

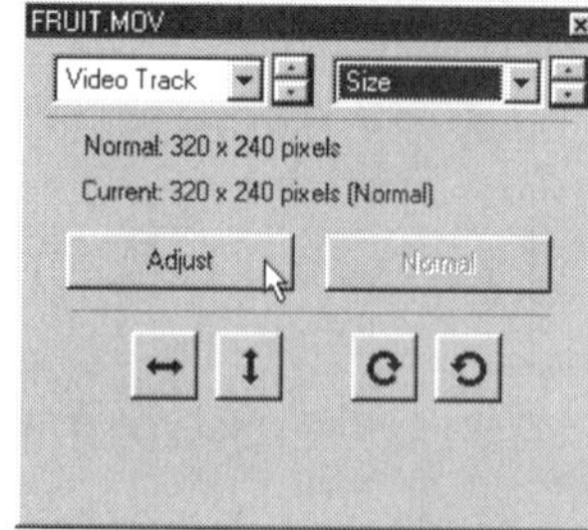

Figure 7.6 Click the Adjust button.

Figure 7.7 Clicking and holding on the red corner marks, drag toward the center of the image to shrink or away from the center of the image to stretch.

Figure 7.8 Use the red marks on the image's edge to skew.

Figure 7.9 Drag from the red circle in the center to rotate the image.

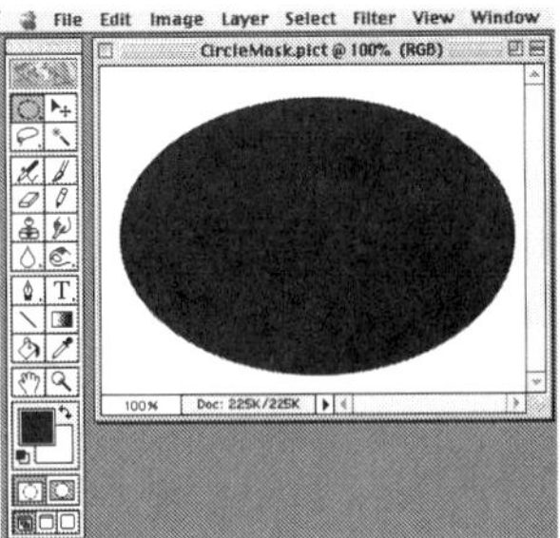

Figure 7.10 You need to first create a black-and-white graphic of the mask in your favorite graphics program.

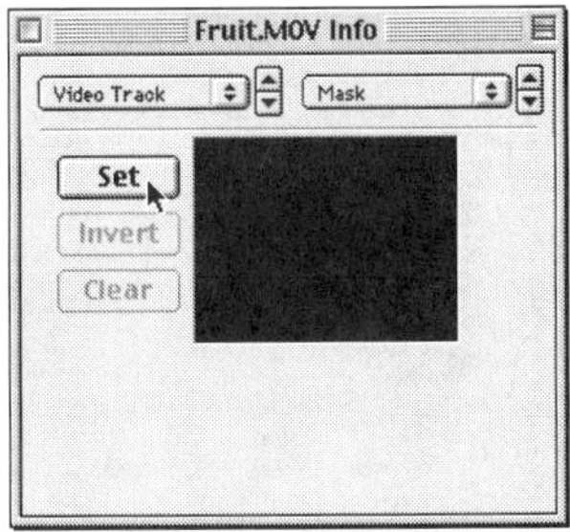

Figure 7.11 In the Mask panel, click the Set button and locate the file containing the mask graphic.

Figure 7.12 The track you are masking appears only in the black areas of the graphic...

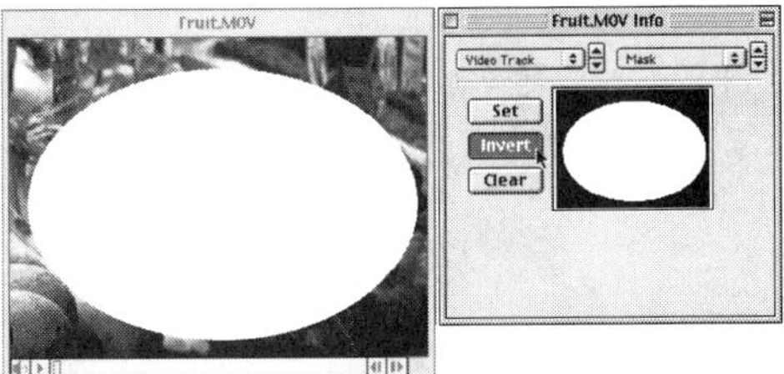

Figure 7.13 ...or only in the white areas if you click the Invert button in the Mask panel.

Masking a visual track

MoviePlayer allows you to put a mask on a visual track so it plays within a non-rectangular shape. This is useful when you have tracks layered on top of each other, as well as when you have a track that you'd like to have play inside a non-rectangular shape on a Web page.

To mask a visual track

1. Using a graphics program, create a black-and-white image of the shape you'd like to use as a mask (**Figure 7.10**). Ideally, make this graphic the same dimensions as the visual track you wish to mask. This graphic is your mask.
2. In MoviePlayer, in the movie's Info window (opened by choosing Get Info from the Movie menu), choose the track you'd like to mask in the left pop-up menu, and Mask in the right pop-up menu.
3. Click the Set button in the Mask panel (**Figure 7.11**).
4. In the Open dialog box, locate and select the file created in step 1, and click Open.
5. The image appears in the Info window and the visual track shows in the movie window only in the black areas of the shape (**Figure 7.12**).

   If the dimensions of the mask used do not match those of the track you are masking, the mask is resized and reproportioned to match those dimensions.
6. If you'd prefer to have the visual track show in the area defined by the white region of the image, click the Invert button (**Figure 7.13**).

Placing visual tracks side by side

It is sometimes useful, particularly when analyzing visual data, to show two visual tracks side by side. To do this using MoviePlayer, you simply put the two tracks in the same movie and position them appropriately. We've covered these tasks already, but here's a review of the steps to take:

To put visual tracks side by side

1. Open two movies, select data from one, and copy that data.
2. Click in the other movie, move the slider to the far left of the playber, and add to it the data you copied from the first movie: Hold down the Option key (Mac) or Ctrl and Alt keys (Windows), and choose Add from the Edit menu (**Figure 7.14**).

   The added visual data is layered on top of the visual data that was there previously.
3. Open the Size panel in the Info window by choosing Get Info from the Movie menu, then choosing the added visual track—the one lower in the list—in the left pop-up menu and Size in the right pop-up menu.
4. Click the Adjust button (**Figure 7.15**) and then click in the movie window to make it active.
5. Click on any part of the added image except one of the red markings and drag to the right or left to position the image next to the image from the original track (**Figure 7.16**).

   The movie window expands to fit both images.
6. Click in the Info window and click Done.

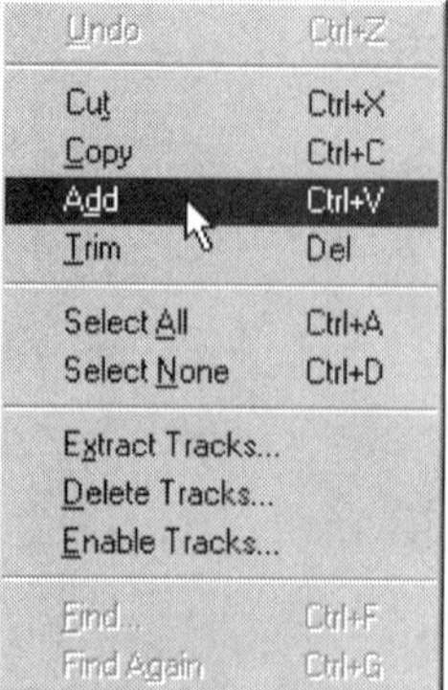

Figure 7.14 Use the Add command to put two visual tracks in the same movie.

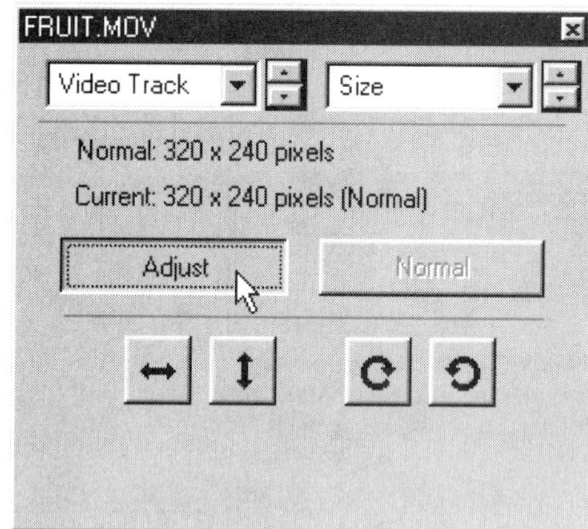

Figure 7.15 In the Size panel of the Info window, click Adjust.

Figure 7.16 Drag the track on top to the right or left.

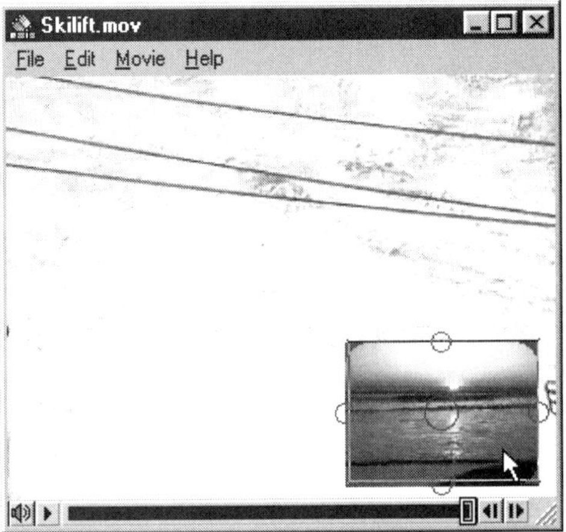

Figure 7.17 After changing the size, drag the image to your desired location.

Figure 7.18 A picture-in-a-picture can be non-rectangular if a mask is applied to the track.

Creating a picture-in-a-picture effect

Another interesting MoviePlayer effect, this one adapted from television, is the picture-in-a-picture. This, too, can be accomplished using techniques already covered.

To create a picture-in-a-picture effect

1. As we did in *Placing video tracks side-by-side*, open two movies, select data from one, copy that data and add it to the other.
2. Click the **Adjust** button and then click in the movie window to make it active.
3. Click on one of the red markings in the corners of the image and drag toward the center of the image to shrink it.
4. If you want to change the location of the image, click anywhere except on a red mark and drag to your desired location (**Figure 7.17**).

✔ Tip

- By applying a mask (as described in *Masking a visual track*), you can make the inner image non-rectangular; an oval is a commonly used shape (**Figure 7.18**).

Relayering tracks

You may accidentally add visual tracks to a movie in the wrong order, so that one track is layered on top of another when you really want it to be behind. (Each added track is placed on top of any tracks that were already there.) MoviePlayer provides you with a way to fix this by changing the layering of tracks.

To change the layer of a track

1. In the movie's Info window, choose the track in the left pop-up menu and choose Layer in the right pop-up menu.
2. In the Layer panel (**Figure 7.19**), click the downward-pointing arrow to decrease the layer number, or click the upward-pointing arrow to increase the layer number.

   The thing to remember here is precisely what it says in the Info window: "Smaller layer numbers are further forward."

   Thus, if you want a track to be behind all other tracks, you'll want to make sure that its layer number is greater than any other track's. If you want it to be the frontmost track, its layer number should be smaller than any other track's; this may be a negative number.

   If you have many visual tracks, you may have to click one of the arrow buttons multiple times to get a track correctly positioned.

✔ Tip

- When a new track is added to a movie, it gets a number one less than the lowest number already there and is thus placed in front of any existing tracks. Think of the Layer panel as the place to change the layer numbers given by default.

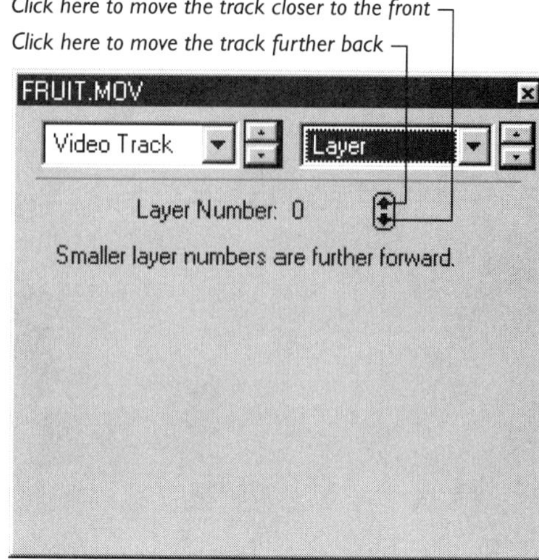

Figure 7.19 The Layer panel

Figure 7.20 After selecting "transparent" in the scrolling list, click the Color button to bring up a Color Picker dialog box.

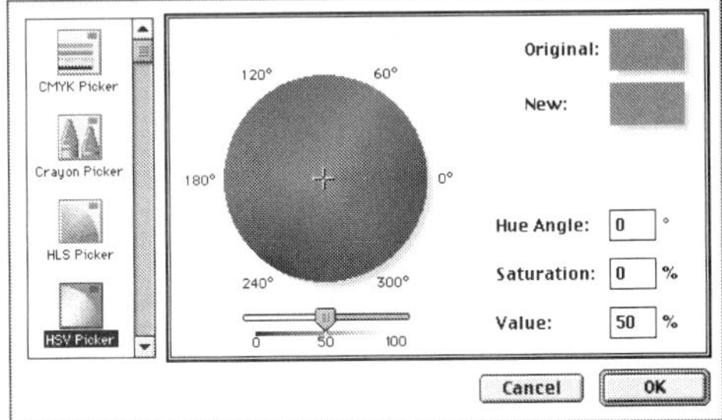

Figure 7.21 This is a Mac OS Color Picker dialog box.

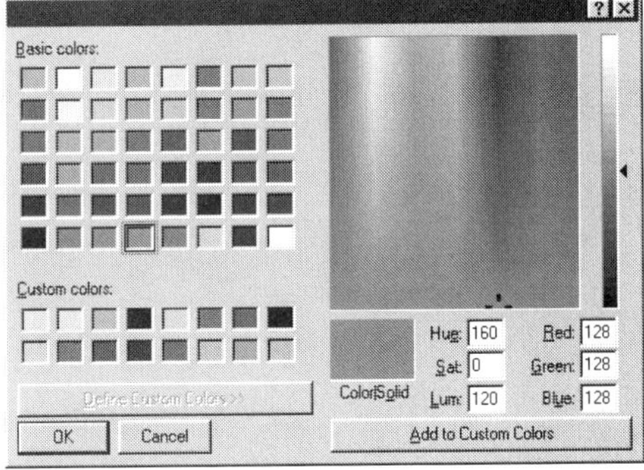

Figure 7.22 This is a Windows Color Picker dialog box.

Figure 7.23 The color chosen in the Color Picker dialog box becomes transparent in the track selected in the Info window.

Making a color in a track transparent

When you have a track layered on top of another, you can define a particular color in the image to be transparent. This works best with images that have solid areas of color—computer-generated images or animations, rather than photographic images.

To make a color in the track transparent

1. Choose **Get Info** from the Movie menu.
2. In the Info window, choose a visual track from the left pop-up menu and choose **Graphics Mode** from the right pop-up menu.

   You'll see a scrolling list.
3. Choose **transparent** from the scrolling list.
4. Click the **Color** button (**Figure 7.20**).
5. A Color Picker dialog box appears (**Figures 7.21** and **Figure 7.22**). Pick the color that you want to make transparent and click **OK**.

   Any portions of the image that are in the color you selected become transparent (**Figure 7.23**).

Picking the right color

Yes, we know that it's not always easy to identify the color that should be transparent. Users of Mac OS 8 or later can hold down the Option key to get an eyedropper pointer; you can then click anywhere on the screen and the color under the cursor will automatically be selected in the Color Picker dialog box. Other users may need to open the image (or a frame from the track) in a program like Adobe Photoshop in order to obtain the numeric values that identify a particular color.

Blending tracks

When you have a track layered on top of another, you can make the top track partially transparent, so it looks like the tracks are blended together.

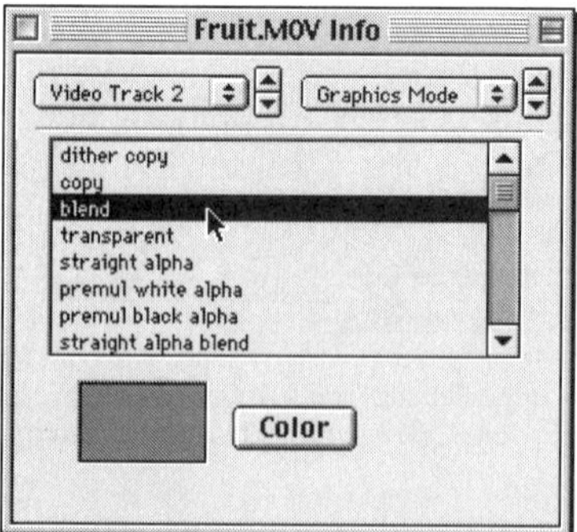

Figure 7.24 Choose "blend" for a track you want to be translucent.

To make a track partially transparent

1. In the Info window (accessed by choosing **Get Info** from the Movie menu), choose your top track in the left pop-up menu and **Graphics Mode** in the right pop-up menu.
2. Choose **blend** from the scrolling list (**Figure 7.24**).

   You'll be able to see through the selected track to tracks below (**Figure 7.25**).
3. If the degree of translucency isn't what you want or you want a tinted effect, click the **Color** button.

   In the Color Picker dialog, choose a light tone to make the track less translucent or a dark tone to make the track more translucent. Gray tones remove all colors from the image equally; if you pick a color, you'll find that the image is colorized.

Figure 7.25 You can see through the track to others behind it.

The copy modes

There are three "copy" modes listed in the Graphics Mode panel: dither copy, copy, and composition (dither copy). Choose one of these modes if you want no part of the image to be transparent. Dither copy is the default mode for most tracks and is usually the best copy choice. The difference between dither copy and copy is only apparent when your system is in 256-color mode; dithering is the adjusting of adjacent pixels of different colors to give the illusion of a color that's not in the set of available 256 colors. Dithered images look better, but copy mode may provide better performance.

Composition (dither copy) is more appropriate for certain files (usually animated GIF files); these are automatically assigned composition mode when opened in MoviePlayer.

Figure 7.26
Here's an image.

Figure 7.27
Here's the image's alpha channel. (It was created from the image using an image processing tool like Photoshop.)

Figure 7.28
Here's the image after being imported into MoviePlayer and composited with another track using one of the alpha channel modes.

Creating tracks with alpha channels

Only certain programs create alpha channels. When you save in such a program, be sure to save the file appropriately; this means saving it as a 32-bit image. With many file formats that MoviePlayer can open, the alpha channel is maintained. However, if you import a PICT file, compression is applied; you must make sure to choose a compressor that supports 32-bit color (Animation, None, or Planar RGB). See Chapter 8 for more info.

Using alpha channels

Alpha channels are used by graphic artists when they need sophisticated transparency effects. An alpha channel is a type of mask, but can include partially transparent pixels so that when the image containing the alpha channel is layered on top of another image, the transition between the two is less abrupt and thus looks more seamless. (See **Figures 7.26** and **7.27** for an example of an image and its alpha channel.)

To use alpha channels

1. You'll need to first create an image with an alpha channel.
2. Open or import the image with the alpha channel and add it to another track. Then, in the Graphics Mode panel, choose one of the alpha channel modes in the scrolling list—straight alpha, premul white alpha, or premul black alpha—depending on how the file was created. (That is, only choose one of the "premul" modes if the graphic was created with a premultiplied alpha channel. The premul white alpha choice is for images created on a white background, and the premul black alpha choice is for those created on a black background. If you don't know if the image has a premultiplied alpha channel, try each of the modes and pick the one that looks best.)

   The black area of the alpha channel allows the image below to show completely through (**Figure 7.28**).

   Straight alpha blend is a combination of straight alpha and blend, so the masked areas will be transparent, and the non-transparent areas will be translucent. As with blending, you can use the color picker to alter the degree of translucency.

Adding visual data to QuickTime VR movies

There's not a lot you can do to alter QuickTime VR movies using MoviePlayer, but you can bring in extra visual data by adding any visual track to your QuickTime VR movie. We'll first cover the general technique for adding data to a QuickTime VR movie, and then list some specific effects that you can apply.

To add tracks to a QuickTime VR movie

1. In the Info window (accessed by choosing Get Info from the Movie menu), choose Movie from the left pop-up menu and Controller from the right pop-up menu.

   A list of controller names appears. The controller currently selected depends on which version of QuickTime VR was used to create the movie as well as whether the movie is a panorama or object. You should remember which controller is selected.

2. Select Movie Controller in the list (**Figure 7.29**).

   Switching to the Movie Controller gives you access to MoviePlayer's editing features.

3. Use the Add or Add Scaled commands to add visual data as described in Chapter 6. Manipulate the added data in ways described earlier in this chapter—resize, reposition, apply a mask, use transparencies, etc.—to achieve a desired effect.

4. In the Info window, choose the VR controller that was selected prior to switching to the Movie Controller.

✔ Tip

- You can use the masking technique described in *Masking a visual track* to add a black-and-white copyright mark to a QuickTime VR movie.

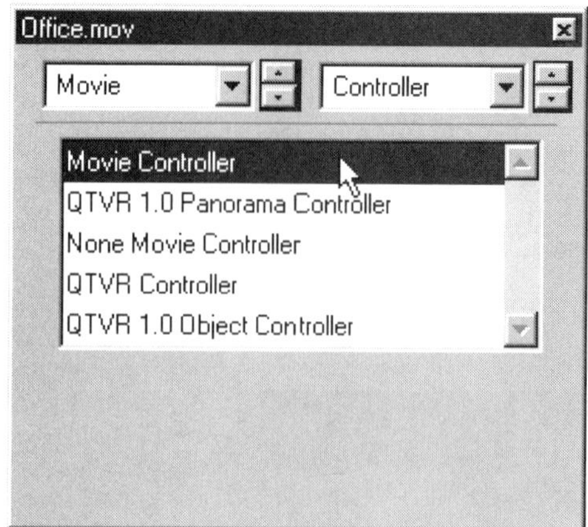

Figure 7.29 The trick to adding data to a QuickTime VR movie is to switch to the movie controller.

Figure 7.30 A VR panorama or object can have a graphic (such as this logo) that is always visible.

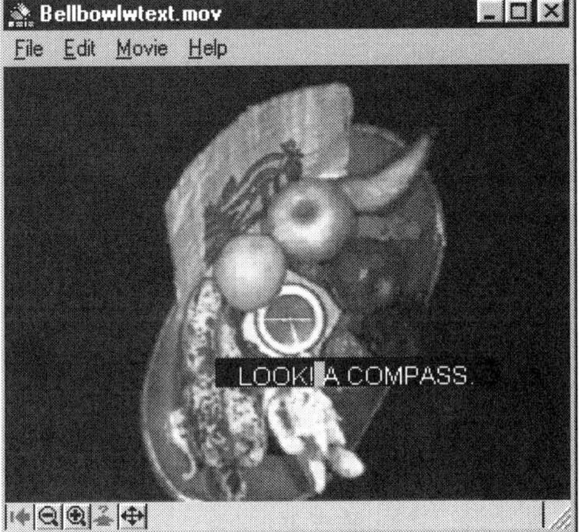

Figure 7.31 A VR object movie can have different graphics or text on different frames.

What you can accomplish by adding data to a VR movie

- By using the Add Scaled command to add data to the entire movie, you can give your panorama or object movie a logo, frame, or caption that always appears in the movie window (**Figure 7.30**).
- By adding data to selected frames in an object movie, you can have graphics or text that appear only when the object is in a certain position (**Figure 7.31**). If it is text that you add to selected frames in an object movie, viewers can search for a text string in order to locate a certain viewing angle.
- If you add data that changes over time to multiple frames of an object movie, the data "plays" as you move the object.
- Some object movies have multiple frames per rotational position, providing an animated effect even when the user is not moving the object. If you add data that changes over time (including audio) to one of these files, the data plays even when the object is not being moved.
- If you add data that changes over time to a panorama, users can double-click in the area of the window where this data is visible to make it play. This added data needs to include at least one visual track (something to double-click on), but if audio is added as well, it will also play when the visual track is double-clicked.
- If you add data that changes over time to a multi-node movie, a different image from the added data appears in each node. If there's a one-to-one correspondence between frames in the added data and the nodes, you get one frame to a node. This is a good way to title nodes, or provide a "you are here" map that appears in each node.

Adding a custom color table to a movie

When a movie with visual data consisting of thousands or millions of different colors plays on a computer system that can show only 256 different colors at a time, the end result is often less than ideal. This isn't just because there aren't enough colors, but also because the standard 256 colors that the system uses aren't usually the best colors for that particular movie. Standard system colors on both platforms, for example, don't have many flesh tones or earth tones.

Fortunately, you can designate a custom set of 256 colors that are more appropriate for your movie. This way, when the movie plays on a system that can show only 256 colors, the computer uses the colors you've specified. A movie with a custom color table playing on a 256-color computer still doesn't look as good as it would on a system that can show more colors, but it looks better than it would using the standard system colors.

To add a custom color table to your movie

1. Open the Colors panel of the movie's Info window by choosing **Movie** from the left pop-up menu and **Colors** from the right pop-up menu (**Figure 7.32**).
2. Click **Set** and locate the file that has the custom color table you want.
3. The colors of the selected color table will appear to the left of the Set button (**Figure 7.33**).

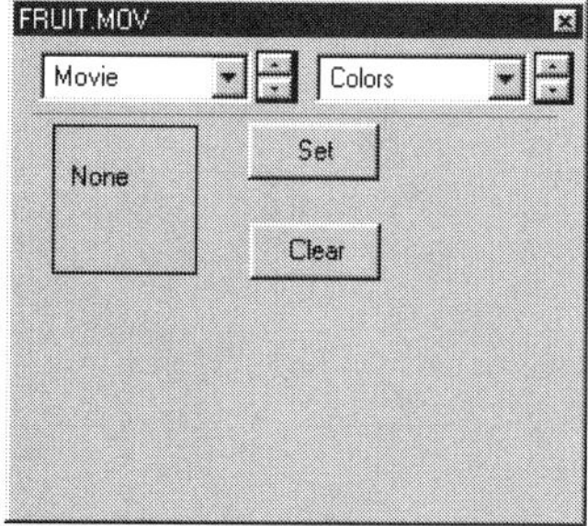

Figure 7.32 Click the Set button in the movie's Colors panel and locate the file that has the color table you wish to use.

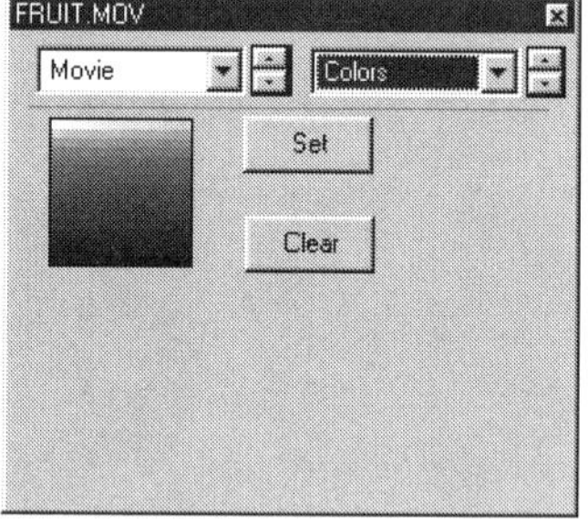

Figure 7.33 The color table is displayed in the window. (Sorry you can't see the colors in this grayscale image.)

Where to get a custom color table

If you have an existing file that has a custom color table, you can attach that table to your movie. Files that may already include a custom color table include graphics files (such as GIFs).

To define a custom color table for your own movie, you need software that can analyze your movie and figure out which 256 colors to use. DeBabelizer and Media Cleaner Pro are examples of commercial products that can create custom color tables for QuickTime movies.

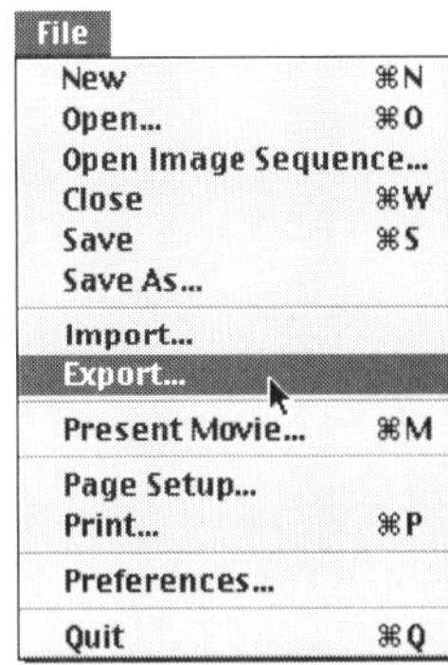

Figure 7.34 To create a still image from the current image in the movie window, choose Export from the File menu.

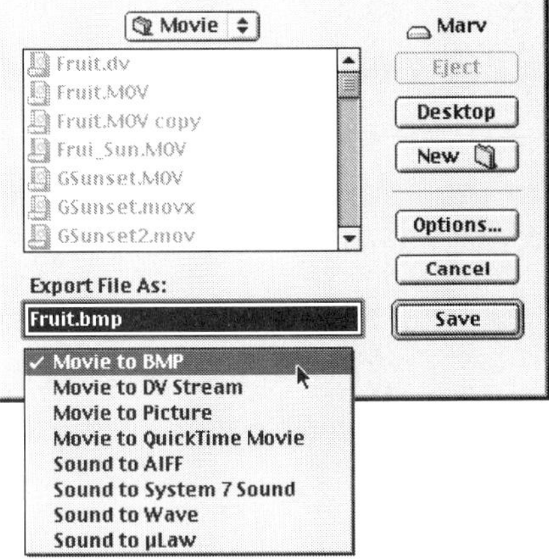

Figure 7.35 Then choose either Movie to BMP or Movie to Picture, depending on whether you want a BMP or PICT file.

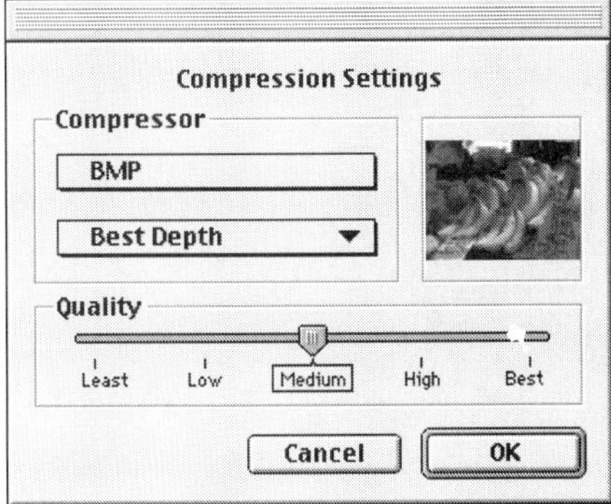

Figure 7.36 If you click the Options button, a dialog box in which you can choose compression settings appears. We'll look at compression settings in the next chapter.

Creating a still image file from any image in a movie

Whenever you have a movie window with a visual element, you can create a still image file of what appears in that window in the BMP or PICT formats.

To export an image as a PICT or BMP

1. Move the slider until the image you want to use is on your screen.
2. Choose **Export** from the File menu (**Figure 7.34**).
3. In the pop-up menu at the bottom of the window, choose either **Movie to Picture** (for a PICT file) or **Movie to BMP** (**Figure 7.35**).
4. Click **Save**.

   You can click the **Options** button before clicking **Save** to open a Compression Settings dialog box (**Figure 7.36**) where you can choose compression settings for the image. (Please see Chapter 8 for a discussion of compression settings.) In general, however, the default settings are fine.

   Regardless of whether you switch compression settings or not, the image is compressed when it is saved. In general, any system on which you want to open the image must have QuickTime installed in order to decompress the image. (BMP files, however, will open on any Windows machine, even without QuickTime installed; there are also several Mac OS apps which will read BMPs without QuickTime.)

   The exported image contains everything that is visible in the current frame, even if the image is composed of data from multiple tracks.

✔ Tip

- Recall from Chapter 5 that you can always copy from the MoviePlayer window and paste into a graphics application; use this technique if you need a still image in a format other than BMP or PICT. However, exporting has the advantage that you get a file without requiring some other application.

8

VIDEO AND MPEG TRACKS

Video tracks are the most commonly seen type of track in QuickTime movies and are what most people associate with QuickTime.

Since video tracks are almost always compressed, in this chapter we'll first provide some background information about video compression. We'll then look at the Compression Settings dialog box, which comes up in a few places in this chapter as well as in some later chapters concerning movie delivery.

Many video tracks are created by capturing video from a camcorder or VCR into a QuickTime file. MoviePlayer doesn't have capture functions, so we won't cover that here. However, you can use MoviePlayer to create video tracks when you have existing still image, video, or animation files, so we will cover those techniques.

For Mac users, we'll also go over how you can create a QuickTime file from an MPEG movie file, in which case an MPEG track rather than a video track is created.

In this chapter we'll cover only those aspects of QuickTime and MoviePlayer that apply to video and MPEG tracks and not to any other track types. To learn about additional techniques for manipulating video and MPEG tracks, make sure to read Chapter 7, *Working with Visual Tracks.*

Understanding video compression

What is compression? Essentially, compression is a method of cheating: Though viewers may see what looks like many megabytes of information per second, the data that has actually been stored and is being seen is much smaller, thanks to various techniques for reducing the amount of data necessary to display images and for efficiently representing that information.

Compression is crucial to the video track, particularly for movies with a high frame rate. An individual full-screen image is about 1 MB in size, which means that full-screen video at 30 frames per second—what you're used to seeing on television—would contain close to 30 MB of information per second of video. (We could also say that it has a *data rate* of 30 MB per second.) You wouldn't want to store more than a few seconds of data at that size. Besides, unless you had special hardware, your computer couldn't move that much data to your screen quickly enough. And it's way too much to move over modems, which have speeds of far less than 1 MB per second. Even if you use only a portion of the screen and lower the frame rate, as with many QuickTime movies, without compression it's still too much information.

Thus, just about all QuickTime video tracks are compressed in some way. QuickTime gives you access to a wide variety of compressors, each of which works slightly differently and is appropriate for different types of media. (Many compressors come with QuickTime; see Table 8.1 for a list. You can also obtain additional compressors; we'll talk about some of these in Chapters 15 and 17.)

There are two basic ways that compressors do their jobs. They do *spatial compression* and *temporal compression*.

Table 8.1

Video Compressors Included with QuickTime 3

Compressor Name	Comments
Animation	Works best on computer-generated animations with broad areas of flat color. Doesn't work well when the scene has lots of color changes.
BMP	Used for still images when exporting in the BMP format. Does minimal compression. Inappropriate for video-based movie playback.
Cinepak	Commonly used for video movies that require CD-ROM playback. Compresses very slowly.
Component Video	A high-quality compressor. Good for capture on AV Macs and as an intermediate storage format. Low compression ratios (larger files).
DV-NTSC, DV-PAL	Used with Digital Video cameras.
Graphics	Good for 8-bit graphics files. Usually better than the Animation compressor in 8-bits. Slower to decompress than Animation.
H.263	Designed originally for video conferencing. Very high compression ratios. Only works at window sizes of 352x288, 176x144, or 128x96.
Intel Indeo Video Interactive	Very high image quality. Requires a Pentium for compression and decompression. No Mac OS version.
Motion JPEG A, Motion JPEG B	Used to decompress files made with certain hardware Motion-JPEG cards when the card isn't available, or to compress in a format that can be played by certain hardware Motion-JPEG cards.
None	Good for capture only. Does almost no compression.
Photo JPEG	Ideal for high-quality compressed still images. Also useful as an intermediate storage format for movies and for QuickTime VR panoramas. Decompresses too slowly for video-based playback.
Planar RGB	For importing images with an alpha channel (Photoshop stores it's files in a format which requires the use of this code to be imported properly).
Sorenson Video	Very high compression ratios and high quality. Excellent for Web and CD-ROM. On Mac OS computers, requires a PowerPC processor for compression.
Video	Very fast video compression and decompression. Decent compression ratios. Good for real-time capture of video, particularly when hard disk space is at a premium. Good for testing clips. OK for hard-disk playback. Image quality is poor when compressing enough for CD-ROM playback.

When a compressor does spatial compression, it essentially throws out redundant data from individual frames.

When a compressor does temporal compression, it throws out information that is repeated from one frame to the next. It saves a single frame in its entirety, but for subsequent frames, it saves only the parts of the picture that have changed. The first frame is called a *key frame*; and the subsequent frames are referred to as *difference frames*.

Since you generally won't use MoviePlayer to apply compression to your movies until it's time to distribute them, we won't go into the details of the process until Chapter 13. There will be a few places in this chapter, however, where you'll have to make some compression choices, so it's a good idea to have a sense of what compression is.

✔ Tip

- Compressors are also called *codecs*, for *compressors-decompressors*; if a file has been compressed, a decompressor is necessary during playback.

The Compression Settings dialog box

There's an important dialog box—the Compression Settings dialog box (**Figure 8.1**)—that you may see when working with video tracks in MoviePlayer, so let's preview it now.

The area in the top right of the dialog box shows a sample frame from the movie. As you make changes in the dialog box, the sample frame reflects the effects of those changes. You can zoom in on the image by holding down the Option key (Mac OS) or Ctrl and Alt keys (Windows) and clicking. You can zoom out by adding the Shift key to the key or keys you hold down for zooming in. You can click and drag in the image to move it around when it is zoomed in.

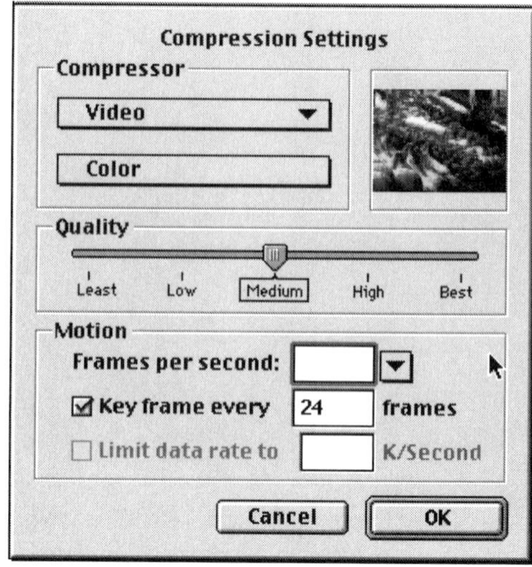

Figure 8.1 The Compression Settings dialog box is used frequently in MoviePlayer and other QuickTime applications to choose compression settings for video tracks.

You can use the top pop-up menu in the Compression Settings dialog box (**Figure 8.2**) to choose a particular compressor (codec); all built-in compressors as well as any added compressors appear in this list.

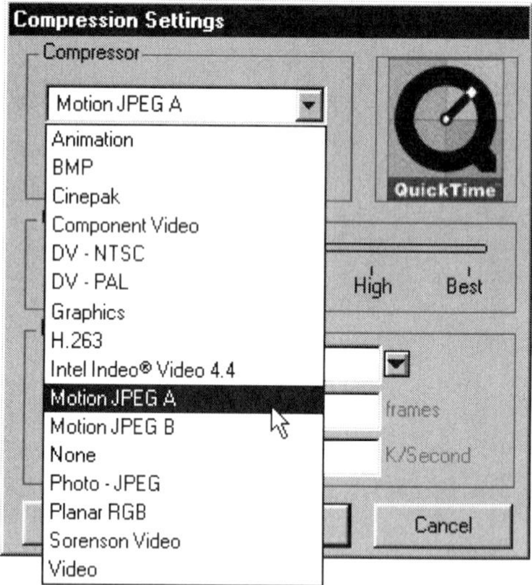

Figure 8.2 You can choose any of the compressors available to QuickTime.

Depending on the compressor selected, you can use the pop-up menu below that to choose how many different colors should be used to represent the image. (For some compressors you aren't given a choice.)

You can use the slider in the area in the middle of the dialog box (labeled "Quality") to indicate the image quality you'd like. While your first instinct might be to always choose the highest quality, you should be aware that higher quality means less compression and therefore larger files and higher data rates.

The bottom area of the window (labeled "Motion") enables you to choose settings that impact how smoothly the movie plays. You can specify frame rate, key frame rate, and, for some compressors, data rate. We'll make suggestions on specific settings for each

Figure 8.3 For some compressors, you'll see an Options button at the bottom of the window that provides access to additional settings and information.

of these in the specific situations we describe in this chapter and later chapters.

In some cases, depending on the compressor you've chosen, you may see an Options button in the bottom left of the window (**Figure 8.3**). Click this button to view information or set additional options specific to the compressor.

✔ Tip

- The Compression Settings dialog is part of QuickTime itself, so many other applications use it, too. Thus, what we've covered here will apply to other tools and situations.

Determining how a video track was compressed

Now that you know that video tracks can be compressed with different compressors, you may be interested in knowing how a particular video track was compressed. (In rare cases, when a video track has been compressed with a codec not included with QuickTime, the movie will open but show no image. An error message appears stating that "the required compressor can not be found". You can check to see the name of the compressor used,though it won't necessarily tell you where to find the appropriate codec.).

To determine how a video track was compressed

1. Choose Get Info from the Movie menu (**Figure 8.4**).
2. In the Info window, choose the video track in the left pop-up menu and choose Format in the right pop-up menu.

   The third line in the Format panel (**Figure 8.5**) shows the number of colors in the image.

   The fourth line, the one labeled "Data Format," generally tells you how the track was compressed.

   In some cases, such as when the track is created by importing a still image and is not compressed using a QuickTime codec, the Data Format instead lists the file format, such as GIF or TIFF.

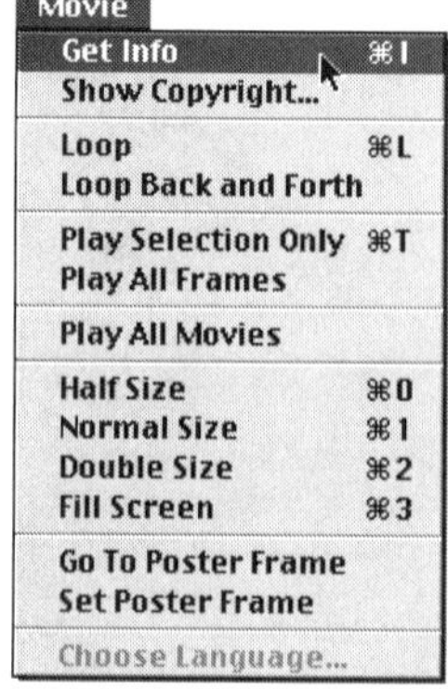

Figure 8.4 Choose Get Info from the Movie menu to open the Info window for the movie.

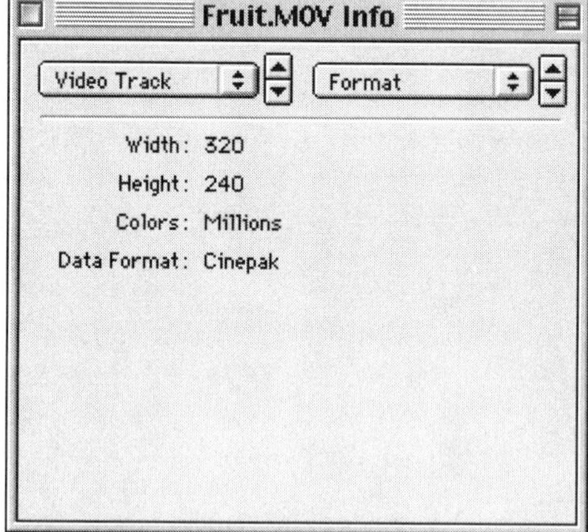

Figure 8.5 Colors tells you the number of colors used in the image. Data Format indicates how the movie was compressed (if it was compressed).

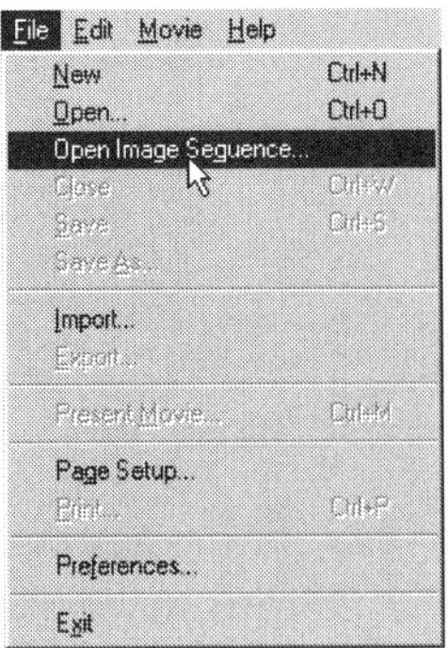

Figure 8.6 When you have a numbered sequence of images that you want to turn into a QuickTime movie, choose Open Image Sequence from the File menu.

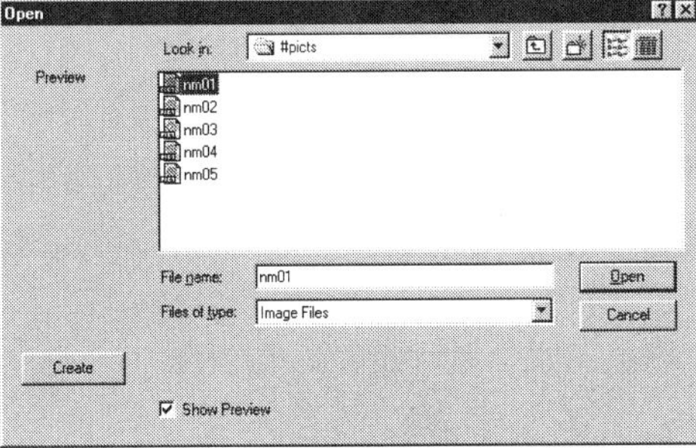

Figure 8.7 Select any of the files in the sequence and click Open.

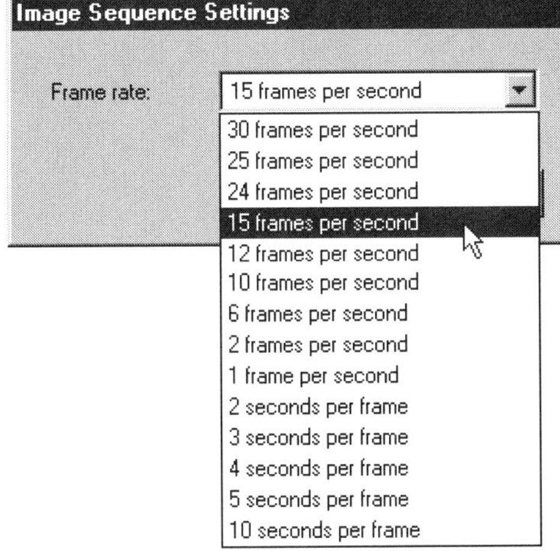

Figure 8.8 Pick a frame rate in the Image Sequence Settings dialog box—choices at the bottom of the list are best for slide shows and choices at the top are best for conveying a sense of motion.

Creating video tracks from a sequence of still images

Since video tracks are normally composed of a sequence of images, it makes sense that you can create one by putting together a bunch of still images. You might want to do this if you have a bunch of images you want in a slide show. Or you might have animation program that doesn't support QuickTime, but that will export an animation as a sequence of still images.

To create a video track from a sequence of still images

1. Name the still image files so that they have a common name with sequential numbers appended to this name (e.g. picture1, picture2, picture3, etc.). Put them all in the same folder.
2. Choose Open Image Sequence from the File menu (**Figure 8.6**).
3. In the Open dialog box, locate and select any of the files that have been sequentially named and click Open (**Figure 8.7**).
4. In the Image Sequence Settings dialog box that appears, specify a frame rate for the movie. You have a large number of choices, as shown in **Figure 8.8**. In general, a frame rate of less than two seconds per frame is best if you want a slide-show effect; a frame rate of at least six frames per second is usually necessary for conveying a sense of motion.
5. Click OK.

   A new movie window appears. The movie contains the images you numbered sequentially, and plays at the frame rate you specified.

Creating a video track from a single still image

You can also create a single-frame video track from a single still image; you might want to do this if you want to merge the still image with other QuickTime tracks. It's also useful for creating a poster movie to be used on the Web, as we'll discuss in Chapter 15.

The procedure you follow to create a video track from a still image varies depending on whether or not the file is a PICT file. (Most still image formats can be opened directly, whereas PICT is one of the file formats that must be imported, as described in Chapter 2.)

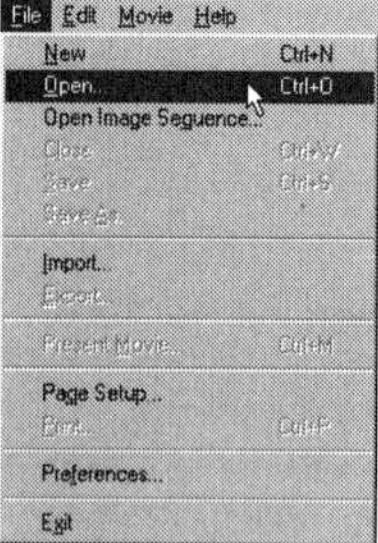

Figure 8.9 You open most still image files as you would any QuickTime movie.

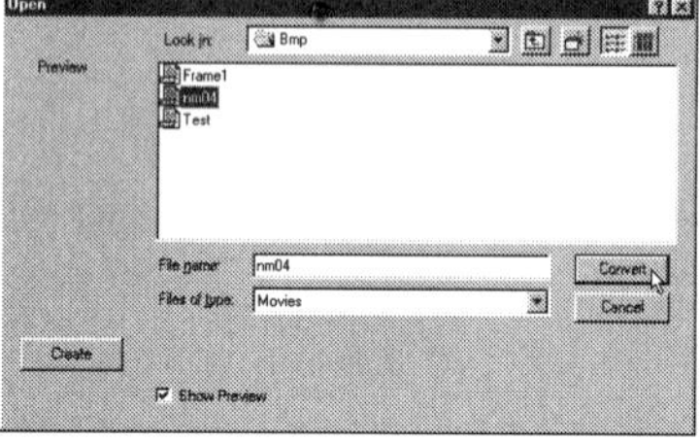

Figure 8.10 The only difference is that there's a Convert button rather than an Open button.

To create a video track from a single still image in any format but PICT

1. Choose **Open** from the File menu (**Figure 8.9**).
2. In the Open dialog box, locate the still image file and click the **Convert** button (**Figure 8.10**).

   The image that you selected appears in a new movie window (**Figure 8.11**). The title of the window is the same as the name of the file you opened.

   If you click the Play button, the slider will move to the end of the play bar, but the image won't change; the movie is a single frame that has a duration of 2/30ths of a second (indicated as 00:00:00.02 in the Time panel of the Info window; see **Figure 8.12**).

   The data in this movie can be copied and pasted or added to other QuickTime movies. However, you have not actually created a QuickTime movie *file* until you save. If you quit MoviePlayer without saving, the file remains in its original still image format.

Figure 8.11 The image opens in a movie window.

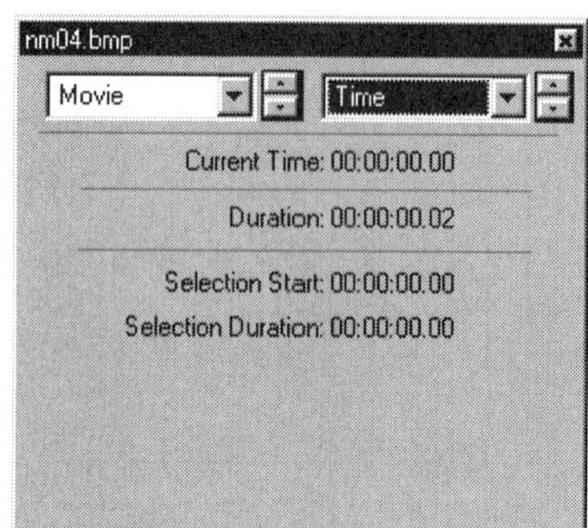

Figure 8.12 You get a very short movie; its duration is 2/30ths of a second.

Figure 8.13 For PICT files, choose Import rather than Open.

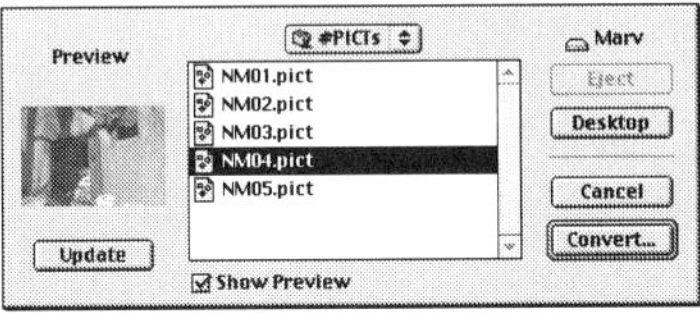

Figure 8.14 When you click on a PICT file, the Open button changes to a Convert button. (The ellipses indicate that there will be another step.)

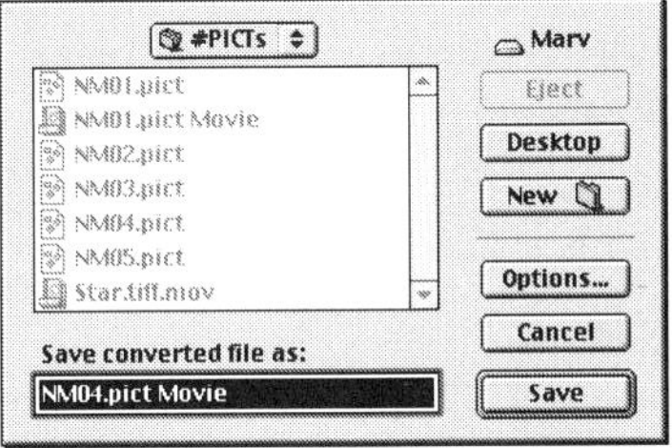

Figure 8.15 The next step is to save the file.

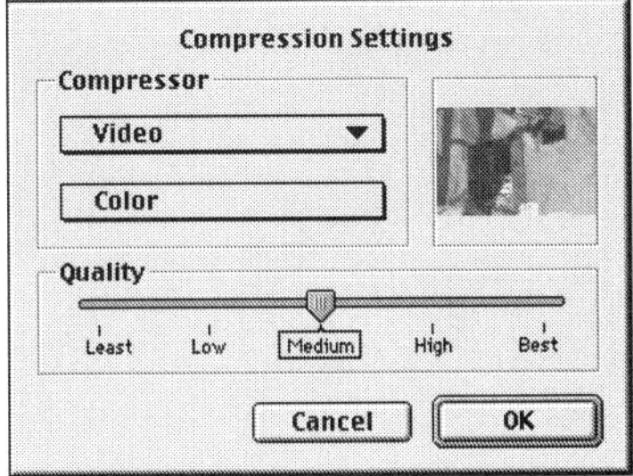

Figure 8.16 If you click the Options button in the Save dialog box before saving, you can alter the compression settings of the single-frame movie that will be created.

To create a video track from a single PICT file

1. Choose **Import** from the File menu (**Figure 8.13**).
2. In the Open dialog box, locate the PICT file and click the **Convert** button (**Figure 8.14**).

   A Save dialog box appears (**Figure 8.15**), since you need to create a new file.
3. If you know specific compression settings you want to apply to this image, click the **Options** button. You'll get a Compression Settings dialog box without the motion settings area; see **Figure 8.16**. However, we recommend leaving the default settings because they generally work fine.
4. If desired, change the name and location for the file to be created.
5. Click **Save**.

   A new window opens, containing a movie consisting of a single frame with a duration of 2/30ths of a second.

   Since a new file has been created, you don't need to save this movie unless you alter it.

Creating video tracks from non-QuickTime animation and video files

As with still image files, the file format of a time-based file dictates the process you follow to create a video track from the file. You can directly open Animated GIF files (a standard animation format on the Web) and FLI/FLC files (the standard Windows animation format). You can also directly open AVI files (the format for Microsoft's Video for Windows) and DV files (the new digital video standard). However, you must import PICS animations (the standard Mac format), converting and saving the file before it can be viewed.

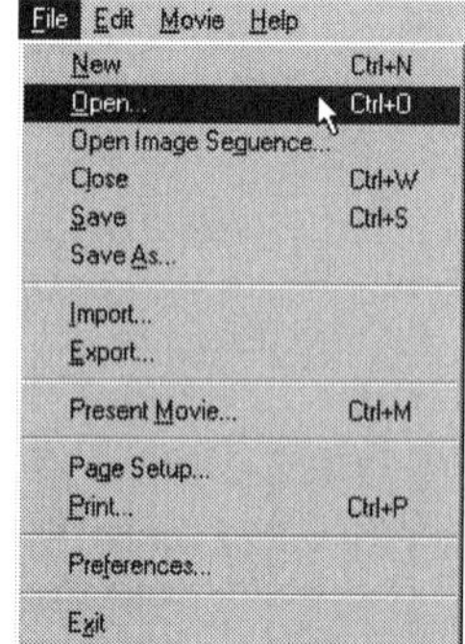

Figure 8.17 You open Animated GIF, FLI/FLC, AVI, and DV files just like any QuickTime file.

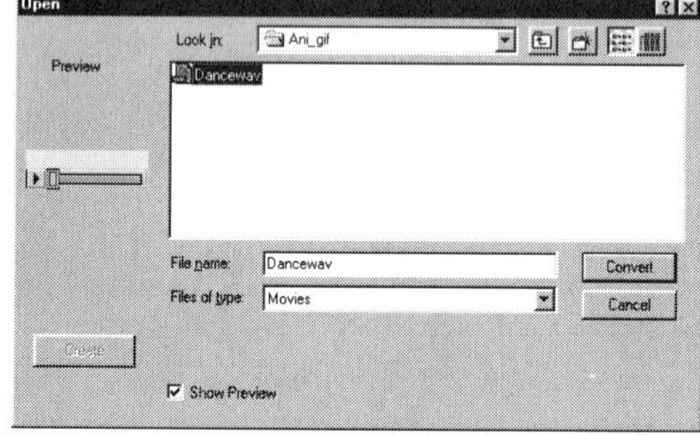

Figure 8.18 When you click on one of these files, the Open button changes to a Convert button.

To create a video track from an Animated GIF, FLI/FLC, AVI, or DV file

1. Choose **Open** from the File menu (**Figure 8.17**).
2. In the Open dialog box, locate the animation or video file and click the **Convert** button (**Figure 8.18**).

   A new movie window appears with a title the same as the name of the file you selected.

   When played, the animation or video should behave as it did in its original format.

   The data in this movie can be copied and pasted or added to other QuickTime movies. However, you have not actually created a QuickTime movie *file* until you save. If you quit MoviePlayer without saving, the file remains in its original format.

Problems with AVI files

Just as QuickTime files can be compressed with a variety of compressors, so can AVI files. Sometimes when you try to open an .avi file you'll get an error message saying "You may experience problems playing a video track in 'yourmovie.avi' because the required compressor could not be found." This is because the file was compressed using a codec that's not currently available in QuickTime.

Figure 8.19 Choose Import when you have a PICS animation file that you want to turn into a QuickTime movie.

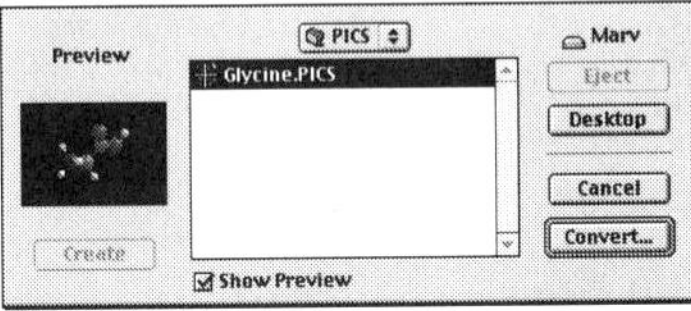

Figure 8.20 When you click on a PICS file, the Open button changes to a Convert button. (The ellipses indicate that there will another step.)

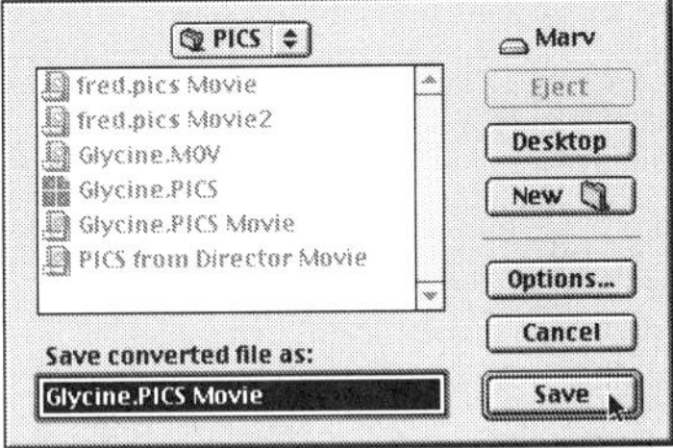

Figure 8.21 The next step is to save the file.

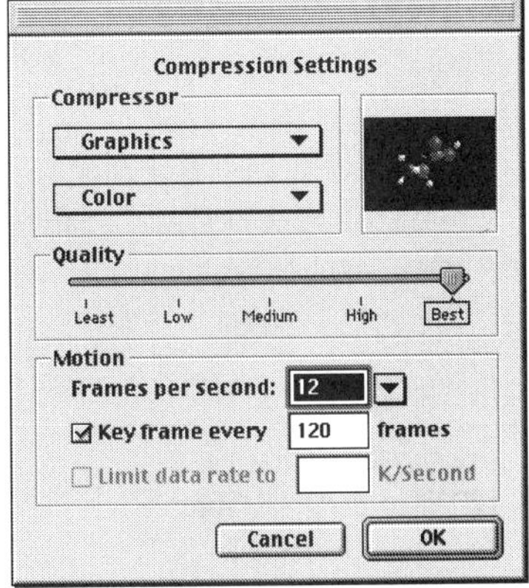

Figure 8.22 If you click the Options button before saving the file, you'll get a standard Compression Settings dialog in which you can specify compression settings.

To create a video track from a PICS animation file

1. Choose **Import** from the File menu (**Figure 8.19**).
2. In the Open dialog box, locate the PICS file and click **Convert** (**Figure 8.20**).
3. A Save dialog box appears in which you can click **Save** to create a new QuickTime file (**Figure 8.21**).

   If you wish to specify compression settings, click the **Options** button to open the Compression Settings dialog box (**Figure 8.22**) before clicking the **Save** button.

✔ Tip

- If you have problems creating QuickTime movies from PICS files on a Windows computer, we recommend doing it on a Mac OS computer and then copying the resulting QuickTime movies to a Windows computer.

Adding images to an existing movie

Just as you can use the Paste command to insert a graphic from another application into a movie (as described in Chapter 5), you can also use the Add or Add Scaled commands (as described in Chapter 6) to add a copied graphic so that it is layered over other visual tracks.

A common reason to do this is to add some kind of visual element, such as a logo, to a corner of the movie window, as you see on many programs on television.

Adding a graphic is a way to create a new video track. (Contrast this with pasting, in which case the graphic is appended to the existing video track. No new video track is created.)

To add a small graphic from another application to a movie

1. Select and copy the image from the graphics application.
2. In MoviePlayer, with the movie to which you want to add the graphic open, choose Select All from the Edit menu, or select the portion of the movie to which you want to add the graphic.
3. Hold down the Shift and Option keys (Mac) or Shift, Ctrl, and Alt keys (Windows) and choose Add Scaled from the Edit menu (**Figure 8.23**).

   When you play the movie, the graphic appears during the part of the movie you selected.

   The movie now contains an additional video track; you can verify this in the Info window (**Figure 8.24**).

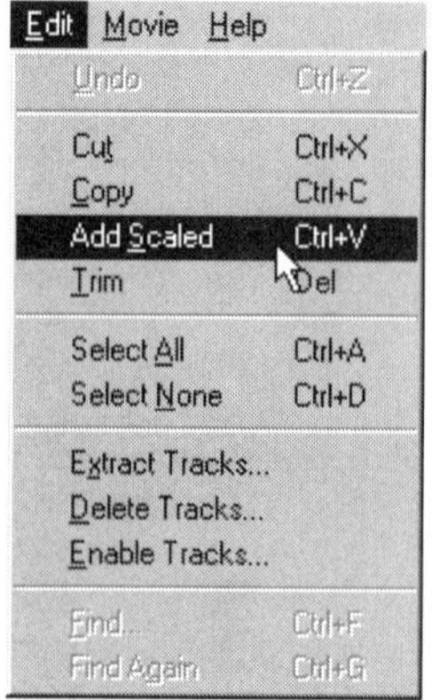

Figure 8.23 Choose Add Scaled to add a graphic so it appears for the duration of the selection. You'll need to hold down the Shift and Option keys (Mac) or Shift, Ctrl, and Alt keys (Windows) to get this choice.

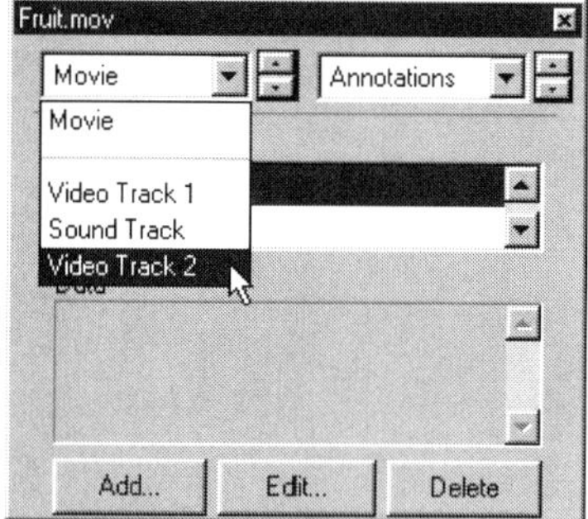

Figure 8.24 You can see in the Info window that an additional video track has been added.

✔ Tip (Mac only)

- If you hold down the Control key when you're adding data, a Compression Settings dialog appears so you can specify the compressor, number of colors, and quality for the new track. Otherwise, defaults are chosen depending on the format of the image.

Graphic too large or in the wrong place?

Use the Size panel in the Info window, as described in Chapter 7, to move the graphic to the correct location or to resize it.

Figure 8.25 You can open an MPEG file in MoviePlayer using the Open command.

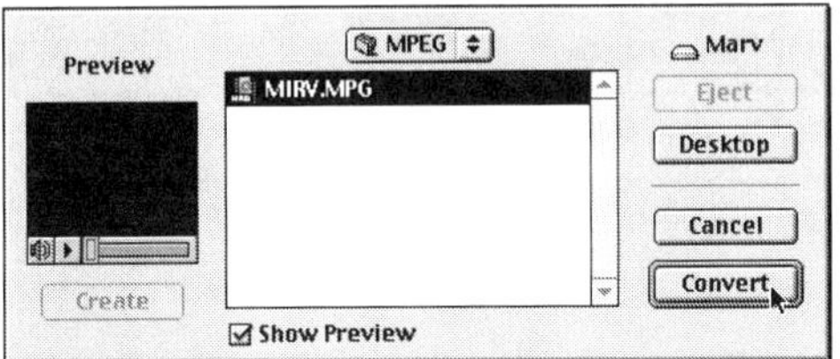

Figure 8.26 When you select an MPEG file, the Open button changes to a Convert button. Click it to open the file.

Seeing black lines?

Normally, when you double the window size for an MPEG movie, the pixels are doubled horizontally but not vertically. Instead, black lines are added for every other line of pixels. Since the computer doesn't have to display every other horizontal line, it performs better, allowing the movie to play back more smoothly. MoviePlayer allows you to specify not to use this black-lining technique, but rather to double the pixels both horizontally and vertically. To do this, use the Info window, choosing the MPEG track in the left pop-up menu and **High Quality** in the right pop-up menu. Then select the **High Quality Enabled** checkbox. (Note that there's a High Quality option available for other tracks as well, but most of these do not produce obvious results. One exception is the text track; see Chapter 9.)

Creating MPEG tracks from MPEG files (Mac only)

MPEG (which stands for Motion Picture Experts Group) is a commonly used video and audio standard. Apple's QuickTime MPEG extension allows the import of MPEG-1 (the most common MPEG format) data into a QuickTime movie. Rather than going into a standard video track, the data goes into a special MPEG track that contains both audio and video.

Once it's in a QuickTime track, MPEG data can be played back and edited like any other QuickTime data type. It can also be combined with other track types.

Unlike other QuickTime track types, however, when you copy and paste selected portions of an MPEG track, the data from the entire track comes along; the data you didn't explicitly copy doesn't play, but it's still in the file. In the same way, when you delete data from an MPEG track, the data doesn't really go away—it's just not played. Thus, files with edited MPEG tracks can be much larger than you might think from viewing the movie.

Currently, the MPEG extension to QuickTime works only on Mac OS-based computers with PowerPC microprocessors, but Apple has plans to release a Windows version; by the time you read this it may be available. It is also likely that they'll release a new version that works with other formats of MPEG.

To create an MPEG track from an MPEG file

1. Choose **Open** from the File menu (**Figure 8.25**).
2. Locate the MPEG file you would like to open, and click **Convert** (**Figure 8.26**).

   The file is opened like any other QuickTime movie. When you check the movie composition in the Info window, however, you'll see that there is a single MPEG track (**Figure 8.27**).

✔ Notes

- MPEG audio tracks are a different matter. We'll cover these in Chapter 12.
- Tracks on a Video CD (a format designed to play on CD-i players that never really made it) are actually MPEG-1 tracks and thus can be opened by MoviePlayer. On the Video CD the files have a table of contents that can be used to jump to specific predesignated points in the video. When opened in MoviePlayer, the entries in the table of contents show as a chapter list (see *Using Chapter Lists* in Chapter 3.)

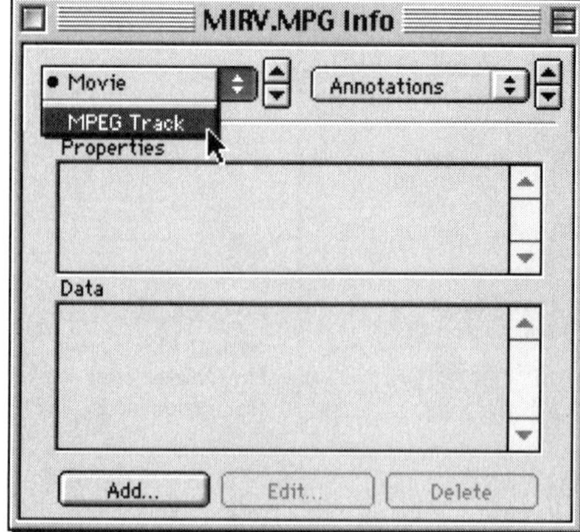

Figure 8.27 When you open an MPEG file in MoviePlayer, you create a single MPEG track, even if the file also contains audio.

Text Tracks

Of all the QuickTime track types, text tracks are perhaps the least used, yet they have tremendous potential. Not only do they allow you to caption a movie, but because they are searchable they add a level of interactivity to movies.

Text tracks are easy to create from scratch, requiring no special tools other than a simple text processor or word processor (in conjunction with MoviePlayer).

In this chapter, we'll show you how to create text tracks and how to alter their appearance and behavior. Once you have a text track you can combine it with other tracks as described in Chapter 6; you can also change its position and appearance as described in Chapter 7.

Creating a text track by importing a text file

It's a simple matter to create a text track, as long as you have a text or word processor.

To create a text track from a text file

1. In a text or word processor, type the text that you'd like to have in a text track, with Return characters separating material that you'd like to see in different frames (**Figure 9.1**). Save this file as text only.
2. In MoviePlayer, choose Import from the File menu (**Figure 9.2**).
3. Locate and select the text file you created, and click the Convert button.
4. In the Save dialog box that appears, provide a name for the file, navigate to the location where you'd like it saved, and click Save.

   A new window appears, containing a text track with your text in it (**Figure 9.3**).

   The resulting track has centered, white text on a black background; each line of text in the file is a frame with a duration of two seconds. (On subsequent pages we'll show you how to change these defaults.)

✔ Tip

- We have seen random text characters in the text track when we've imported text files on the Windows platform. When this happens, we generally have luck getting a "clean" text track if we retype the text, including return characters, and import again.

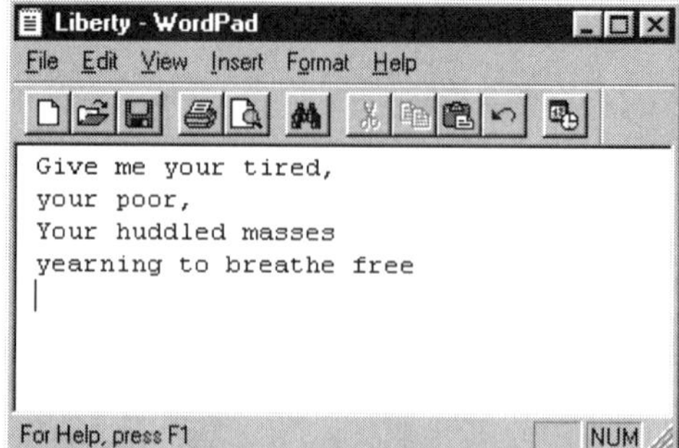

Figure 9.1 Type return-separated text in your word or text processor.

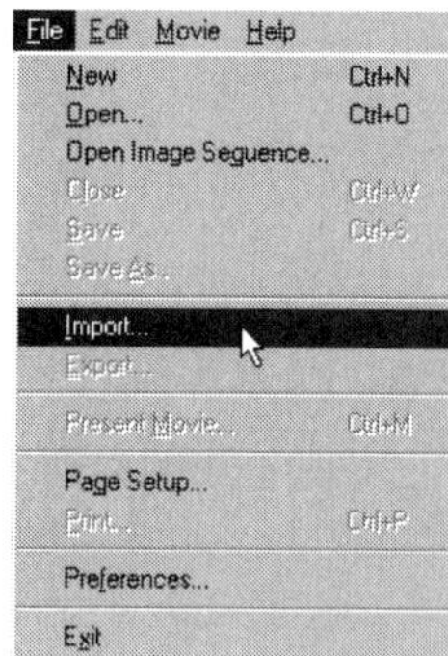

Figure 9.2 Use MoviePlayer's Import command to import the text file.

Figure 9.3 The resulting track is centered white text on a black background. Each line of text is a different frame.

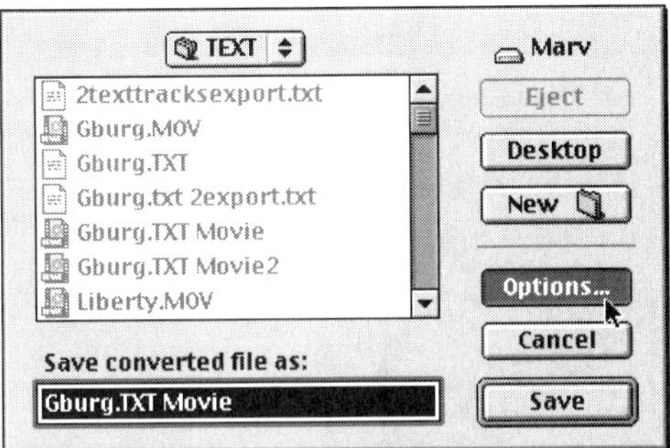

Figure 9.4 Click the Options button in the Save dialog box to change text settings.

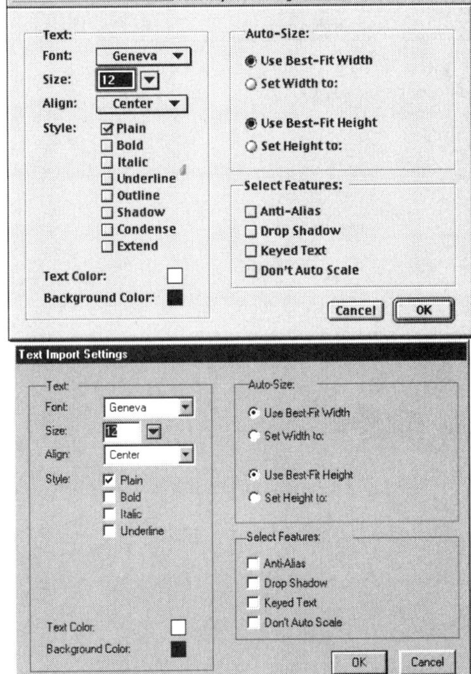

Figure 9.5 The Text Import Settings dialog box—which is slightly different for the Mac OS (top) and Windows— lets you change a number of properties.

Specifying text track appearance when you import

When you import your text, you can specify such characteristics as the text's font, size, and color, as well as the track's width and height.

To change text features

1. Import the text as described on the previous page, but before clicking the Save button, click the Options button (**Figure 9.4**).

   The Text Import Settings dialog box appears (**Figure 9.5**).

2. Make your changes:

   Use the Font, Size, and Align pop-up menus and the Style options to change basic text properties.

   To select a text color or a background color for the text track, click the square next to Text Color or Background Color and use the dialog box that appears. (Click OK to return to the Text Import Settings dialog box.)

   Select Use Best-Fit Width and Use Best-Fit Height or enter your own values for width and/or height. Best-fit width and height result in a movie that is 160 pixels wide-and tall enough to fit the longest line of text being imported.

   Select Anti-Alias to fuzz the edges of the characters. (This makes them look smoother when they're displayed in a large font size.)

   Select Drop Shadow to place a drop shadow behind the text.

   Select Keyed Text to specify a transparent background.

   Select Don't Auto-Scale if you want the text to remain the size you defined even if the movie window is resized.

3. Click **OK** to close the Text Import Settings dialog box and return to the Save dialog box, where you can click **Save** to create your new text track movie (**Figure 9.6**).

✔ Warning

- Anti-aliased, drop-shadowed, and keyed text can look quite nice when the text is placed over a video track. However, these features require a lot of computing power to work, which will result in poor performance on all but the fastest computers.

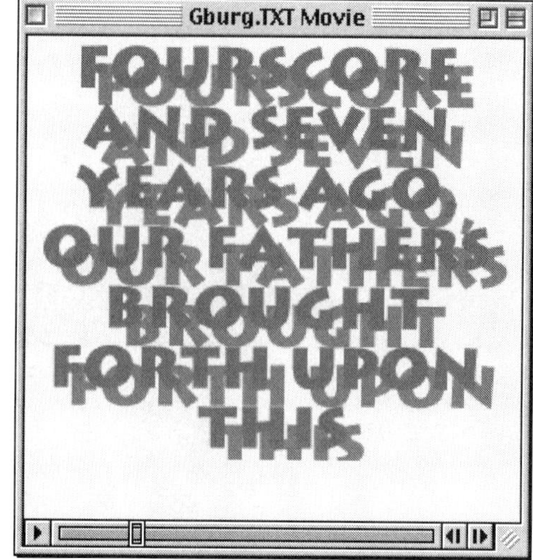

Figure 9.6 The resulting text track can be quite different than the default.

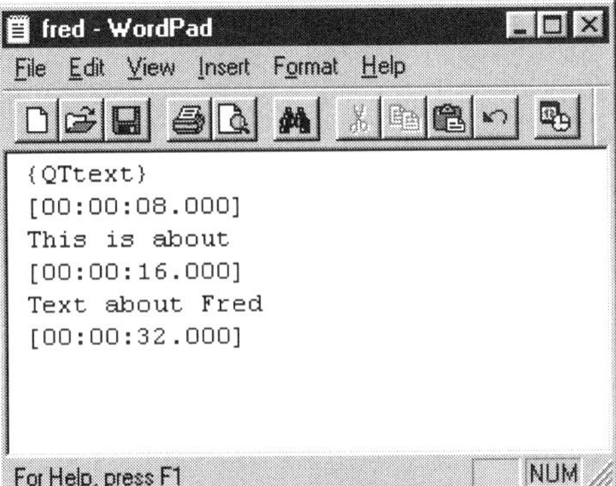

Figure 9.7 Here's a file that can be imported into MoviePlayer.

Alternative ways to specify time stamps

You can, if it works better for you, type time stamps after each line of text that indicate how long the frame should stay on the screen, rather than when the frame should end. You'll need to put {timestamps:relative} before any time stamps, and put [00:00:00.000] before the first line of text, too.

You can also specify time stamps with a final number that is a fraction of a second other than 1/600ths, using a special timescale tag. For example, if you put {timescale: 30} at the top of the file, the final number will be read as 1/30ths of a second.

Specifying the duration and appearance of individual frames of text

By adding some commands to a text file *before* you import, you gain control over how long the text appears and how it looks *in each frame*. **Figure 9.7** shows an example text file containing such commands.

To create a text track in which the duration and appearance of individual frames are specified

1. Open a text or word processor, and on the first line of your text file, enter {QTtext}.

   This signifies that the file is one which will contain special commands to process when imported, rather than just straight text.

2. Type your text, adding additional time stamps and text descriptors as described below.

3. Save and import the file into MoviePlayer as described in *Creating a text track by importing a text file*, earlier in this chapter.

To use time stamps to specify a duration for individual frames of text

1. Before each line of text, enter a time stamp value in square brackets (e.g. [00:00:08.000]), indicating when the frame containing that line of text should appear. (You can put the time stamp immediately preceding the text, but for readability we suggest you put it on a separate line.)

   Time stamps are specified as hours: minutes:seconds.1/600ths of a second.

2. After the last line of text type a final time stamp followed by a return. (Note that this last time stamp not only designates

when the last frame ends, but also the duration of the text track movie which will be created when this file is imported).

To use text descriptors to specify the appearance of the text in individual frames

- Before individual lines (either in a line of its own or on the same line as the text string), add text tags such as **font** and **size**, as in the example file shown in **Figure 9.8**. These are called *text descriptors*. They can also be put at the top of the file, in the same line as the {QTtext} tag. Text descriptors affect all subsequent text in the file up to the point in the file where a new value for that descriptor is specified. See **Table 9.1** for some other tags you can use.

✔ Tip

- You'll probably find it easier to create a file like this if you follow the steps in the next task.

✔ Warnings

- Be careful to use valid and logical time stamps and descriptors in your file, or MoviePlayer won't be able to import it. (An example of a bad time stamp is one that's formatted incorrectly, or one that specifies a time earlier than a previous time stamp. An example of a bad text descriptor is one that's mispelled or that has an inappropriate value.)
- There's a bug in the release of QuickTime that's available as we write this; some text descriptors don't work unless there is at least one additional command in the first line after {QTtext}; this command can be anything as long as it is enclosed in curly brackets. This bug may be fixed by the time you read this, however.

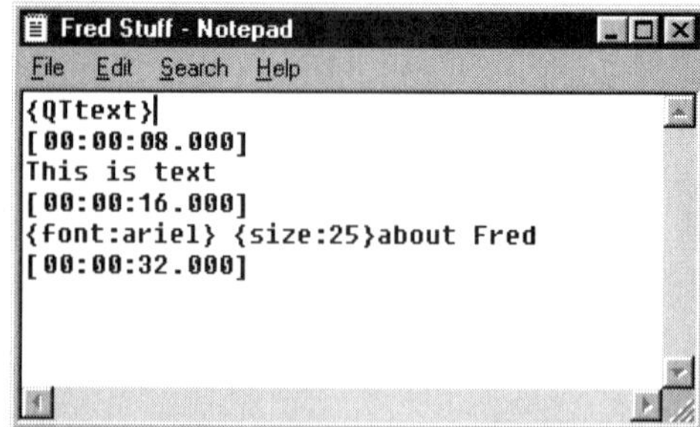

Figure 9.8 This file will change the font and size of the last line.

Table 9.1

Some Text Descriptors That Can Be Used for Individual Lines of Text

Descriptor	Possible Values	Examples
{font: fontname}	Any fontname	{font: Courier}, {font: Ariel}
{fontstyle}	plain, bold, italic, underline	{italic}
{size: pointsize}	Numbers representing the font size	{size: 14}
{justify: alignment}	left, right, center	{justify: right}
{textColor: redvalue, greenvalue, bluevalue}	Numbers between 0 and 65535, representing how much of each color should be used.	{textColor: 0,65535,0} (this value represents pure green)
{backColor: redvalue, greenvalue, bluevalue}	Numbers between 0 and 65535, representing how much of each color should be used.	{backColor: 65535,0,65535} (this value represents magenta)
{scrollIn:onOrOff}	on,off	{scrollIn:on}
{scrollOut:onOrOff}	on,off	{scrollOut:on}

These and additional text descriptors are documented more completely at http://www.apple.com/quicktime/authors/textdesc.html

Figure 9.9 Choose Export from the File menu.

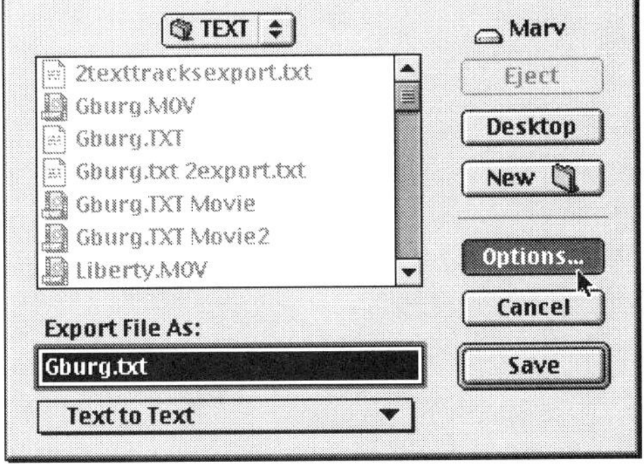

Figure 9.10 Choose Text to Text and click the Options button.

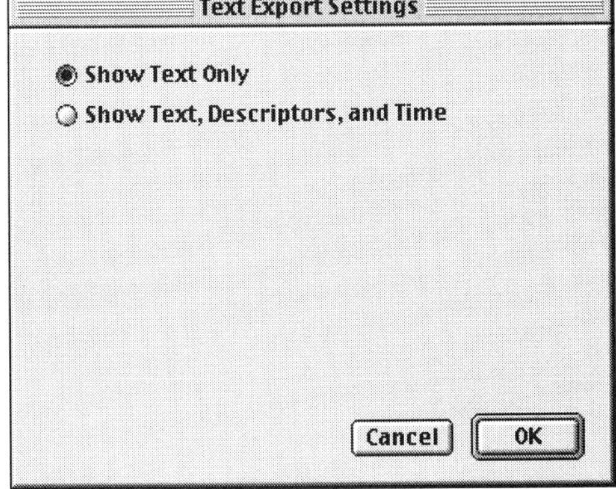

Figure 9.11 A simple Text Export Settings dialog box appears.

Exporting a text track with text descriptors and time stamps

Now that you know how to create a text track with all the extra codes by hand, we'll show you an easier way. This involves exporting a text track in a way that includes the codes so that you can simply edit those codes, rather than typing them all in yourself.

To create a text file with text descriptors and time stamps

1. If your text isn't already in a text track, create a text track by importing a text file as described in *Creating a text track by importing a text file* earlier in this chapter. (Use the Import command in MoviePlayer's File menu.) Don't worry about any timing or styling issues at this point.
2. With the movie containing the text track open, choose Export from the File menu (**Figure 9.9**).
3. Choose Text to Text in the pop-up menu at the bottom of the dialog box and click the Options button (**Figure 9.10**).
4. In the Text Export Settings dialog box (**Figure 9.11**), click the Show Text, Descriptors, and Time button.

   More options appear (**Figure 9.12**).
5. In general, you can leave the options as they are and click OK.

   To match your personal editing preferences, however, you may want to change the time stamps so they are shown relative to the start of the sample; this means that each time stamp indicates the amount of time for which the preceding line of text will appear. If you prefer to view fractions of seconds as something other than the default of 1/600, enter a different number in the field at the bottom. (The reason that the default is 1/600 is that 600 is the smallest number into which 30, 25, and 24 divide evenly. These are the frame rates of the different formats of video and film used today.)

The file created can be opened in a text or word processor, edited as described on the previous pages, and then re-imported. Compared to typing it all yourself, this method saves you time and decreases the likelihood of errors, since you only have to edit specific items, rather than type everything from scratch.

✔ Tip

- You can also export a text track without the text descriptors or time stamps if you need to have a text file with the words from your text track.

Figure 9.12 Click the Show Text, Descriptors, and Time button. Additional options appear. Click OK. The file can then be edited and re-imported.

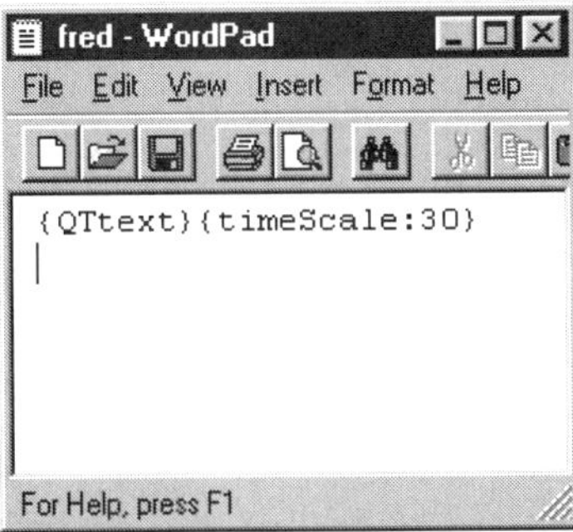

Figure 9.13 Start your file by entering this line of text.

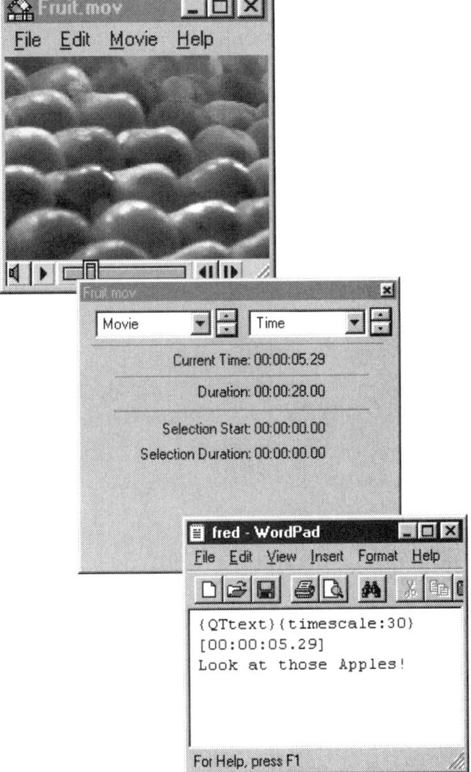

Figure 9.14 In the text file, type the current time (listed in the Info window) and then, on the next line, type the text that you want to appear at that time.

Creating a text track that's synched to other tracks

If you have a large amount of text to add to a movie, and it needs to appear at precise times in the movie, you may find the following technique to be an efficient way to make sure that you create a properly-timed text track, which, when added to the movie, shows the right text at the right time.

To create a text track that's synched to other tracks

1. With the movie to which you want to add text open, choose Get Info from the Movie menu to open the Info window and choose Time in the right pop-up menu. (The left pop-up should have Movie chosen.)
2. Open your word processor and set up your screen so you can see the movie, the Info window, and the word-processing window all at the same time.
3. Type {QTtext}{timeScale:30} in the first line of the word-processing window (**Figure 9.13**).

   ({timeScale:30} indicates that your values are entered as thirtieths of a second. You'll want to enter values this way, since this is how the Info window shows time, and you'll be copying values from there.)
4. Click on the movie you're indexing, and move the slider to a location where you'd like text to appear.
5. Click in the word-processing window and on the next line, type (in brackets) the current time as it appears in the Info window, a return, and the text that you want to appear at this point in time (**Figure 9.14**).
6. Repeat the two previous steps for each point at which you want to add text. After

the last word, type a return, and enter (in brackets) the value that's listed for Duration in the Info window.

7. Save the text file (as text-only), then import it into MoviePlayer.

8. In the text movie, choose **Select All** and then **Copy** from the Edit menu.

9. In the movie to which you want to add the text, move the slider to the beginning of the movie and then, holding down the **Option** key (Mac OS) or **Ctrl** and **Alt** keys (Windows) choose **Add** from the Edit menu to add the text.

✔ Tip

- If you create a text track in this way and then disable it (as described in Chapter 5), the movie can still be searched. This is a good way to create an index to a movie.

Chapter lists

We briefly covered chapter lists in Chapter 3 (*Using Chapter Lists*). In order to create a chapter list, you must first create a text track appropriately synchronized to the video. However, in order to turn the text track into a chapter list, you'll need a tool other than MoviePlayer. One tool that allows you to do this is Terran's Media Cleaner Pro. There's also a freeware, Mac-only tool called Chapter List Maker (available at http://www.dvision.se/CLM_Download.html).

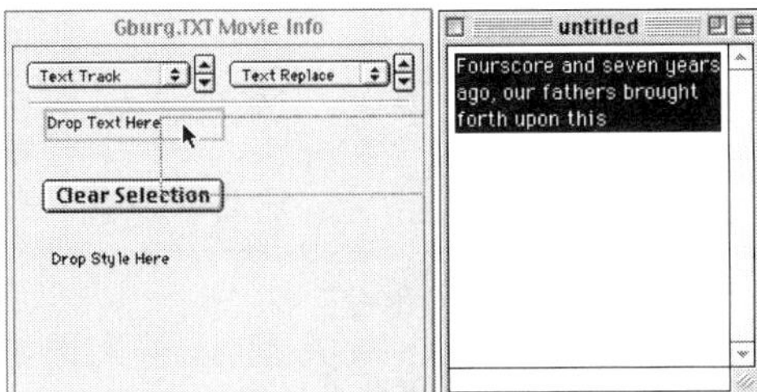

Figure 9.15 To replace words in a text track, drag to the area labeled "Drop Text Here."

Changing text that's already in a text track (Mac OS only)

You can replace selected text that's already in a movie using drag-and-drop editing. You can also change the style of the text.

To replace existing text

1. Select the portion of the movie that has the text you want to replace.
2. In a text editor or word processor, type the text that you want to replace the existing text in your text track. (You must be able to drag and drop text from the text editor or word processor. Apple's SimpleText works.)
3. In the movie's Info window (accessed by choosing **Get Info** from the Movie menu), choose the text track from the left pop-up menu, and choose **Text Replace** from the right pop-up menu.
4. Select and drag the replacement text from the text processor to where the words "Drop Text Here" appear in the Info window, as shown in **Figure 9.15**. (A border appears around the words when your cursor is in the right location to drop the text.)

   The selected text in the movie changes to the text you dropped.

To change the font, size, and style of the text in a text track

1. Select the portion of the movie in which the text to which you want to apply a new font, size, or style is displayed.
2. In a text editor or word processor that enables you to style individual elements of text, type any text and set it to your desired font, size, and style.
3. In the Text Replace panel, select and drag the styled text from the text processor to where the words "Drop Style Here" appear in the Info window (**Figure 9.16**).

   The selected text in the movie changes to match the style of the text you dropped. (The content of the text is unaffected.)

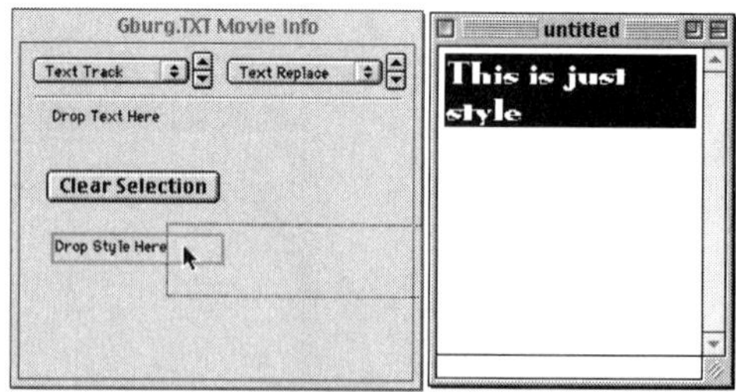

Figure 9.16 To change the font, size, or style of text in a text track, drag any styled text to the area labeled "Drop Style Here."

To delete portions of text from a text track

1. Select the portion of the movie in which the text you want to clear is displayed.
2. In the Text Replace panel in the Info window, click Clear Selection

✔ Warning

- You cannot use the Undo command to undo changes made in the Text Replace panel.

Anti-aliasing text

Normally, text in a text track is not anti-aliased unless this option is chosen when the text is imported (see *Specifying text track appearance when you import* earlier in the chapter). However, there is a panel in the Info window that allows you to switch to anti-aliased text. To do this, use the Info window, choosing the text track in the left pop-up menu and High Quality in the right pop-up menu. Then select the High Quality Enabled checkbox. (Note that there's a High Quality option available for other tracks as well, but most of these do not produce obvious results. One exception is the MPEG track; see Chapter 8.)

Figure 9.17 If you've copied text from a word processor, you can use the Add command to add it to a movie. (You can also use the Add Scaled command.)

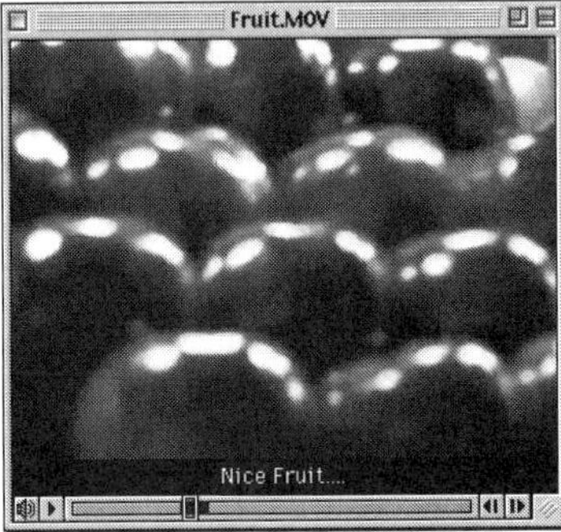

Figure 9.18 The text track is added below the other tracks.

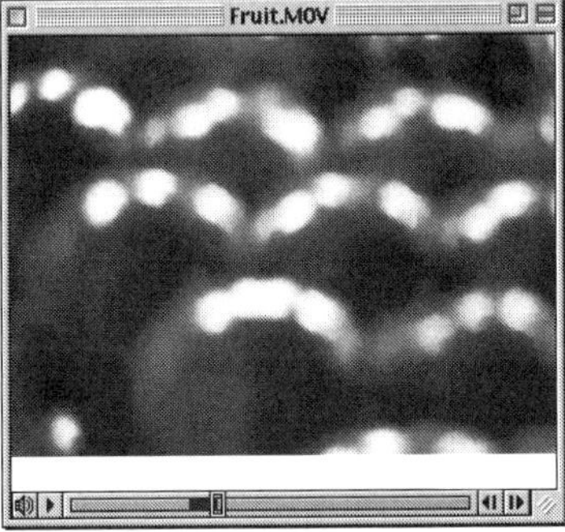

Figure 9.19 During portions of the movie where no text was added, white shows at the bottom of the window.

✔ Tip (Mac OS only)

- If you want to change the text's properties, hold down the Control key while you add the text. The Text Settings dialog box (described in *Specifying text track appearance when you import*) appears so you can specify your choices.

Adding small amounts of text

By far the simplest method of getting small amounts of text into a movie is to add the text directly to the movie where you'd like it to appear. You don't need to first create a separate text track and then add it to the other tracks.

To add small amounts of text to a movie

1. In a text or word processor, type the text you want to add, select it, and copy it.
2. In the movie to which you want to add the text, move the slider to the point where you want the text to first appear.
3. If you want the text to last two seconds, hold down the Option key (Mac OS) or the Ctrl and Alt keys (Windows) and choose Add from the Edit menu (**Figure 9.17**).

   If you want the text to last for a duration other than two seconds, select the duration you'd like in the play bar, and use the Add Scaled command (add the Shift key to the keys used for the Add command).

   A text track is added below the visual data that's already visible in the window; the window is stretched to accommodate it (**Figure 9.18**). However, portions of the movie that don't include text are white in the text track area (**Figure 9.19**). The only way to make that area black is to add empty text for those portions. In general, we recommend adding text this way only if you will add text for the duration of the movie or if the text track will be disabled. Note also that each time you add text like this, a new text track is created; thus it is not a good technique when you need to add a lot of text.

Searching a text track

If you have a movie that contains a text track, you can navigate through the movie by searching for specific text strings. This is particularly useful as a method of random access for long movies which don't have significant visual changes, perhaps a video of a lecture or even an audio-only movie.

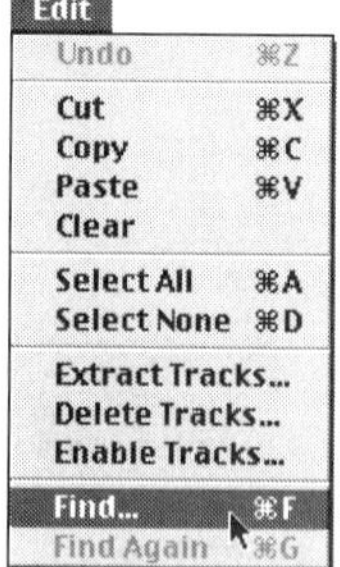

Figure 9.20 Choose Find from the Edit menu.

To search for text in a text track

1. Choose Find from the Edit menu (**Figure 9.20**).
2. Type the text string you want to find and click the Find button (**Figure 9.21**).

   The movie jumps to the first point in time after the location of the slider where the text is located. The specific string you typed is highlighted if the text track is visible (**Figure 9.22**).

   If the specified text is not found in the text track, you'll hear an alert sound, regardless of whether the text track is visible or not.

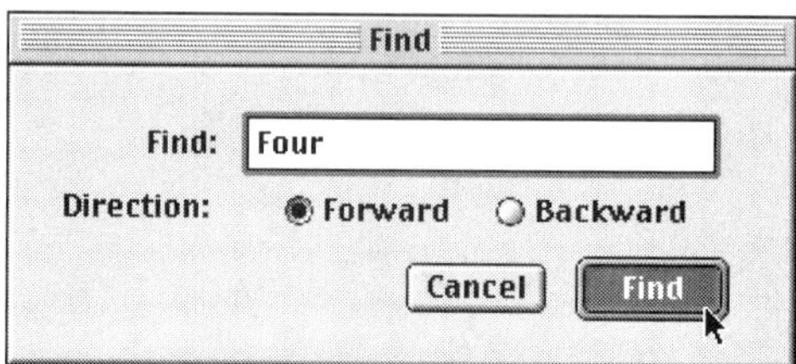

Figure 9.21 Type a text string.

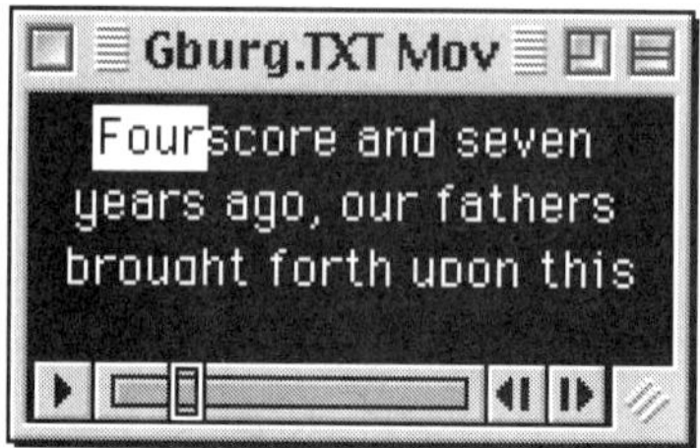

Figure 9.22 The movie jumps to the point where the text is located; the string you typed is highlighted.

To search for a repeat occurrence of the text

- Choose Find Again from the Edit menu (**Figure 9.23**).

To find a previous instance of the text

1. Choose Find from the Edit menu.
2. In the Find dialog box, click the Backward button before clicking the Find button.

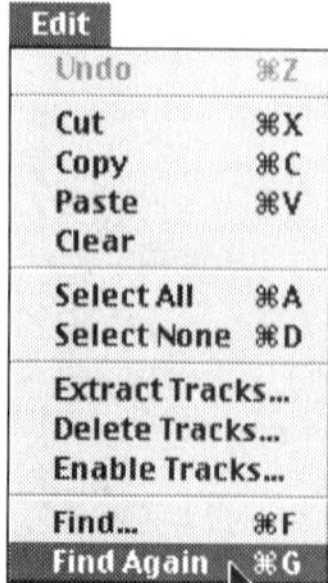

Figure 9.23 Find Again lets you locate a repeat occurrence of the text.

10

Sprite and 3D tracks

As with other QuickTime track types, you can use MoviePlayer to copy and paste data from 3D and sprite tracks, as well as do the other things we covered in Chapter 7.

However, there are essentially no methods for creating useful sprite and 3D tracks with MoviePlayer. (One exception: We'll show you how you can open a still 3D image.)

So you'll need to either obtain sprite or 3D tracks that have already been created or use commercial tools to create them. (For creating sprite tracks—including wired sprites—look into Lari Software's Electrifier Pro, Totally Hip Software's WebPainter, and Paceworks' ObjectDancer. There's also Apple's free, unsupported Sprite Export Xtra for Macromedia Director, but this won't currently create wired sprites. For creating 3D tracks, you can use Strata VideoShop 4.0/3D or a free, unsupported tool from Apple called 3D Movie Maker; both let you animate 3D objects created using 3D modeling software.)

Once you have a sprite or 3D track, however, there are fun and potentially useful changes you can make with MoviePlayer. We'll cover these in this chapter.

Attaching a graphic or video sequence to a sprite

Typically a sprite is a static graphical object that moves across the screen in a particular way. However, MoviePlayer provides a mechanism by which you can replace a sprite's graphic with data from a QuickTime track. This can be a video track, giving you an animated sprite.

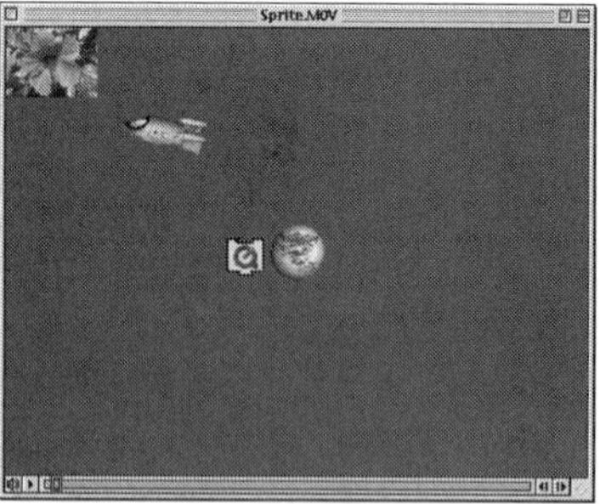

Figure 10.1 Start by adding a visual track to a movie with a sprite track. (In this case, the added track is a video track of a flower blowing in the wind. The sprite track contains three graphics that move around in the window.)

To replace a sprite's graphic with another QuickTime track

1. Add the track you want to use as a replacement to the movie containing the sprite track. (You'll want the added track to have the same duration as the sprite track, so use the Add Scaled command, as described in Chapter 6. For dynamic tracks, make sure the track is the right duration before adding it, or it will play in fast or slow motion.)

   Don't worry about the track's location in the Movie window (**Figure 10.1**).

2. In the Info window (accessed by choosing Get Info from the Movie window), choose the sprite track from the left pop-up menu and Image Overrides from the right pop-up menu.

3. Select the sprite that you want to change and click the Select Override Track button (**Figure 10.2**).

4. In the Select Override Track dialog box, select the added track, and click OK (**Figure 10.3**).

   The sprite's original graphic is replaced by the data from the added track (**Figure 10.4**).

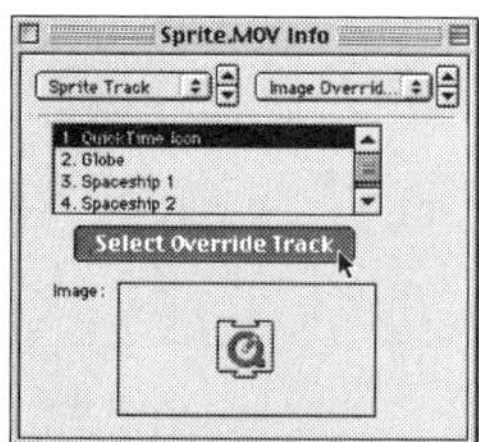

Figure 10.2 In the Image Override panel in the Info window, select a sprite and click the Select Override Track button.

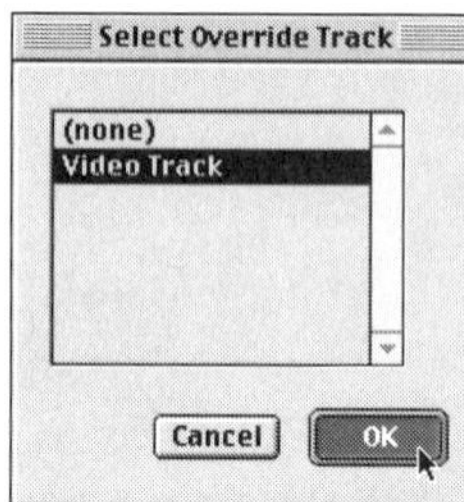

Figure 10.3 Select the track you added.

Figure 10.4 The sprite's graphic is now the track you added. (The flower video now moves around in the window, following the path the QuickTime icon did previously.)

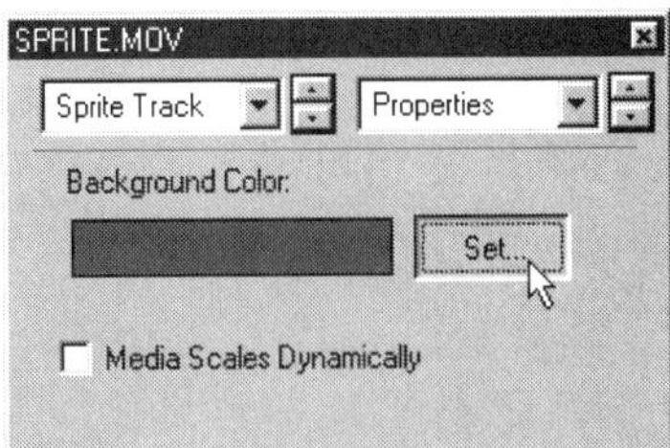

Figure 10.5 Click the Set button in the Sprite Properties panel of the Info window.

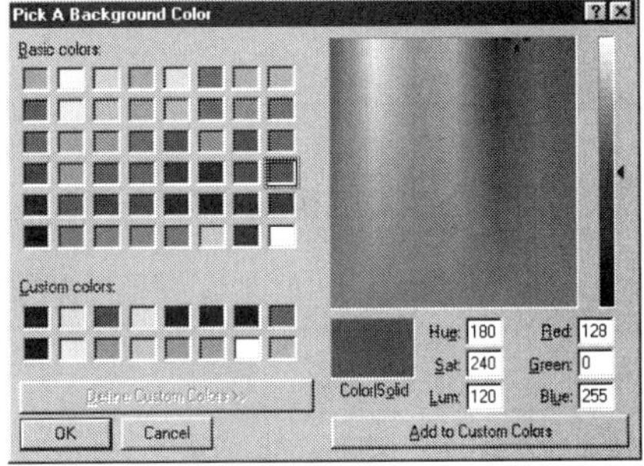

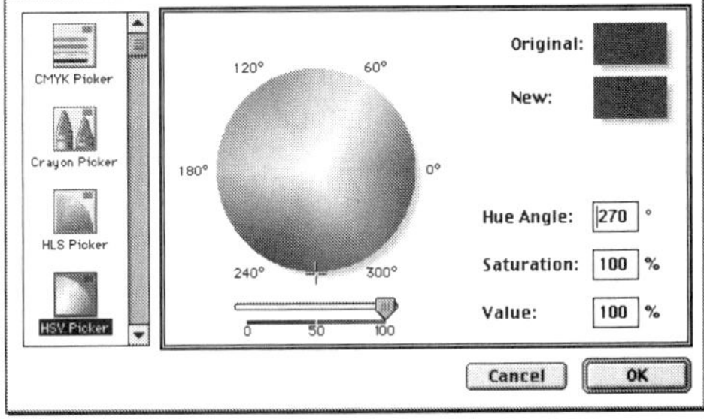

Figure 10.6 Use a Color Picker dialog box to choose a new background color (top is a Windows color picker; bottom is a Mac OS color picker).

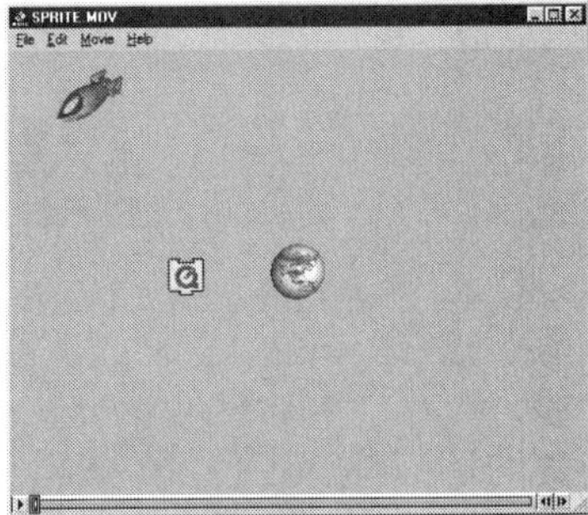

Figure 10.7 The color you select becomes the background color.

Changing the background color of a sprite track

Sprite tracks have a background color. It's very easy to change this color if you're so inclined.

To change a sprite track's background color

1. In the movie's Info window, choose the sprite track from the left pop-up menu and **Properties** from the right pop-up menu.

   The current background color appears in the bar below the words "Background Color."

2. Click the **Set** button to the right of the colored bar (**Figure 10.5**).

   A Color Picker dialog box appears.

3. Choose a color and close the Color Picker dialog box by clicking **OK** (**Figure 10.6**).

   The background color of the sprite track is now the color you picked (**Figure 10.7**).

Creating a static 3D track from a 3D file

MoviePlayer can directly open 3D files in the 3DMF format. Keep in mind, however, that these have no motion defined for them; they're static 3D objects.

However, if you do want to create a track with a still 3D image (perhaps to combine with other data), the steps are the same as those for opening many other media files.

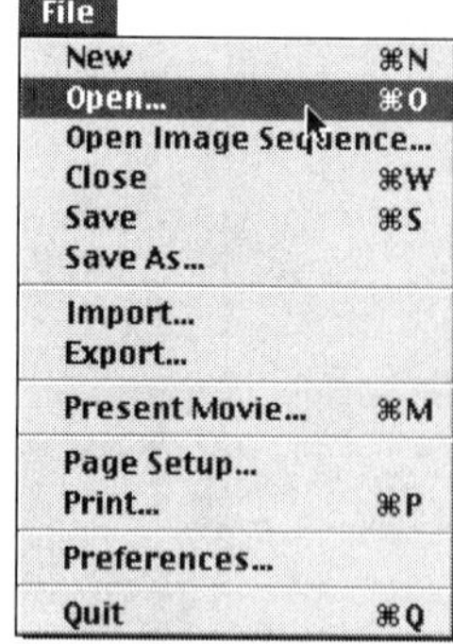

Figure 10.8 Choose Open from the File menu.

To create a 3D track from a 3DMF file

1. Choose **Open** from the File menu (**Figure 10.8**).
2. Select a 3D file.

   The Open button becomes a Convert button (**Figure 10.9**).
3. Click the **Convert** button.

   The file is opened, and the visual data appears in a standard QuickTime movie window. The movie contains one 3D track (**Figure 10.10**).

   The original 3D file is not changed unless you save this movie with the same name as the 3D file.

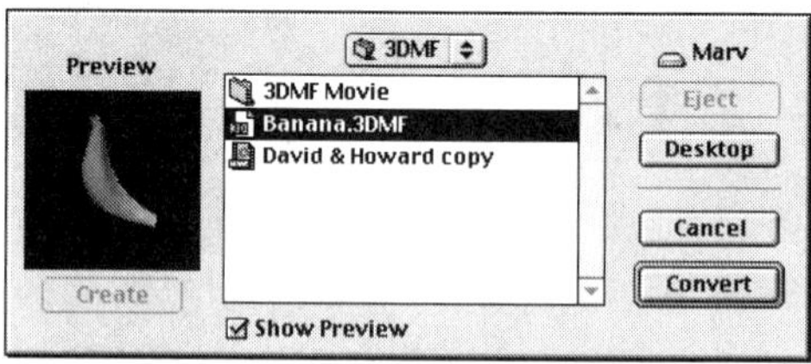

Figure 10.9 Select a 3D file and click Convert.

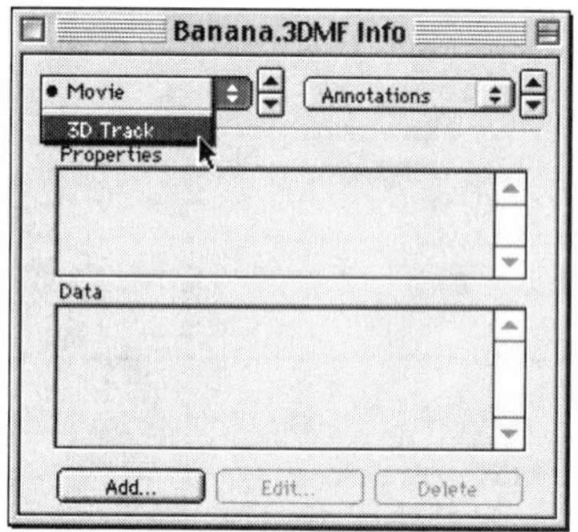

Figure 10.10 You've created a QuickTime movie with a single 3D track.

Creating dynamic 3D tracks

To animate an object in a 3D track, you need a tween track to define the object's motion. The application VideoShop is one tool that can be used to associate a tween track with objects in a 3D track. A free tool from Apple called 3D Movie Maker can also be used to associate some pre-defined tween tracks with 3D objects. (Both of these tools are currently Mac OS only, but we recommend checking Apple's QuickTime site for Windows versions). You can't do this in MoviePlayer, however.

Figure 10.11 Start by adding a visual track to a movie with a 3D track that contains objects with a texture map. (In this case, a beach at sunset is the added video track.)

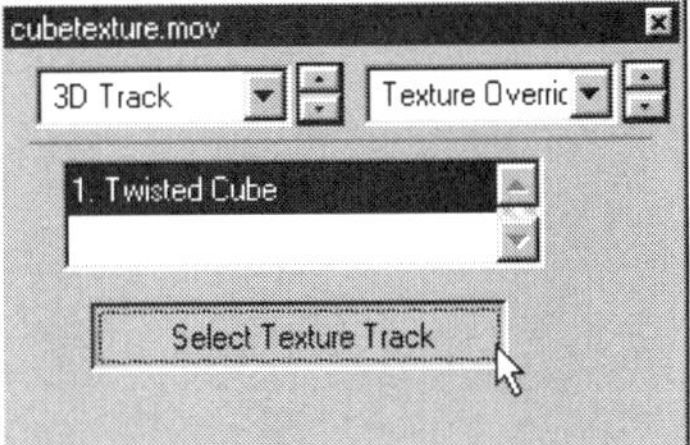

Figure 10.12 Select the object to which you want to apply a new texture and click Select Texture Track.

Figure 10.13 Select the track you want to map onto the object (i.e. the track you added).

Changing texture mapping for a 3D track

Some QuickTime 3D tracks have 3D objects with a *texture map* defined. (A texture map is an image used to define the surface of the object.)

If you have such a movie, you can use MoviePlayer to replace the texture currently mapped to the 3D object with your own visual track.

To determine if an object in a 3D track has a texture map

1. In the Info window (accessed by choosing Get Info from the Movie menu), choose the 3D track from the left pop-up menu, and choose Texture Overrides from the right pop-up menu.
2. If any objects are listed (as in **Figure 10.12**), they contain a texture map that you can replace.

To change the image mapped onto a 3D object with a texture map

1. Add to your movie the visual track you want to map onto the 3D object. Use the Add Scaled command, so the track has a duration equal to the 3D track.

   The added track will likely be layered over other tracks (**Figure 10.11**). Don't worry about this; it's temporary.
2. In the Texture Overrides panel (**Figure 10.12**), click to select the object to which you want to apply a new texture and then click the Select Texture Track button.
3. In the Select Texture Track dialog box that appears, choose the track you added in step 1 and click OK (**Figure 10.13**).

   The track selected is now mapped onto the object. The name of the object as listed in the Texture Overrides panel now has the name of the mapped visual track appended to it.

4. If your movie contained a track which was previously being used as a texture it may become an independent track again, probably layered over other tracks. If this is the case, you can use the Delete Tracks command in the Edit menu to get rid of this extra track.

   Now you can see the 3D object with your track mapped onto it (**Figure 10.14**).

Figure 10.14 The track you selected is mapped onto the object.

Creating 3D tracks with texture maps

You can create a 3D model with a texture map using almost any QuickDraw 3D modeling tool.

If you want to animate it with 3D Movie Maker or open it as a static graphic directly in MoviePlayer, but still be able to alter the texture, as described here, you'll first need to run it through a $50 commercial tool called 3DMF Optimizer, from Pangea Software.

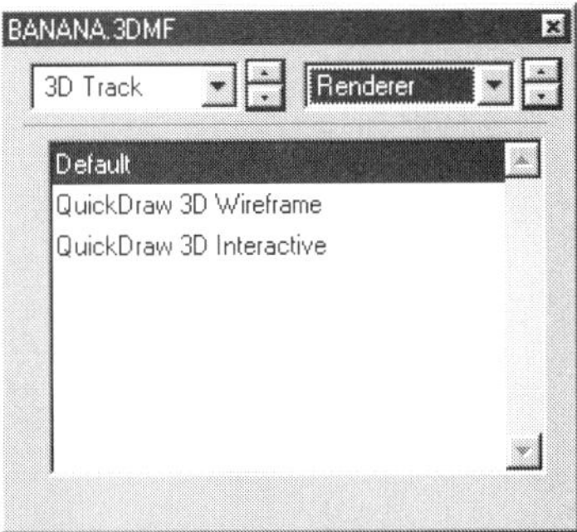

Figure 10.15 Use the Renderer panel in the Info window to choose a renderer.

Figure 10.16 A 3D object rendered by the default renderer.

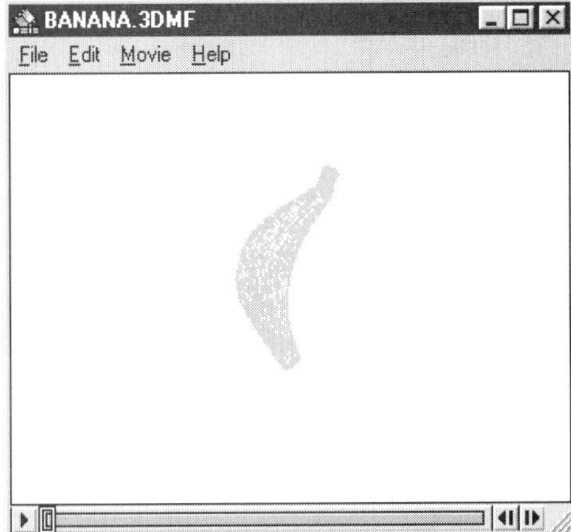

Figure 10.17 A 3D object rendered by the wire frame renderer.

Changing the renderer for a 3D track

3D objects can be rendered using a variety of different techniques. By specifying which technique is used to render an object, you determine how it looks. MoviePlayer lets you choose a renderer for objects in 3D tracks.

To change the renderer for a 3D track

1. In the Info window, choose the 3D track from the left pop-up menu and choose Renderer from the right pop-up menu.
2. In the Renderer panel (**Figure 10.15**), choose a renderer.

   The QuickDraw 3D Interactive renderer shows solid surfaces for the 3D objects (**Figure 10.16**). The default option is the same as the interactive renderer unless the original 3D file specified some other renderer as its default.

   The wire frame renderer removes any textures from the model, leaving only the wire frame defining the geometry of the object (**Figure 10.17**).

✓ Tip

- It's possible for programmers to create plug-in renderers for QuickDraw 3D, the 3D technology that works with QuickTime. Currently, none of these are available for sale on their own. However, some come as part of 3D modeling software; for example, one is part of Electric Cafe's ModelShop 3. Others may be available in the future from such companies as Lightwork Design and Viewpoint Datalabs. If you install one of these plug-in renderers, you will see additional choices in the Renderer panel.

11

Working with Audio Tracks

Don't forget about the audio! Audio is an often-overlooked component of multimedia; many people are so excited to see the video image that they forget all about the sound. However, sound makes a big difference: It's been shown that better sound often makes people think that the video image is better.

When we use the term *audio*, we're referring to tracks that you can hear. QuickTime has two major types of audio tracks. There are those tracks that contain digitized sound. The most common of these are *sound tracks*. In addition there are *MPEG audio tracks*, which also contain digitized sound. *Music tracks*, on the other hand, are composed of a sequence of commands that tell QuickTime how to play sounds called *instruments*. (Music tracks are based on the MIDI standard.)

In this chapter we'll cover techniques that apply to all types of audio tracks—combining them with video or still images and altering the volume and balance.

In the chapters that follow, we'll cover sound and music tracks individually.

Adding new audio to a movie

If you have read Chapter 6 you may be able to guess at this point how you'd add new audio to a movie, but we'll show you the specific steps here anyway. Remember that a QuickTime file can have multiple tracks of the same type, so you can add new audio even if your file already contains an audio track. This technique is often used to add narration or background sound or music to a movie that already has audio.

To add new audio to a video file

1. If your audio isn't already a QuickTime sound or music track, open or import the file containing the audio. (Details are in Chapters 12 and 13.)
2. Select and copy all or part of the audio movie.
3. Open the movie file to which you want to add audio, and move the slider to the point where you want the audio to begin playing.
4. Hold down the **Option** key (Mac OS) or the **Ctrl** and **Alt** keys (Windows) and choose **Add** from the Edit menu (**Figure 11.1**).
5. If the video has a greater duration than the audio, a portion of the play bar, representing the length of the audio, is selected and the slider is positioned at the end of the selection (**Figure 11.2**). Since the slider is positioned at the end of the audio, you can repeat step 4 one or more times to have the audio repeat.
6. If the audio has a greater duration than the video, the window appears white during any time that there's no video for the audio (**Figure 11.3**). You'll probably want to select the portion of the track that is only audio and delete it.

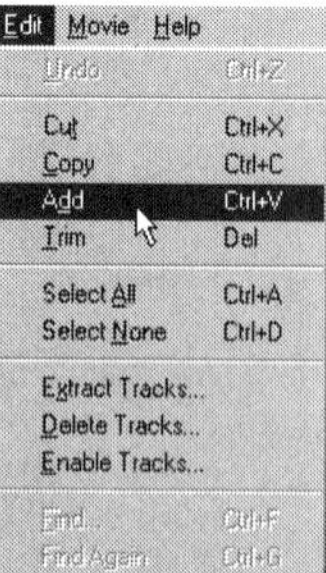

Figure 11.1 Use the Add command to add the audio to the video.

Figure 11.2 If the audio is shorter than the video, after you add only part of the play bar is selected.

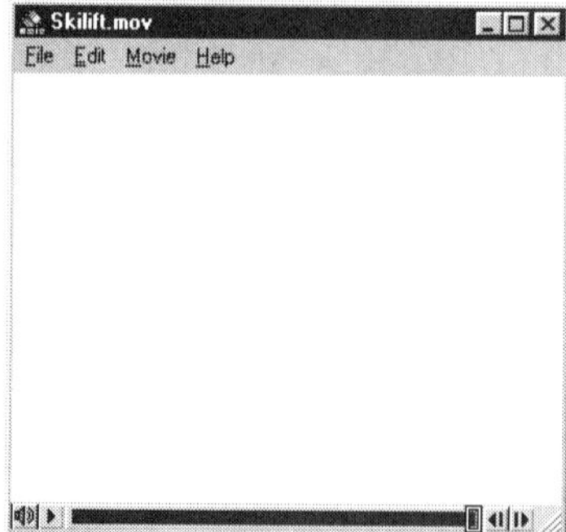

Figure 11.3 If the audio is longer than the video, the window is white where there's only audio.

✔ Tip

- To quickly get rid of audio that extends beyond the video track, you can put your slider at the far right of the play bar, hold down the Shift key, and press the left arrow key or the click the left Step button. This selects the audio-only area; you can then simply delete this selection.

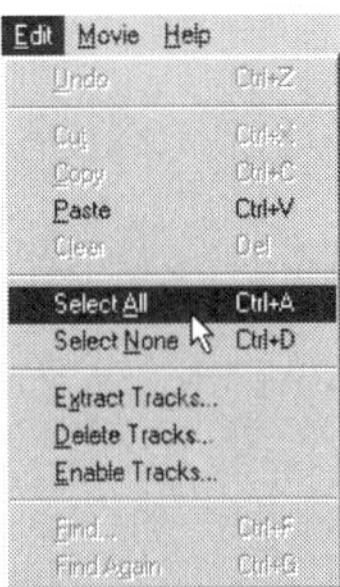

Figure 11.4 In the audio movie, choose Select All from the Edit menu.

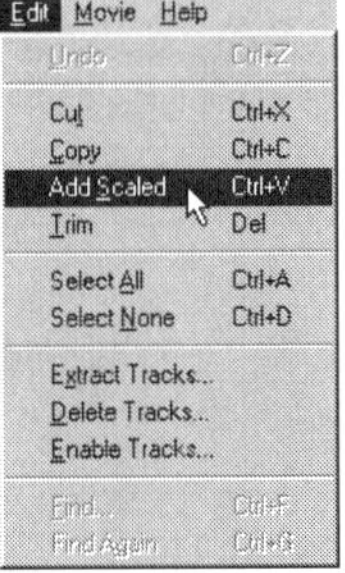

Figure 11.5 Use Add Scaled to add previously copied image data. (You'll need to hold down the modifier keys—Shift and Option for the Mac; Shift, Ctrl, and Alt for Windows—to make this choice available.)

Figure 11.6 The graphic is added to the sound file, and appears for the duration of the sound.

Adding a still image to an audio track

The technique for merging audio with still images differs only in that you can take advantage of MoviePlayer's ability to scale in time; this makes it easy to match the duration of the still image to the duration of the audio.

To add a still image to an audio track

1. Open or import your audio file.
2. Open or import your still image file and choose Copy from the Edit menu. (With nothing selected, the current—and only—frame is copied.)

   Or open the image in your graphics application and copy it from there.
3. Click in the window for the sound movie and choose Select All from the Edit menu (**Figure 11.4**).
4. Hold down the Shift and Option keys (Mac OS) or the Shift, Ctrl, and Alt keys (Windows) and choose Add Scaled from the Edit menu (**Figure 11.5**).

   The sound movie's window expands to fit the graphic (**Figure 11.6**).
5. Save the movie containing both the sound and the graphic as a self-contained file.

Having audio play when the movie isn't in front

You can decide whether or not you want to be able to hear movie files when they are in the background, either because some application other than MoviePlayer is active, or because some other Movie window in MoviePlayer is active.

To have audio play when a movie is in the background

1. Choose Preferences from the File menu (**Figure 11.7**).

   The Preferences dialog box appears (**Figure 11.8**).

2. If you want to be able to hear the audio from your movies even when some other application is open, check Play sound in background.

3. If you want to be able to hear the audio from multiple movies at the same time, make sure that Only front movie plays sound is not checked.

Figure 11.7 Choose Preferences from the File menu.

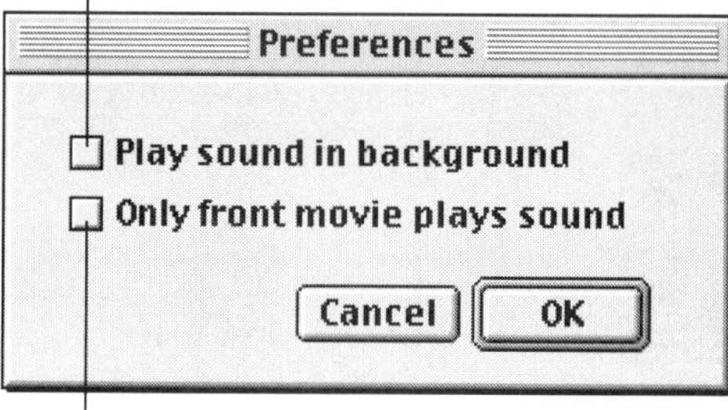

Figure 11.8 MoviePlayer's Preferences dialog box contains options that affect whether audio is heard in movies that are not in the front.

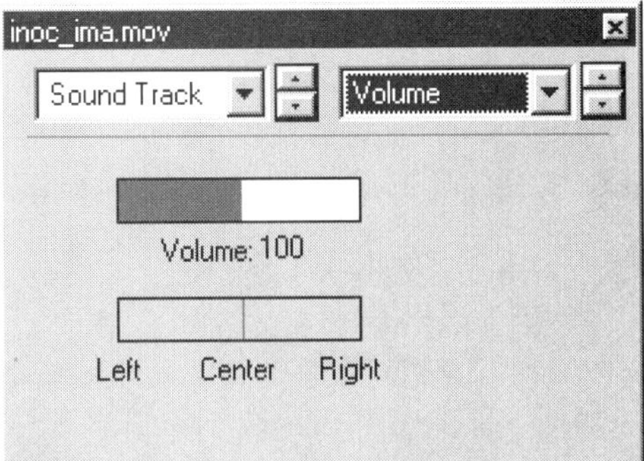

Figure 11.9 The Volume panel; drag in the top bar to change the track's default volume. Drag in the bottom bar to change how much sound is directed to each speaker.

✔ Tip

- Hold down the Option key (Mac OS) or Ctrl and Alt keys (Windows) when you click in the volume rectangle to make the indicator bar snap to numerical values that are increments of 25. Hold down the same key(s) when you click in the balance rectangle to make the little green line snap to Left, halfway between Left and Center, Center, halfway between Center and Right, and Right.

Changing the default volume and balance of an audio track

If you'd like, you can change the default volume at which your audio track plays. You can also adjust the balance, making the audio louder on the left or on the right (assuming it's played back in stereo, of course).

To change the default volume of an audio track

1. In the Info window (accessed by choosing Get Info from the Movie menu), choose the audio track for which you'd like to change volume from the left pop-up menu, and choose Volume from the right pop-up menu.

   The Volume panel appears (**Figure 11.9**)

2. Drag the bar in the top rectangle (or click in the rectangle to automatically have the bar extend to the point clicked). The farther to the right the bar extends, the louder the volume. The number below the bar shows the percentage of normal volume. (If you set the volume beyond 100 percent of normal, the part of the bar to the right of center turns red to warn you that the sound may become distorted.)

To change the balance of an audio track

1. Open the Volume panel, as described previously.
2. Click in the lower rectangle (labeled "Left", "Center", and "Right"). Clicking to the right of center directs more sound to the right speaker and clicking to the left of center directs more sound to the left speaker.

12 Sound and MPEG Audio Tracks

QuickTime sound tracks are composed of digitized audio. Like video tracks, sound tracks have certain properties associated with them—properties over which you have some amount of control.

In this chapter, we'll start by providing a basic introduction to the characteristics of digital sound, looking at the dialog box that gives you some access to these properties and the info panel that lets you check what they are. Then we'll cover various methods for creating sound tracks. (In addition, we'll cover importing MPEG audio files to create MPEG audio tracks; this works only if you have the QuickTime MPEG Extension, which is available only on Mac OS until the fall of 1998.) Finally, we'll show you how you can use MoviePlayer as a sound conversion utility.

Understanding the characteristics of digitized sound

In many ways it helps to think of digitized sound as being analogous to digitized video.

Digitized sound is actually composed of a sequence of individual sound samples. The number of samples per second is called the *sample rate* and is very much like a video track's frame rate. The more sound samples per second, the higher the quality of the resulting sound. However, more sound samples also take up more space on disk and mean that more data needs to be processed during every second of playback. (As we mentioned when discussing video in Chapter 8, the amount of data that must be processed every second is called the *data rate*.)

Sound samples can be different sizes. Just as you can reproduce a photograph more faithfully by storing it as a 24-bit (full-color) image than as an 8-bit image, 16-bit sound samples represent audio more accurately than 8-bit sound samples. We refer to the size of those samples as a sound's *sample size*. As with the sampling rate, a larger sample size increases the accuracy of the sound at the expense of more storage space and a higher data rate.

Like video, sound can be compressed using some specific techniques designed to represent the sound data more efficiently and lower the data rate. You can choose from a large number of sound compressors when you compress a QuickTime sound track. (See **Table 12.1**) And, as you can for video tracks, you can add additional sound compressors.

One additional property of a sound track is the number of channels it contains: one (mono) or two (stereo).

Table 12.1

Audio Compressors Included with QuickTime 3

Compressor Name	Comments
24-bit Integer, 32-bit Integer	Increases the sample size to 24 or 32 bits (but will be converted to 8- or 16-bit to play on current hardware).
32-bit Floating Point, Floating Point	Actually increases the sample size of 64-bit the audio (to 32 or 64 bits), which allows for more accurate conversion to other sample sizes and the application of effects. (Playback on current systems, however, is still 8- or 16-bit.)
ALaw 2:1	Internet standard for compressed audio in Europe and everywhere else except the United States and Japan. Low compression ratio and low quality. Generally not recommended.
IMA 4:1	Very good for music and other audio content. Must be 16-bit ; relatively low compression ratio.
MACE 3:1, MACE 6:1	Outdated Macintosh compressors. Low quality. Not generally recommended.
QDesign Music Codec	Excellent for music content intended for the Web. Extremely low compression ratio.
QUALCOMM PureVoice	Excellent for voice content intended for the Web. Extremely low compression ratio.
uLaw 2:1	Internet standard for compressed audio in the United States and Japan. Low compression ratio and low quality. Generally not recommended.

This table lists the compressors you can choose when compressing sound tracks; there are others, such as DV, PCM, and IMA ADPCM, that QuickTime uses internally when importing or exporting certain file formats. You may see one of these listed in the Format panel for the audio track of a DV or AVI file that you've opened in MoviePlayer.

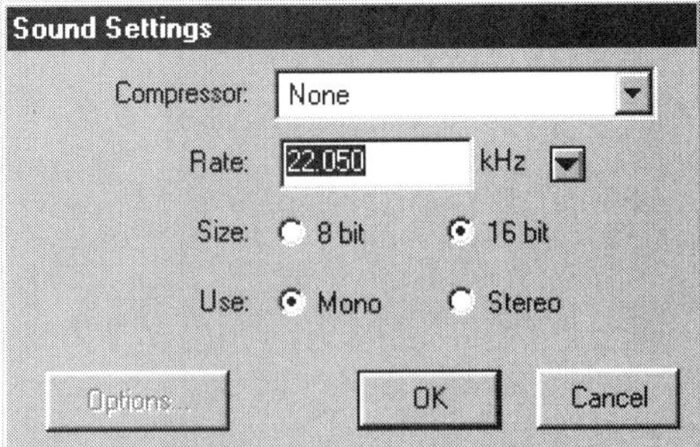

Figure 12.1 The Sound Settings dialog box.

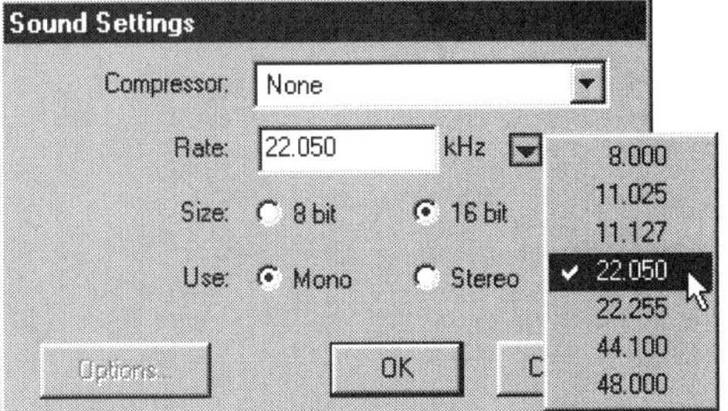

Figure 12.2 It's best to choose from the Rate pop-up menu.

The Sound Settings dialog box

You access the properties of a sound file via the Sound Settings dialog box (**Figure 12.1**). As with the Compression Settings dialog box for video, this dialog box is used for a few different tasks in MoviePlayer, as well as in many other QuickTime applications.

Your options in the Sound Settings dialog box include:

- **Compressor:** Depending on the sound format chosen, you'll have different choices for a compressor. When you choose certain compressors, an Options button at the bottom of the dialog box becomes available, giving you access to additional features of the compressor.
- **Rate:** You can either type in a sample rate directly or use the pop-up menu (**Figure 12.2**). It's best to use one of the choices in the pop-up menu, as these are optimal choices for today's computer sound cards. In general, rates of 22.050 kHz or 11.025 kHz (22,050 samples per second or 11,025 samples per second) usually result in very good quality sound. (It's best to avoid the 11.127 and the 22.125 choices, as these may not perform well on Windows computers.)
- **Size:** You have a choice of 8-bit or 16-bit. For some compressors, the 8-bit choice will be unavailable. (8-bit sound provides for 256 possible values, whereas 16-bit sound provides for 65536 possible values.)
- **Use:** This refers to the number of channels. You have a choice of Mono or Stereo. Mono is the usual choice; most audio files you work with will be recorded in mono, anyway. On the rare occasion when you have a stereo file and you want to retain its quality, it may make sense to select Stereo.

Checking the characteristics of a sound track

If you want or need to know the properties of a sound track in a movie you have, you can check in the movie's Info window.

To check the characteristics of a sound track

1. Choose **Get Info** from the File menu to bring up the Info window.
2. From the left pop-up menu, choose the sound track, and from the right pop-up menu, choose **Format**.

   The Format panel shows the file's sample rate, the number of channels, its sample size, and how it was compressed (**Figure 12.3**).

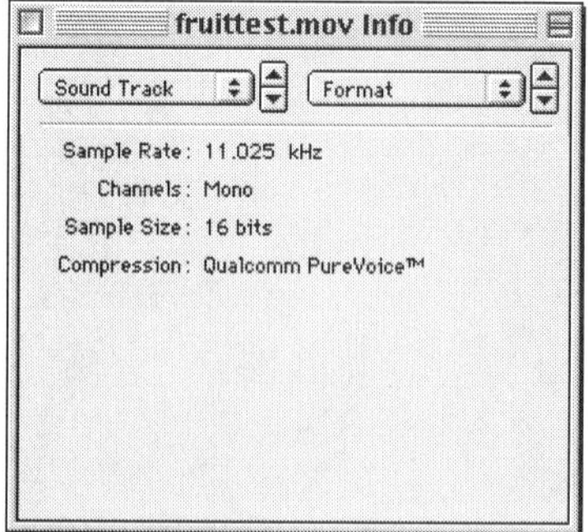

Figure 12.3 The Format panel for a sound track.

✔ Note

- This panel lists those characteristics of a sound track that are relevant only to digitized sound. Remember that there are other properties of audio tracks in general; see *Changing the default volume and balance of an audio track* in Chapter 11.

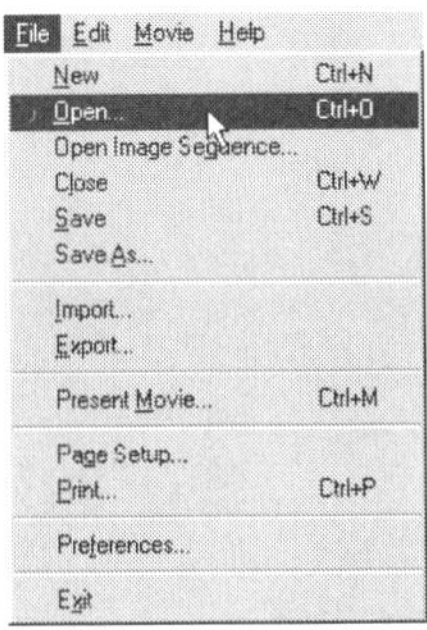

Figure 12.4 You open most sound files as you would any QuickTime movie.

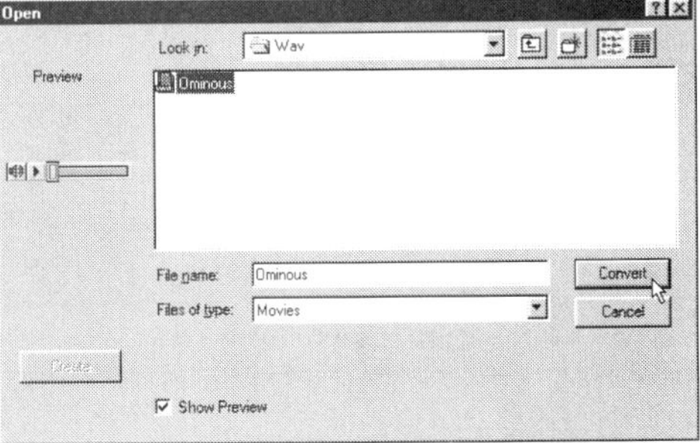

Figure 12.5 The only difference is that when you click on the Open button it turns into a Convert button.

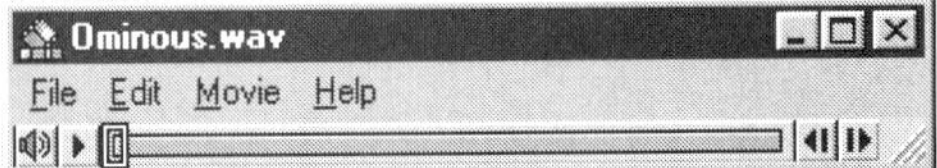

Figure 12.6 The resulting movie has no visual component; you see only a play bar.

Creating a sound track from a sound file

You can create a QuickTime sound track from an existing sound file in another audio format by opening it in MoviePlayer. Most audio files—including AIFF/AIFC, Sound Designer 2, WAV, and µLaw (au) files—open directly in MoviePlayer. Macintosh System 7 sound files need to be imported, however.

To create a sound track from a sound file in most sound formats

1. Choose **Open** or **Import** from the File menu (**Figure 12.4**).
2. In the Open dialog box, locate the sound file and click the **Convert** button (**Figure 12.5**).

   A new movie window containing no image appears (**Figure 12.6**). The title of the window is the same as the name of the file you opened.

   The sound data in this movie can be combined with other QuickTime movies. However, you have not actually created a QuickTime movie *file* until you save. If you quit MoviePlayer without saving, the file remains in its original format.

✔ Note

- You also create a sound track, along with a video track, when you open DV or AVI files in MoviePlayer. If all you need is the audio, you can simply delete the video track as described in *Deleting tracks* in Chapter 6.

To create a sound track from a System 7 sound file

1. Choose Import from the File menu (**Figure 12.7**).
2. In the Open dialog box, locate and select the System 7 sound file and click the Convert button (**Figure 12.8**).

   A Save dialog box appears (**Figure 12.9**), since you need to create a new file in order to open the System 7 file.
3. If desired, change the name and location for the file to be created.
4. Click Save.

   A movie window with only a controller in it appears (**Figure 12.10**).

   Since a new file has already been created, you don't need to save this movie unless you alter it.

✔ Tip

- If you have problems creating QuickTime movies from System 7 sound files on a Windows computer, we recommend doing it on a Mac OS computer and then copying the resulting QuickTime movies to a Windows computer.

Figure 12.7 For System 7 sound files, choose Import rather than Open.

Figure 12.8 The Open button changes to a Convert... button. (The ellipses indicate that there will another step.)

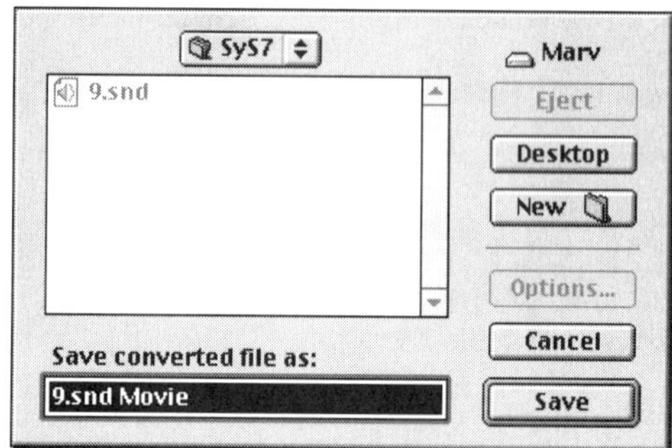

Figure 12.9 The next step is to save the file.

Figure 12.10 A sound-only movie file appears.

Creating a Sound Track from a Sound File

Figure 12.11 Choose Import from the File menu. (Open will work, too.)

Figure 12.12 Select a file from the audio CD and click Convert.

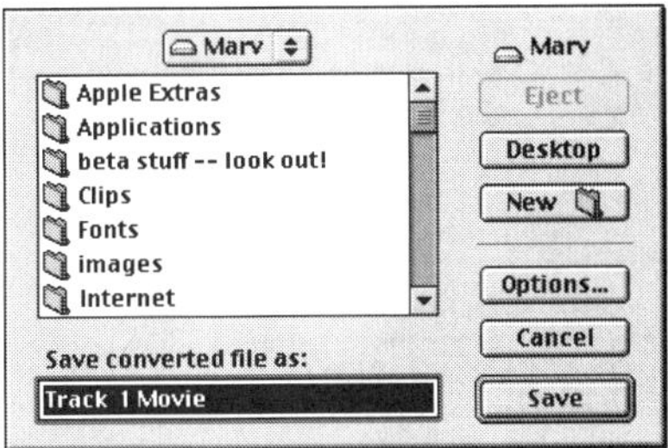

Figure 12.13 You can click Save immediately, or first click the Options button.

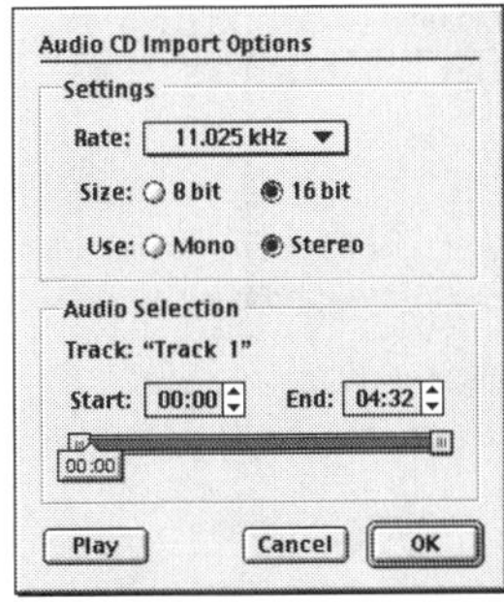

Figure 12.14 If you click the Options button, an Audio CD Import Options dialog box appears.

✔ Warning

- It's not legal or ethical to use other people's music in your productions if they are for anything other than personal use.

Creating a sound track from an audio CD (Mac OS only)

On Mac OS computers you can convert audio from a standard audio CD to a QuickTime sound track. You can then incorporate this music into your QuickTime movie.

To import music from an audio CD

1. Put your audio CD into your CD-ROM drive, as you would any CD.
2. Choose Import or Open from the File menu (**Figure 12.11**).
3. Select one of the files on your audio CD and click the Convert button (**Figure 12.12**).

   (Note that an audio CD is like any other volume on your desktop and is called Audio CD 1 or Audio CD 2 or whatever, depending on how many CDs you've inserted in this session. Each file represents a single song and is called a *track*.)
4. In the Save dialog box that appears (**Figure 12.13**), you can click the Options button to open the Audio CD Import Options dialog box (**Figure 12.14**), where you can set the sample size, rate, and use (stereo or mono) as you would in a standard Sound Settings dialog box. (See *The Sound Settings dialog box*, earlier in this chapter.) You can use the lower part of the window, labeled "Audio Selection", to select only a portion of the track by repositioning the sliders to set start and stop times; use the Play button to verify your selection. Click OK to return to the Save dialog box.
5. Navigate to the location on your hard disk where you want to save the file, provide a new name if you'd like, and click Save.

Creating an MPEG audio track from an MPEG sound file

MPEG sound files are commonly used on the Internet. They come in several flavors—Layer I, Layer II, and Layer III—which differ in how they were encoded. (In theory, the higher the layer number, the better the quality, but this is not always true.) You can open MPEG Layer I and Layer II audio files in MoviePlayer, but QuickTime doesn't yet support MPEG Layer III. You do not, however, create a regular QuickTime sound track; instead you create an MPEG audio track.

The process for opening MPEG sound files is the same as for many other file types.

To create an MPEG audio track

1. Choose Open from the File menu (**Figure 12.15**).
2. Locate and select the MPEG sound file and click Convert (**Figure 12.16**).

   As with any sound file, a new window with only a controller in it appears (**Figure 12.17**). When you check in the Info window, you'll see that the file has a single MPEG audio track (**Figure 12.18**).
3. Make sure to save the file if you want to be able to open it again as a QuickTime movie.

Figure 12.15 Choose Open from the File menu.

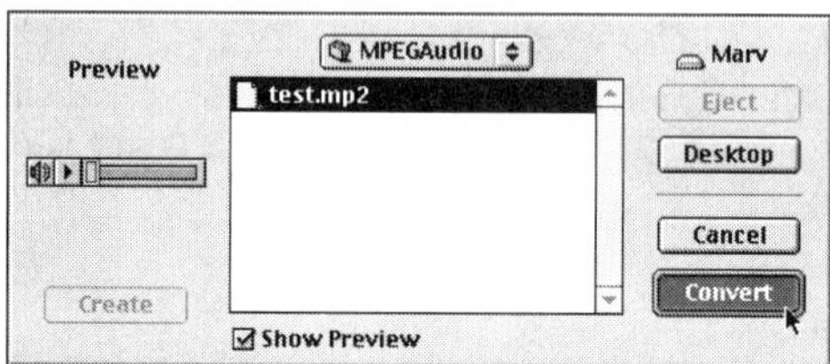

Figure 12.16 Select the file and click Convert.

Figure 12.17 An audio-only file appears.

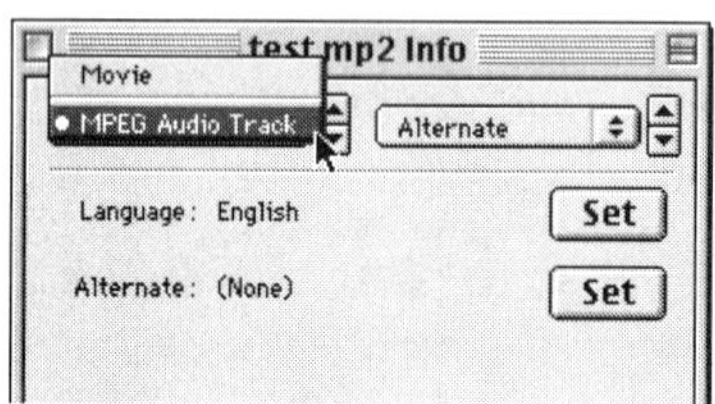

Figure 12.18 It contains an MPEG audio track, rather than a sound track.

✔ Notes

- Like regular MPEG tracks (those containing both video and audio), MPEG audio tracks can be copied and pasted into other QuickTime movies. However, when you select and copy a portion, the data from the entire track is copied. You hear only what you selected, but the file into which you paste will be increased by the full size of the original MPEG audio track.
- There is no Format panel in the Info window for MPEG audio tracks, so you can't use MoviePlayer to access information about the sample rate and sample size of these tracks. Remember, however, that you can see and change properties like volume and balance in the Volume panel.

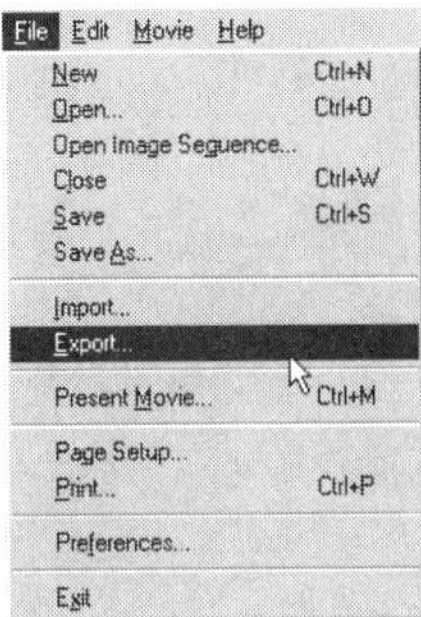

Figure 12.19 Choose Export from the File menu.

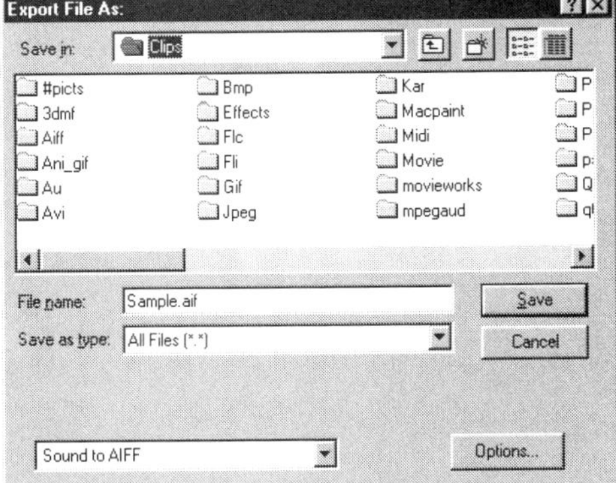

Figure 12.20 Choose Sound to AIFF and click the Options button.

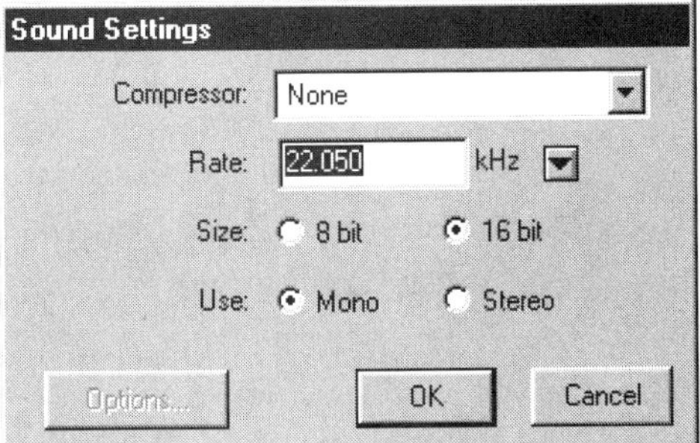

Figure 12.21 In the Sound Settings dialog box, you can change various properties of the sound track.

Changing the characteristics of a sound track

You can use MoviePlayer to change the characteristics of a sound track (but not an MPEG audio track). In general, you will want to do this in order to lower the track's data rate. We'll show you one general technique here. (Another technique is covered in *Compressing selected tracks* in Chapter 14. We'll also talk about specific choices you might make when we discuss preparing movies for the Web in Chapter 15 and when we discuss preparing movies for CD-ROM and kiosk in Chapter 17.)

To change the characteristics of a sound track

1. Choose **Export** from the File menu (**Figure 12.19**).

   (The only way to get to the sound settings dialog box is by exporting.)

2. In the Save dialog box, choose **Sound to AIFF** and click the **Options** button (**Figure 12.20**).

   The Sound Settings dialog box appears (**Figure 12.21**).

3. In the Sound Settings dialog box, make your choices and then click **OK**. (See *The Sound Settings dialog box* earlier in this chapter for an overview, and Chapters 15 and 17 for advice on specific recommendations.)

4. Click **Save** in the Save dialog box to export the file.

5. Open the exported file in MoviePlayer.

   If the sound track was originally accompanied by other tracks, you'll need to delete the original sound track and add the exported track. (Deleting and adding techniques are covered in Chapter 6.)

✔ Warning

- If you have multiple sound tracks in a movie, they will be merged into a single sound track with this technique. See *Compressing selected tracks* in Chapter 14 for an alternative technique.
- The way QuickTime does sample rate and size conversion is very elementary. Thus, changing the rate and size of an audio track using MoviePlayer may not give you the best results. For cleaner sounding audio, you'll want to use a tool designed for audio editing and conversion. One such tool is MacSourcery's BarbaBatch.

Making choices in the Sound Settings dialog box

It doesn't make sense to pick a higher rate, size, or number of channels than is already in the sound track. You'll only increase the amount of data by duplicating what's already there; there won't be any increase in quality. It's also not the best idea to compress a sound file that's already compressed; if you have the original, uncompressed file you should compress that instead.

Figure 12.22 Choose Export from the File menu.

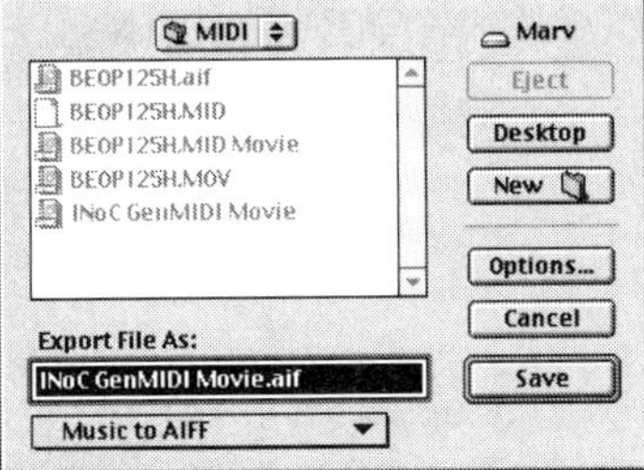

Figure 12.23 Choose Music to AIFF.

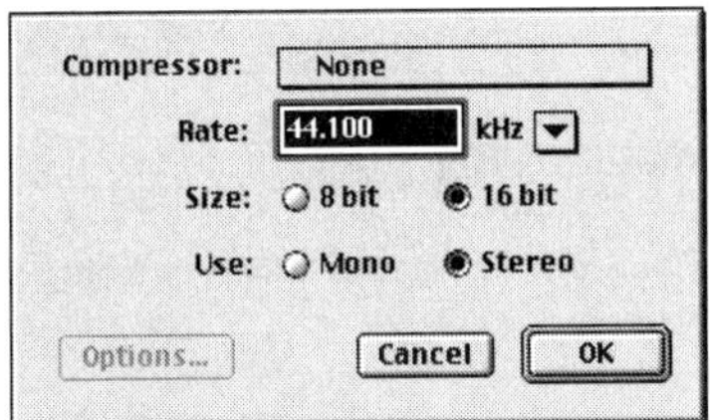

Figure 12.24 If you click the Options button, a Sound Settings dialog box appears, allowing you to specify properties of the sound that will be exported.

✔ Warning

- We generally don't recommend converting a music track to a sound track, since music tracks are so much more efficient. Depending on the settings chosen, the sound track may be hundreds to thousands of times as large as the original music track, and have a correspondingly higher data rate.

Converting a music track to a sound track

It's rare that you'd convert a music track to a sound track, but this is something you'd do if you want to use a QuickTime editor that doesn't handle music tracks. You also might not like the way that music tracks can be altered (see Chapter 13) and thus may prefer the music be converted to digital sound. A converted music track may also sound better because when exporting, the QuickTime music synthesizer can do a better job since it doesn't have to play the music in real time.

Converting a music track to a sound track requires you to first export the music track as a sound file, and then open the exported sound file in MoviePlayer.

To convert a music track to a sound track

1. Choose Export from the File menu (**Figure 12.22**).
2. In the Save dialog box, choose Music to AIFF (**Figure 12.23**).
3. If you want to specify sound format settings, click the Options button.

   A Sound Settings dialog box appears (**Figure 12.24**), in which you can select various sound format options, such as the sample rate and size. (See *The Sound Settings dialog box*, earlier in this chapter.) You cannot, however, pick a compressor when exporting a music track as AIFF.

   When you're done setting sound options, click OK to return to the Save dialog.
4. Click Save.

   It may take a while to export the file.
5. Open the exported sound file as described earlier in this chapter, using the Open command in the File menu.

Using MoviePlayer as a sound conversion utility

Since MoviePlayer can open so many kinds of sound files, you can use it as a sound conversion utility if you want to convert between AIFF, WAV, µLaw, or System 7 Sound formats. (You cannot, however, convert from or to MPEG audio.)

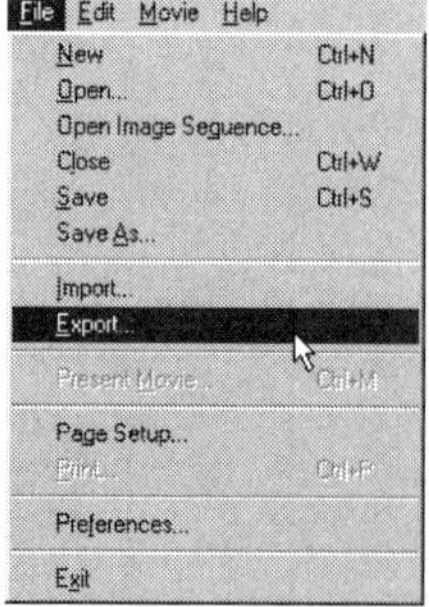

Figure 12.25 After opening or importing your sound file, choose Export from the File menu.

To convert a sound file to a different format

1. Open or Import the file in MoviePlayer.
2. Choose Export from the File menu (**Figure 12.25**).
3. Choose the format to which you'd like to convert: AIFF, WAV, µLaw, or System 7 Sound (**Figure 12.26**).

   If you want to apply compression or change the sample size, rate, or number of channels of the sound, click the Options button to open the Sound Settings dialog box, make your changes, and then click OK. (See the section earlier in this chapter explaining the Sound Settings dialog box.)
4. Click Save (**Figure 12.27**).

Figure 12.26 Choose the format to which you want to convert the file.

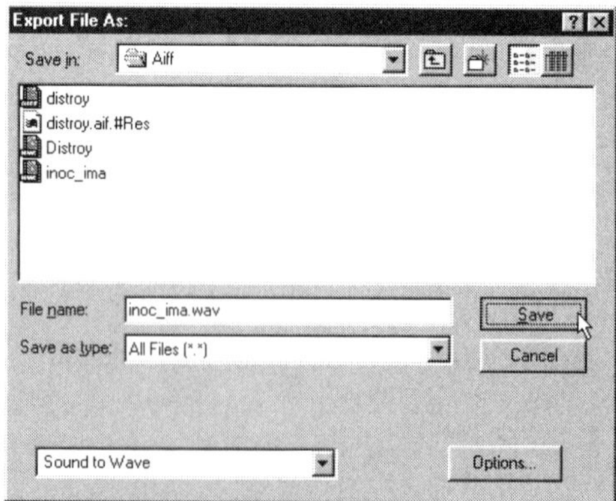

Figure 12.27 Click Save to save the file in the chosen format.

MoviePlayer as Sound Conversion Utility

13

Music Tracks

Music tracks are very similar to MIDI files. MIDI (Musical Instrument Digital Interface) files are a music-industry-standard way to represent music.

Both music tracks and MIDI files consist of a sequence of commands specifying what sounds should be played and how they should be played. The sounds (called *instruments*) are not stored in the file. Rather, the commands are sent to a hardware or software synthesizer. In the case of QuickTime music tracks, QuickTime contains the instruments and works as a software synthesizer.

Related to MIDI files are karaoke files, which are essentially MIDI files with textual lyrics.

In this chapter we'll cover how you import MIDI and karaoke files, the changes you can make to music tracks within MoviePlayer, and how you get QuickTime to use an external synthesizer (such as a MIDI keyboard or sound module). We'll also show you how you can convert a music track back to a MIDI file.

Getting MIDI Files

On the Web, you can find MIDI and karaoke files that QuickTime can import by using your favorite search engine to search for ".MID" and ".KAR" files.

If you're a musician, you may already know about MIDI composition tools that enable you to compose music. There are also a few such tools that let you do this without expensive hardware, by taking advantage of QuickTime's built-in instruments.

Converting MIDI files to QuickTime

QuickTime can import any Standard MIDI file.

To create a music track from a MIDI file

1. Choose **Import** from the File menu (**Figure 13.1**).

   (Or, you can choose **Open** from the File menu; everything will work the same way.)

2. Locate and select the MIDI file and click **Convert** (**Figure 13.2**).

3. In the Save dialog box that appears, you can click the **Options** button (**Figure 13.3**) to open the Standard MIDI Import dialog box (**Figure 13.4**), where you can alter certain properties of the resulting music track.

   If you want your music file to play on computers that still use QuickTime 2.0 or QuickTime 2.1 for Mac OS, check the **Compatible with QuickTime 2.0** checkbox.

   Click **Add silence at end** or **Add silence at beginning** to add one second of silence to the end or beginning of the movie.

   Click the **OK** button to return to the Save dialog box.

4. If desired, change the name and location of the file you are about to create, then click **Save**.

   A new movie file containing a music track is created.

✔ Note

- The QuickTime music synthesizer complies with the General MIDI specification, an industry standard. Though you can import any Standard MIDI file, if the Standard MIDI file isn't also General MIDI compliant, the music will not sound as it's supposed to when played.

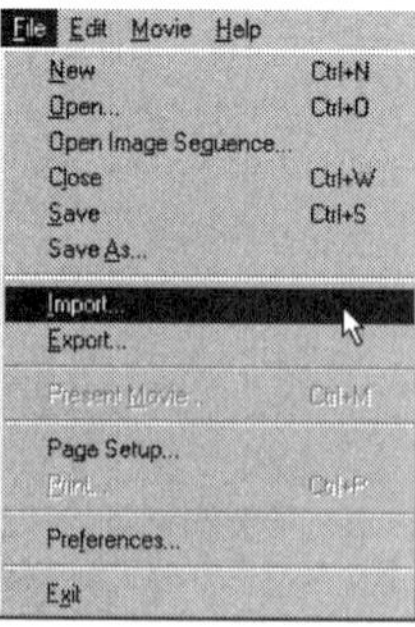

Figure 13.1 Choose Import from the File menu.

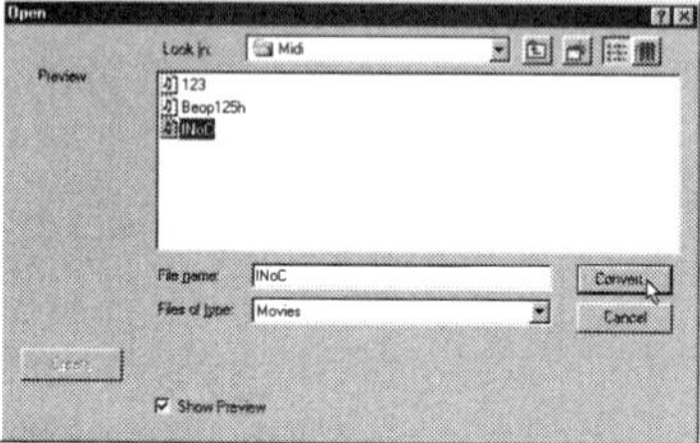

Figure 13.2 Locate a MIDI file and click Convert.

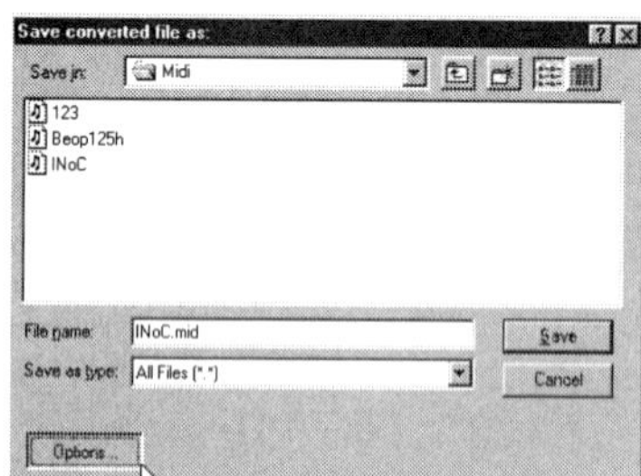

Figure 13.3 Before clicking Save, you may want to click the Options button...

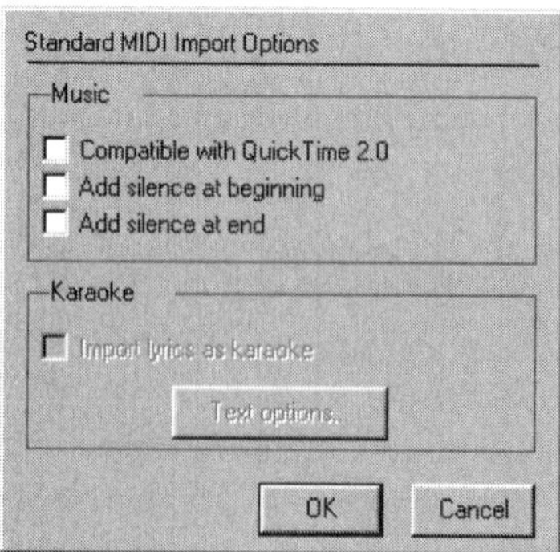

Figure 13.4 ...to open the Standard MIDI Import Options dialog box.

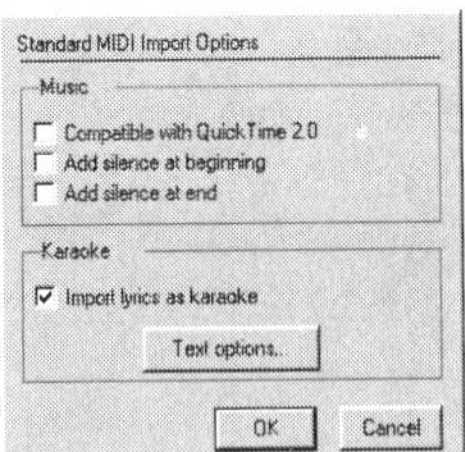

Figure 13.5 When you import a karaoke file, options are available at the bottom of the Standard MIDI Import dialog box.

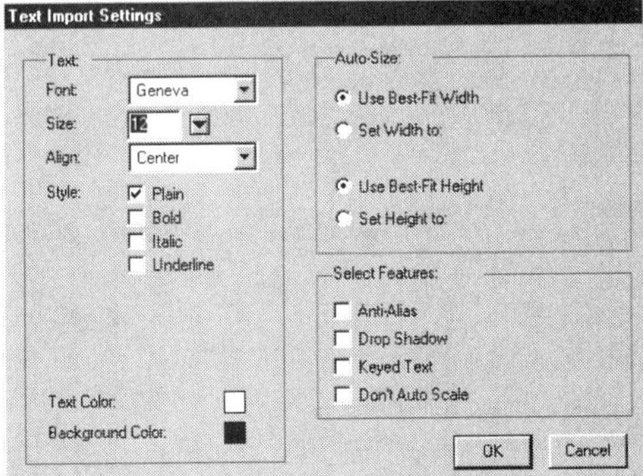

Figure 13.6 If you click the Text Options button in the Standard MIDI Import dialog box, the Text Import Settings dialog appears so you can change the properties of the text track that will be created.

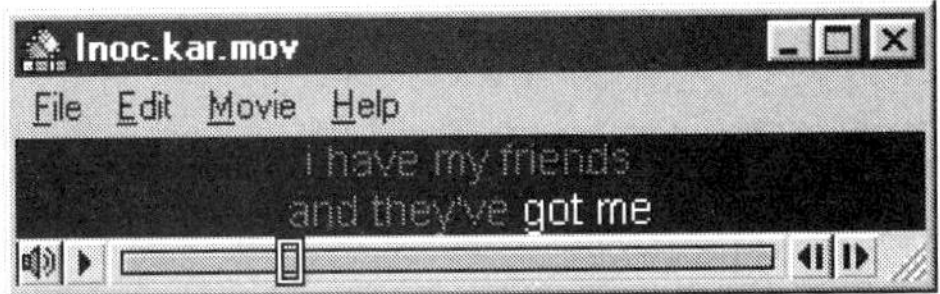

Figure 13.7 An imported karaoke file looks like a text-track movie...

Figure 13.8 ...but it contains both a text track and a music track.

Converting karaoke files to QuickTime

Since karaoke files contain both MIDI and textual data, when converted to QuickTime, they become a movie containing a music and a text track.

To create a music and text track from a karaoke file

1. As with MIDI files, choose **Import** or **Open** from the File menu, locate the file, and click **Convert**.
2. You may also want to click the **Options** button and select any of the options available in the top part of the window (as described on the previous page).

   In addition, the bottom area of the window is not dimmed as it is for MIDI files (**Figure 13.5**). Assuming that you want the text from the file imported make sure that **Import Lyrics as Karaoke** is checked. You can click the **Text options** button to open the Text Import Settings dialog box (**Figure 13.6**). See *Specifying text track appearance when you import* in Chapter 9 for a complete explanation of the options available here.
3. Click **OK** in the Text Import Settings dialog box and/or the Standard MIDI Import dialog box to return to the Save dialog box.
4. Click **Save**.

   A window appears, containing a text track (**Figure 13.7**). If you check in the Info window, you'll see that the movie contains both a text track and a music track (**Figure 13.8**).

✔ Note

- There are actually multiple karaoke file formats. QuickTime handles .KAR files, which are the most popular format.

Changing instruments in a music track

Recall that a music track, like a MIDI file, is composed of a sequence of commands specifying how certain sound samples should be played. These samples are called *instruments*. Most instruments have names and sounds identical to musical instruments in the real world, such as piano, oboe, and bassoon. There are also some instruments that emulate sound effects, such as a telephone ring or a gunshot. In any music track, you can easily switch the instrument used for a certain part of the piece.

To change instruments

1. In the Info window (accessed by choosing Get Info from the Movie menu), choose the music track from the left pop-up menu and Instruments from the right pop-up menu.

   A list of instruments appears in the window (**Figure 13.9**). These are the instruments currently used in the music track.

2. Double-click an instrument in the list.

   An Instrument Picker dialog box with several pop-up menus appears (**Figure 13.10**).

3. Leaving **Best Synthesizer** chosen in the top pop-up menu, change the instrument by changing the item chosen in the Category and/or Instrument pop-up menus.

   Or, to get further choices, choose **QuickTime Music Synthesizer** in the top pop-up menu. The dialog box expands, and you find, in the top part of the window, different choices in the Category and Instrument pop-up menus than were available when Best Synthesizer was chosen (**Figure 13.11**). These sounds are available as long as the QuickTime music software is installed. (This is part of the normal

Figure 13.9 The Instruments panel lists the instruments used in the track.

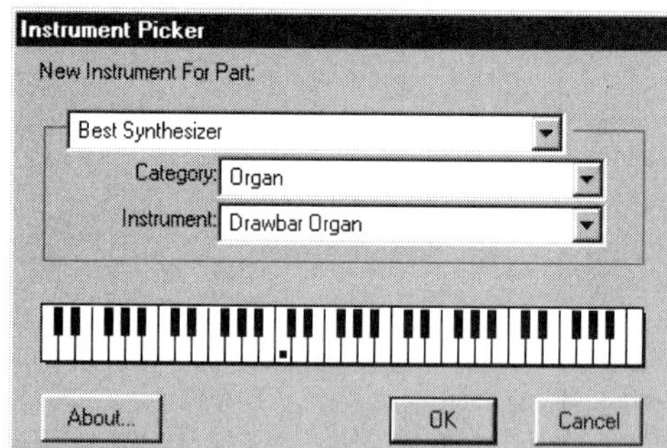

Figure 13.10 When you double-click on an instrument in the Instruments panel, this dialog box appears.

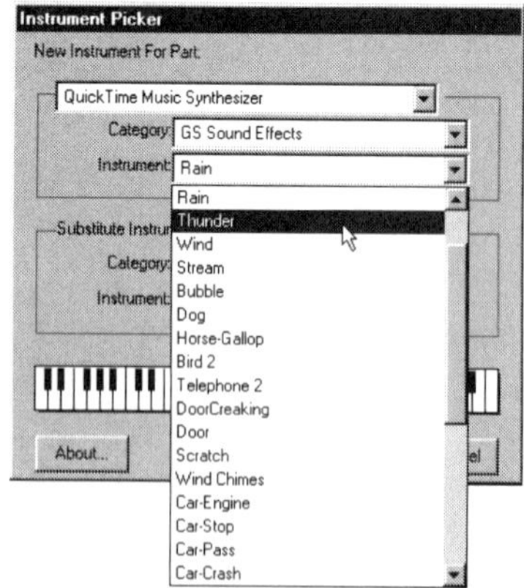

Figure 13.11 When QuickTime Music Synthesizer is chosen, you have some choices that will only work through QuickTime.

QuickTime installation.) If the file happens to be played on a computer that doesn't have the QuickTime music software (very rare) but is connected to an external synthesizer, the instrument selected in the bottom part of the window (labeled "Substitute Instrument") will be used.

✔ Note

- If you have an alternate hardware or software synthesizer it will appear in the top pop-up menu, but we still recommend choosing Best Synthesizer. See *Playing music tracks through a MIDI synthesizer* later in this chapter for an explanation.

Substituting your own custom sound for an instrument in a music track (Mac OS only)

If you've got a music track on a Mac OS computer, you don't have to be satisfied with the sound samples that are built into QuickTime. You can take a sound of your own and use it in place of one of the existing instruments in the music track.

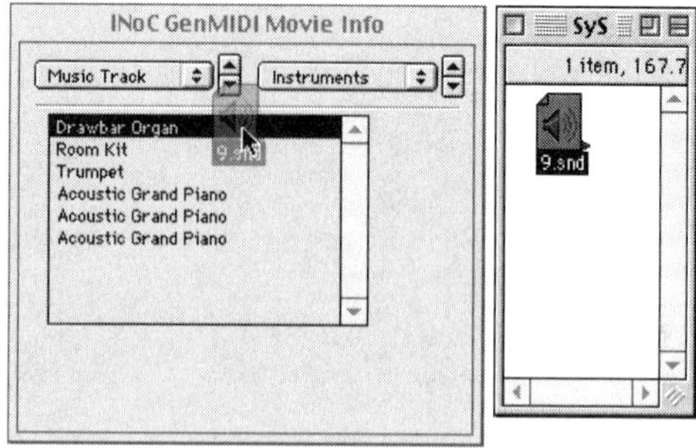

Figure 13.12 Drag a System 7 Sound file over the name of an instrument used in a music track.

To use one of your own sounds in place of an instrument in a music track

1. If your sound isn't a System 7 Sound file, open the file in MoviePlayer and export as a System 7 Sound file. (See Chapter 12 for details.)
2. With your movie containing a music track open in MoviePlayer, open the Info window and choose the music track from the left pop-up menu and Instruments from the right pop-up menu.
3. In the Finder, open the folder that contains the System 7 Sound file, and position the Info window and the folder window so that you can see both.
4. Drag the sound file to the location in the Info window where the instrument you want to replace is shown (**Figure 13.12**).

   The instrument name is replaced by the name of your sound file (**Figure 13.13**).

   When you play the movie, your sound is used instead of the instrument that it replaced.

   The sound data in the sound file becomes part of the QuickTime movie; this can increase the file size of a music-only file considerably.

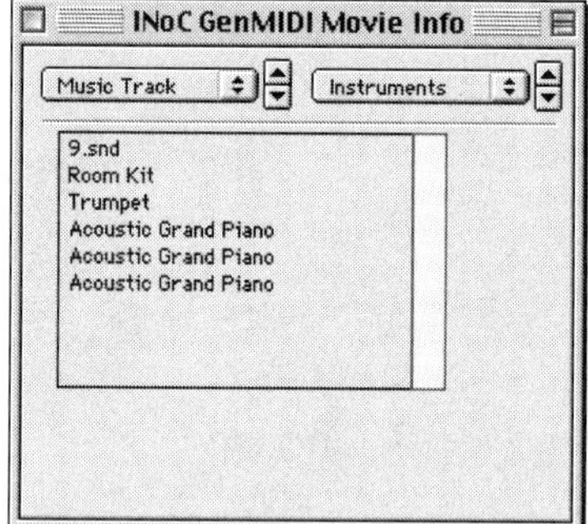

Figure 13.13 The instrument is replaced by your sound.

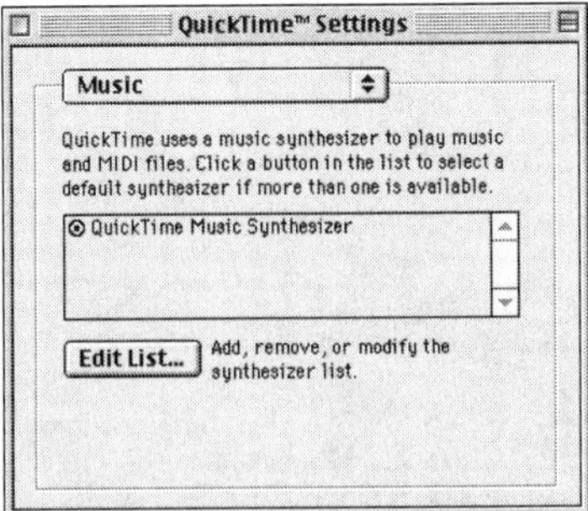

Figure 13.14 The Music panel of the QuickTime Settings control panel lists available synthesizers.

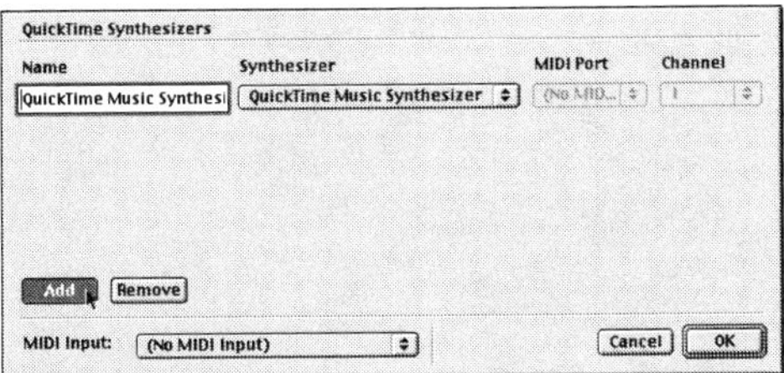

Figure 13.15 If you want to add a new synthesizer, click the Add button.

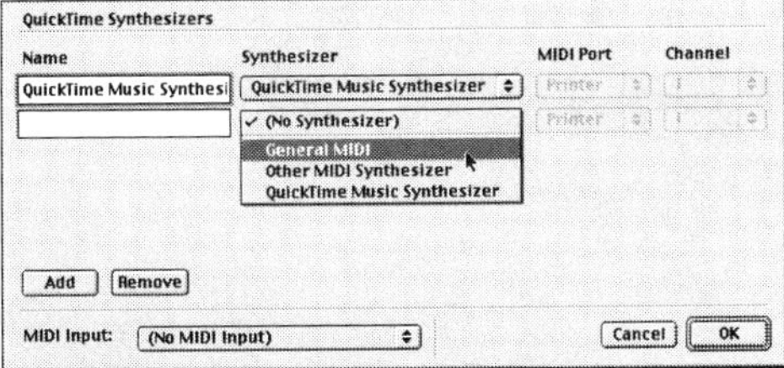

Figure 13.16 When you click the Add button, a new row is created in which you can choose your synthesizer.

Playing music tracks through a MIDI synthesizer (Mac OS only)

While the music synthesizer built into QuickTime is pretty good, you can probably get better audio quality with a hardware synthesizer. If you have a hardware synthesizer —one that meets the General MIDI specification—you can have QuickTime use it to play a music track. You'll also need MIDI system software; some that we know of are Apple's MIDI software, OMS, and FreeMIDI. (See Appendix C for vendor information.)

To have a track played through a MIDI synthesizer connected to your computer

1. Open the QuickTime Settings control panel.
2. Choose Music from the pop-up menu to show the Music panel (**Figure 13.14**).
3. Assuming that you don't see anything but QuickTime Music Synthesizer listed in the scrolling field, click the Edit List button. (If your synthesizer is listed, skip to step 8.)
4. In the QuickTime Synthesizers dialog box (**Figure 13.15**), click the Add button.

   A new row is added.
5. In the pop-up menu in the Synthesizer column for the newly added row, choose your synthesizer (**Figure 13.16**), and then make choices in the MIDI Port and Channel columns, if the pop-up menus are available.

   (We can't tell you exactly what you'll need to choose here because of the large variety of software and hardware available, as well as the many ways that it can be configured. If your synthesizer doesn't appear at all here, it's probably because your MIDI system software is not properly installed and/or configured.)

6. Click **OK**.

7. In the QuickTime Settings control panel, your synthesizer should be listed. Select it by clicking on the radio button for that line in the list (**Figure 13.17**). (Unlike most radio buttons, this one doesn't get selected when you click on the text.)

   Now, when you play movies with music tracks, instruments that are set to Best Synthesizer in the Instrument Picker dialog box will play through your MIDI Synthesizer. (Best Synthesizer is the default.)

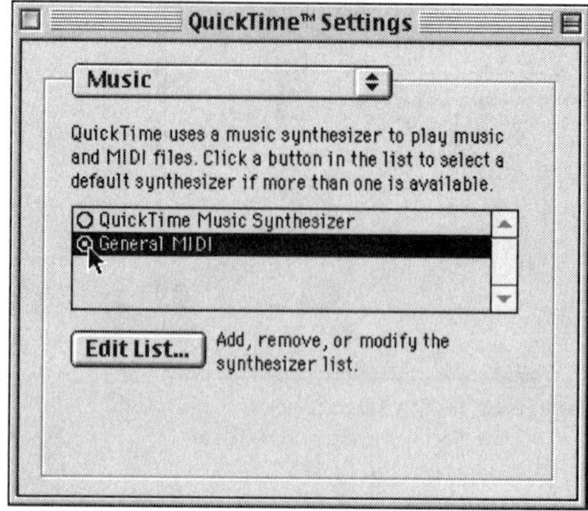

Figure 13.17 The new synthesizer is added to the list of available synthesizers in the Music panel.

✔ Note

- Even though your synthesizer appears in the pop-up menu in the Instrument Picker dialog box, you should leave Best Synthesizer chosen; this way your synthesizer will be used as long as it's available, but if it's not available, the QuickTime synthesizer will be used.

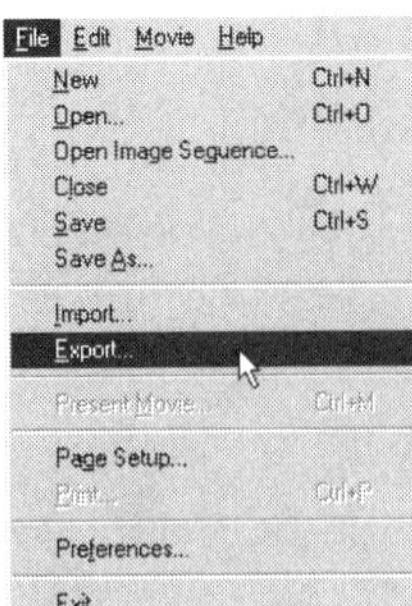

Figure 13.18 Choose Export from the File menu.

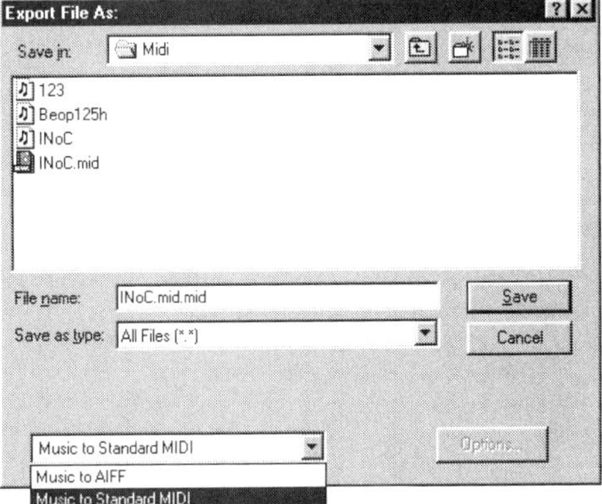

Figure 13.19 Choose Music to Standard MIDI and click Save.

Converting QuickTime music tracks back to MIDI

MoviePlayer's export options let you save a music track as a standard MIDI file. You'd do this if you had MIDI editing software that you wanted to use to alter the music track.

To export a QuickTime music track as a MIDI file

1. Choose **Export** from the File menu (**Figure 13.18**).
2. In the pop-up menu in the lower left corner of the Save dialog box, choose **Music to Standard MIDI** and click **Save** (**Figure 13.19**).

✔ Note

- If your movie contains more than one music track, when you export as MIDI, only the first music track listed in the left pop-up menu in the Info window (usually named "Music Track 1") is exported.

14

Delivery Basics

So you're done editing your movies and you want to distribute them to the world. (Or maybe just to your mother.)

Whether you want to put the movies on the Web, on CD-ROM, or on a hard disk, there are some basic concepts you should understand, and some tasks you'll want to know how to do. In this chapter we'll explain the concepts and show you how to accomplish the tasks.

Understanding data rate and size

The *data rate* of a movie is the average amount of data per second contained in the movie. We mentioned the concept of a video track's data rate in Chapter 8, and a sound track's data rate in Chapter 12. Of course, all tracks have a data rate—it's just that the video and audio tracks' data rates are typically the largest and thus the ones to worry about. The sum of the data rates of all the tracks in the movie is the movie's data rate.

The channel through which your movie is delivered has what's called a *bandwidth*. This is the amount of data per second that it's possible to display using that particular hardware and software.

You need to consider how the data rate of your movie compares to the bandwidth of the system that's presenting that movie. For example, a 4x CD-ROM drive has a theoretical maximum bandwidth of 600 kilobytes per second. If your movie has a data rate greater than that, it will skip and probably will be unwatchable.

Internet bandwidths are very narrow—lower than two kilobytes per second for the slowest modem lines. You want your movie's data rate to be as close to the network bandwidth as possible. How far you can deviate from this depends on how long you're willing to have viewers wait before they can view your movie. (We'll get into details in the next chapter.)

You may also need to be concerned with the *data size* of your movie—the total size of all the data in it (i.e. the data rate multiplied by the duration of the movie). This is because every storage medium—floppy disks, hard drives, CD-ROMs, DVD-ROMs, and even the hard drives to which your Web movies will be downloaded —has a finite amount of space.

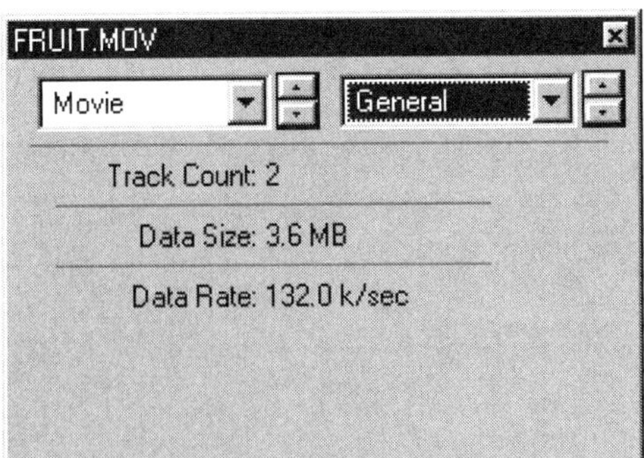

Figure 14.1 The General panel for a movie shows both the data size and the data rate for the movie.

Checking data rate and data size

Since knowing the data size and data rate of a movie can help you predict how well the movie will play on a particular platform, we'll show you how to check these.

To check the data size and data rate of a movie

1. Open the Info window (accessed by choosing **Get Info** from the Movie menu).
2. Choose **Movie** from the left pop-up menu and **General** from the right pop-up menu.

   The General panel (**Figure 14.1**) shows both the data size and the data rate in bytes, kilobytes (k), or megabytes (MB).

✔ Warning

- When you compare the data rate of your file to the bandwidth of your delivery platform you'll need to be careful about your units of measurement. You may have to do some conversions. Kilobytes, for example, are eight times the size of kilobits.

Saving movies for distribution

There are some cases where you need to do nothing more than save your movie to make it ready for distribution. (We described saving in Chapter 5.) Generally, if your movie has a data rate as low or lower than your target bandwidth—as is often the case with text, sprite, 3D, and music track movies—it only needs to be saved. (If you have video and/or audio tracks that need to be compressed you'll have to export; see *Exporting movies as QuickTime movies*.)

Whether you're working on a Mac OS or Windows computer, as long as you use the Save As command, QuickTime 3 automatically saves files so that they are playable on both platforms, and are *fast start* (a format good for the Web, which we describe in the next chapter).

When saving, you usually want to make sure to save your movie as a self-contained file (**Figure 14.2**). Also, if you're saving a movie on a Macintosh, you should give it a .mov extension so Windows computers will recognize it as a QuickTime movie. When you save a movie on a Windows computer, the .mov extension is added automatically.

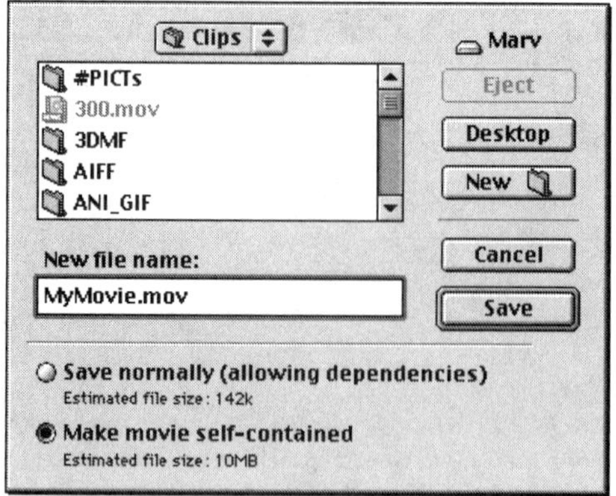

Figure 14.2 In MoviePlayer's Save dialog box, you should save a movie as self-contained unless you have an explicit reason for saving with dependencies.

✔ Note

- Versions of QuickTime previous to 3 did not automatically save movie files so that they were playable on both platforms. If you have older QuickTime movies that were created on a Mac OS computer, and you want to distribute them on both platforms, you may want to open them and save them (with the Save As command) using MoviePlayer and QuickTime 3. (There's no way to check with MoviePlayer to see if they are cross-platform movies or not.)

✔ No guarantees

- There's no tip or rule that we can tell you to guarantee that your movie will play well on all computers. If you want to be *sure* your movies really do play the way you expect them to, you've got to test them on the largest possible variety of computer systems.

Saving double-sized

If you double a movie's window size using the Double Size command in the Movie menu and then save, the movie doesn't increase in file size or data rate, but you get a movie that looks twice as large. QuickTime does an excellent job of playing back movies at double-size. This is an effective technique to use whether you're putting movies on the Web, CD-ROM, kiosk, or outputting to videotape.

Exporting movies as QuickTime movies

In some cases, rather than simply saving your movie, you'll want to export it. MoviePlayer has an export option called "Movie to QuickTime movie," which allows you to do several things that you can't do if you just save a file:

- **Apply compression to video and/or sound tracks:** If you've got a movie with video and sound tracks, you'll probably want to compress those tracks in order to achieve a desired data rate. (This includes changing such characteristics as frame rate and key frame rate for video, and sample rate and sample size for audio.)
- **Combine data in all visual tracks into a single video track, and/or combine data in all sound tracks into a single sound track:** If you've got lower-data-rate visual tracks—3D, sprite, or text—in a movie that also has a video track and you don't need any of the special features of those tracks (e.g. searchability in a text track), you may want to make that data part of the video track—the movie will probably play more smoothly. Also, if the movie has multiple video or sound tracks, combining them into a single video or sound track will almost definitely cause smoother playback. (We're referring here specifically to QuickTime *sound* tracks and not to other types of audio tracks, such as music tracks.)
- **Apply visual filters:** Applying filters may seem like something you'd want to do earlier—say, when you're editing the file—but this is where you do it in MoviePlayer.
- **Permanently reduce the frame size of the movie:** If you reduce the size of the movie's window and then *save* it, the

When not to export

If you have a movie with no video or sound tracks, and only 3D, music, sprite, or text tracks, don't export the movie as a QuickTime movie. Exporting 3D, sprite, or text tracks this way only converts them into video tracks, which have much higher data rates. With QuickTime 3.0, music tracks are ignored if you export as a QuickTime movie; they're not even, as you might expect, converted to sound tracks. You also can't export MPEG tracks, even though the choice is there in the pop-up menu; you get an error message as soon as you hit Save. If you have a movie with a combination of tracks, some of which you'd like to export and some of which should be left alone, see Compressing selected tracks later in this chapter.

movie's data size doesn't change because the movie's default, "normal" window size remains the same. (That is, when you choose Normal from the Movie menu it will return to it's original size.) If you *export* it, however, the movie's normal window size *does* permanently change, reducing the data size considerably. You can always reopen the movie in MoviePlayer, double its size, and resave, if you want something that *looks* big. (See the sidebar *Saving double-sized*, earlier in this chapter.)

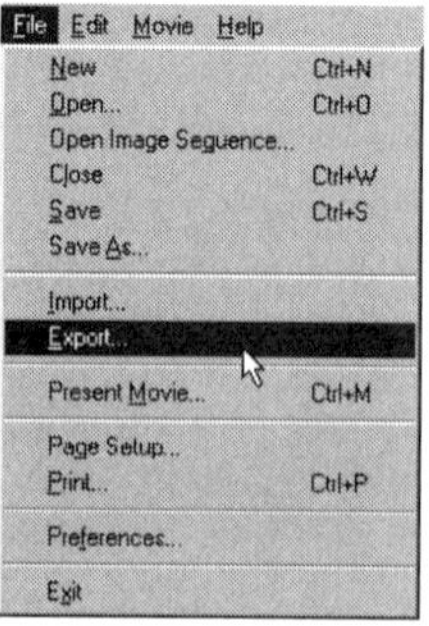

Figure 14.3 Choose Export from the File menu.

To export a movie as a QuickTime movie

1. Choose Export from the File menu (**Figure 14.3**).
2. Choose Movie to QuickTime Movie in the pop-up menu at the bottom of the window (**Figure 14.4**).
3. Click Options.
4. In the Movie Settings dialog box (**Figure 14.5**), make sure that both the Video and Sound checkboxes are selected, unless your movie doesn't contain any visual or sound tracks (or you actually want to make a movie without video or audio).
5. Click the Settings button in either the Video or Sound areas if you want to change any of the settings specified to the right of those buttons. (The default settings are rarely appropriate. We'll offer specific compression recommendations in the following chapters.) When you're done choosing new settings, click OK to return to the Movie Settings dialog box.
6. Click Filter in the Video area of the Movie Settings dialog box if you want to apply a video filter. (See *Applying filters* for more information about filters.) When you're done picking and configuring a filter, click OK to return to the Movie Settings dialog box.

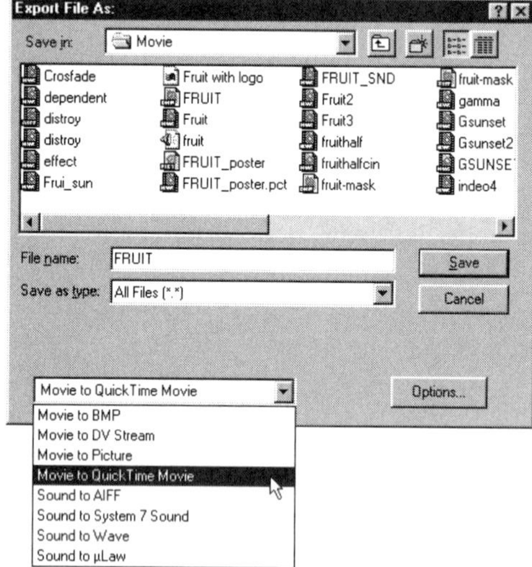

Figure 14.4 Choose Movie to QuickTime Movie.

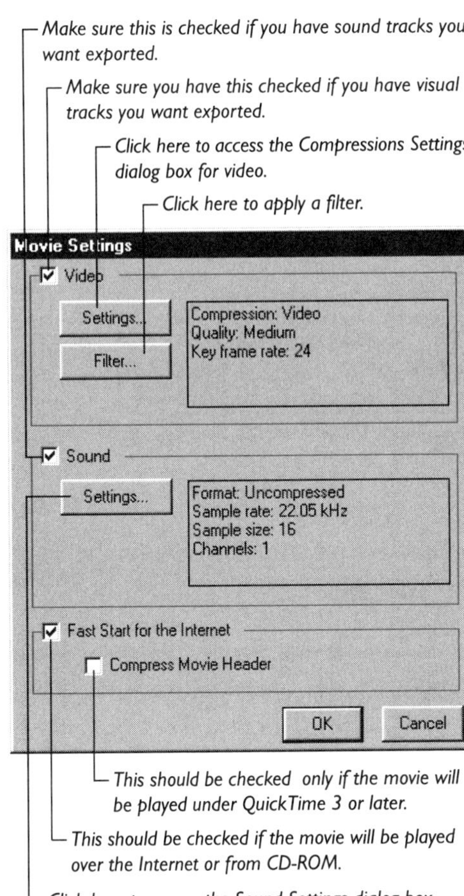

Figure 14.5 The Movie Settings dialog box

7. In most cases, make sure that the **Fast Start for the Internet** checkbox at the bottom of the dialog box is selected. (The next chapter describes fast start in detail. It's actually a good idea to have Fast Start for the Internet checked for CD-ROM and other distribution platforms, as well. The only advantage to not having this selected is that the export may take slightly less time; files exported with the Fast Start for Internet work just fine in non-Internet contexts.)
8. Only select the **Compress Movie Header** checkbox if you are sure the movie will be played with QuickTime 3 or later. (Movies compressed this way will load somewhat faster, but will not work with any version of QuickTime earlier than 3.)
9. Click **OK**.
10. Specify a file name (with a **.mov** extension) and a location and click **Save**.

✔ Tips

- Note that the default settings in the Movie Settings dialog box do not reflect the current status of the video or sound track; to determine those, use the Format panel of the Info window as described in Chapters 8 and 12.
- If at all possible, you should avoid recompressing already-compressed video, since compressors create some visual artifacts (blocky, noisy, or hard-to-discern areas); those artifacts will get considerably worse the second time the clip is compressed. In the same way, you should avoid recompressing audio. You should use the least-compressed version of the movie that you have.

Applying filters

QuickTime 3 includes filters that can be used to alter the appearance of a video track. Using MoviePlayer, you can choose to apply any one of these filters when you export a movie as a QuickTime movie. We'll cover the general process you follow to apply a filter and then provide some examples. In addition, see Table 14.1 for a list of all the filters you can access in MoviePlayer.

To apply a filter

1. Choose **Export** from the Movie menu, choose **Movie to QuickTime Movie**, and click the **Options** button to open the Movie Settings dialog box.
2. Click the **Filter** button (**Figure 14.6**).
3. In the Choose Video Filter dialog box (**Figure 14.7**), click on a filter in the list on the left.

   Depending on the filter selected, you'll be provided on the right with controls and fields to vary certain properties of that filter. (See *Some example filters*, below.)
4. Adjust the settings, using the image sample in the lower left of the window as a guide to ensure that you are achieving the effect you desire. Then click **OK** to return to the Movie Settings dialog box.
5. Click **Save**.

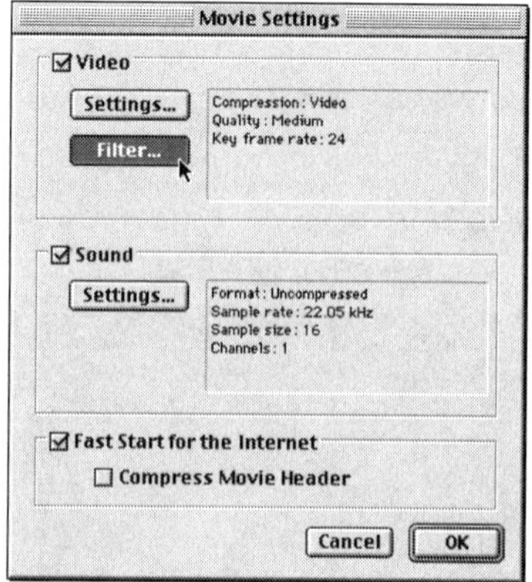

Figure 14.6 In the Movie Settings dialog box, click the Filter button.

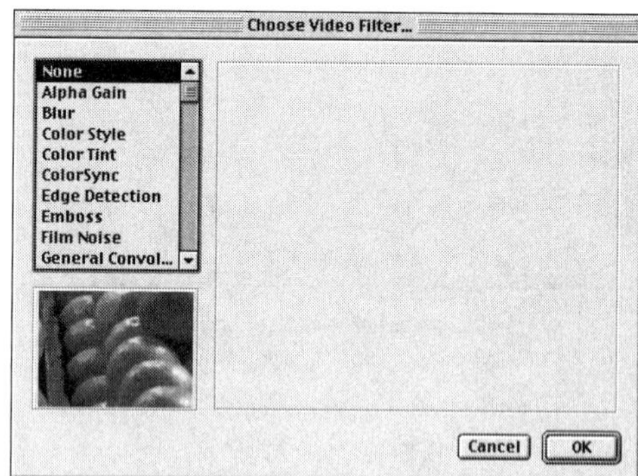

Figure 14.7 The Choose Filter dialog box has a number of filters to choose from. Each has different settings.

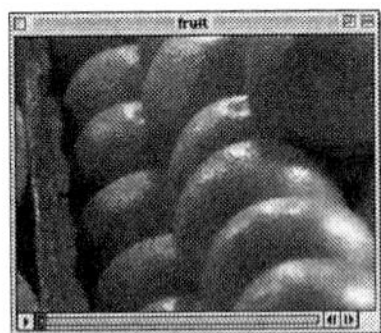
Figure 14.8 Here's an original unfiltered movie image.

Some example filters

Figure 14.8 shows an original, unfiltered movie image. **Figures 14.9, 14.10, and 14.11** show this same image after certain filters have been applied, as well as how the filters were configured in the Choose Filter dialog box.

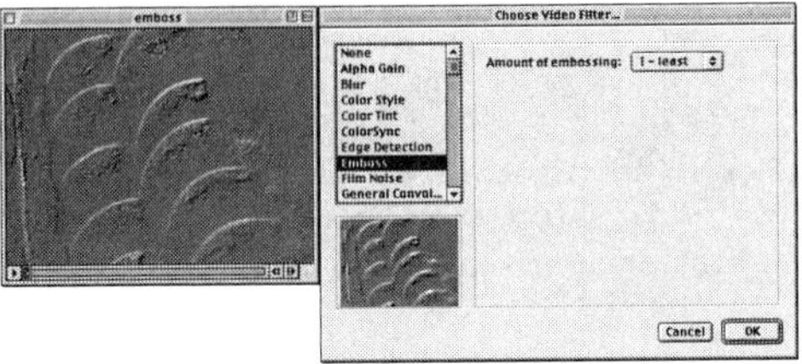
Figure 14.9 The Emboss filter affects the image like this with these settings.

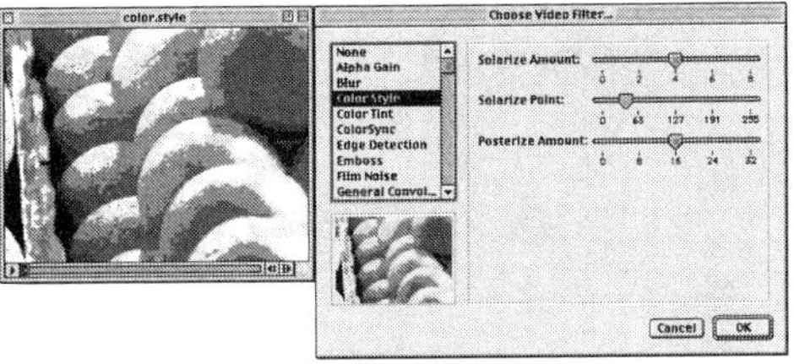
Figure 14.10 The Color Style filter affects the image like this with these settings.

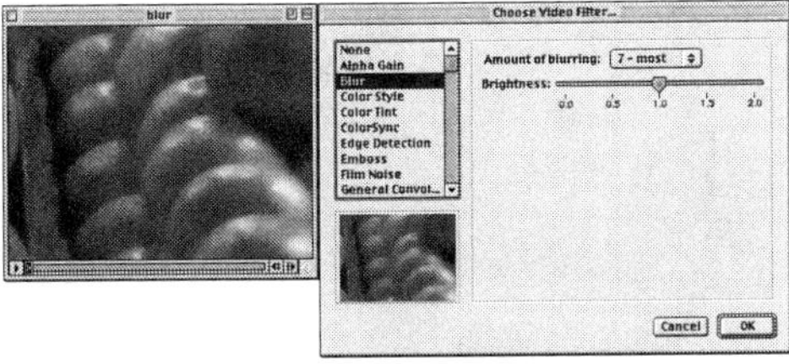
Figure 14.11 The Blur filter affects the image like this with these settings.

Table 14.1

Video Filters

FILTER	COMMENTS
None	Lets you undo any of the other filters in this table.
Alpha Gain	Lets you manipulate the alpha channel of an image.
Blur	Fuzzes the image. You can adjust the amount of blurring and the brightness.
Color Style	Lets you add solarization and posterization effects.
Color Tint	Lets you change the image to black and white, tint it any color, and invert colors.
ColorSync	(Mac OS only) Lets you link the movie's image to a ColorSync profile. You can link to a source and/or a destination profile. Only available if ColorSync system files are installed.
Edge Detection	Finds the edges in the image. You can set the width of the edge and you can also choose to colorize the results.
Emboss	Gives the image a raised, metallic look. You can choose the amount of embossing.
Film Noise	Adds noise to the image so it looks like movie film. You can set various parameters relating to hairs, scratches, dust and fading.
General Convolution	Lets you enter values in a grid to specify a pattern of brightness for the pixels in the image. It's based on a mathematical process called "convolution."
HSL Balance	Lets you alter the look of the image by setting its hue, saturation. and lightness.
RGB Balance	Lets you alter the look of the image by setting its red, green, or blue values.
Sharpen	Sharpens the image. You can set the degree of sharpening and brightness.

Compressing selected tracks

There are times when you want to designate that selected tracks in a movie be compressed while other tracks be left alone. For example, if you have a movie with a text track and a video track, you may want the video track but not the text track compressed. Or, you may just want to lower the data rate of your sound track, leaving other tracks as they are.

While other more expensive tools (such as Media Cleaner Pro) have simple methods for you to designate tracks that should be left alone, there's no correspondingly simple way to do this using MoviePlayer. You'll need to use some combination of techniques covered in this book—copying, pasting, adding, extracting, deleting, exporting, and importing—to achieve the desired result. We'll cover one possibility here. (See *Changing the characteristics of a sound track* in Chapter 12 for an alternative technique.)

To compress only selected tracks in a movie

1. Use the Extract Tracks command in the Edit menu to extract the track(s) you want to compress (**Figure 14.12**).
2. Use the Export command in the File menu (**Figure 14.13**) to export the movie created by the extraction. Apply appropriate compression settings.
3. In the original movie (the one containing all the tracks), use the Delete Tracks command in the Edit menu to delete the track(s) that you extracted in step 1 (**Figure 14.14**).
4. Open the movie exported in step 2 and select and copy the entire movie. (Be careful not to confused the *extracted* movie with the *exported* movie.)

Figure 14.12 Choose Extract Tracks from the Edit menu and extract the tracks that you want to compress.

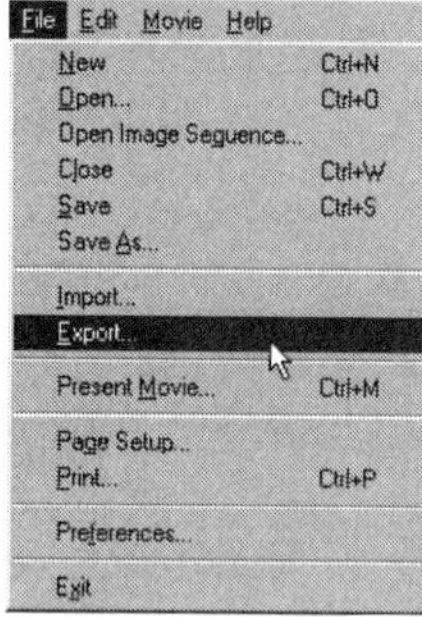

Figure 14.13 Export the movie created by the extraction.

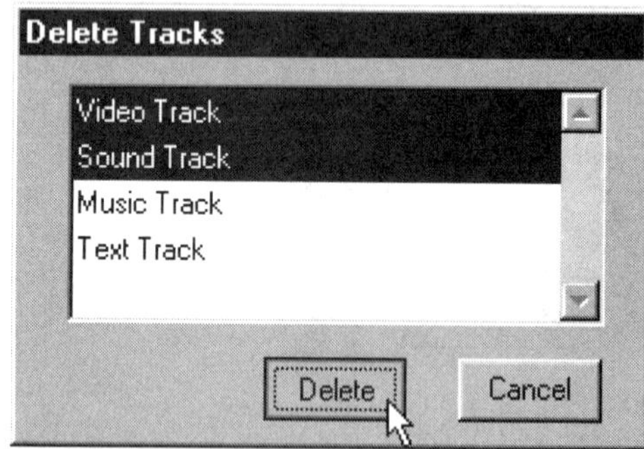

Figure 14.14 Choose Delete Tracks from the Edit menu and delete the same tracks you extracted.

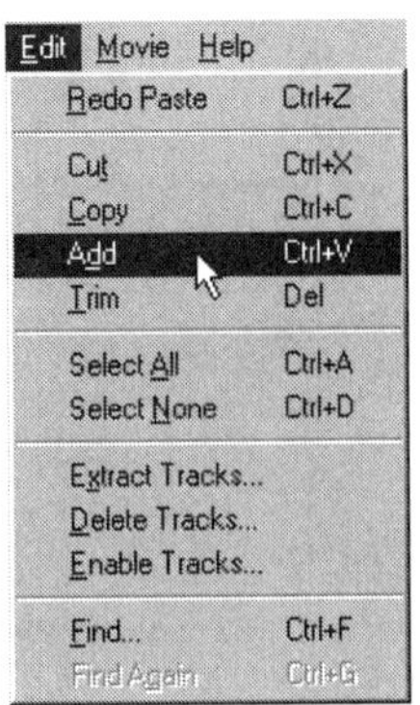

Figure 14.15 Open the exported movie, copy it all, and add it back into the original movie file. (To access the Add command in the Edit menu, Windows users need to hold down the Alt and Ctrl keys; Mac users need to hold down the Option key.)

5. In the original movie, move the slider to the far left of the play bar, hold down the **Option** key (Mac OS) or **Ctrl** and **Alt** keys (Windows), and choose **Add** from the Edit menu (**Figure 14.15**). The tracks you extracted are now added back in their compressed form.

✔ Warning

- We recommend making a copy of your original movie before following this procedure, since deleted tracks can't be restored once the movie is saved.

Better tools

While we'll show you the basics of what you need to know to prepare your movies for distribution using MoviePlayer, it's important to know that you can use other tools to accomplish the same tasks. In particular, Media Cleaner Pro from Terran Interactive is generally considered a must-have in the toolbox of most multimedia developers that are processing QuickTime movies for final delivery. (Media Cleaner Pro generally does an optimal job of compression and has a wizard that helps you to make decisions. It also allows you to do a number of things that you can't do with MoviePlayer, such as cropping movies before compressing them and batch processing many movies at once, rather than doing one at a time.)

Checking the dimensions of a movie

Whether you intend to put your movie on a Web page or use it in an interactive presentation created using a multimedia authoring tool you'll probably need to know your movie's frame size. (This will help you plan screen layout and/or write your HTML code.)

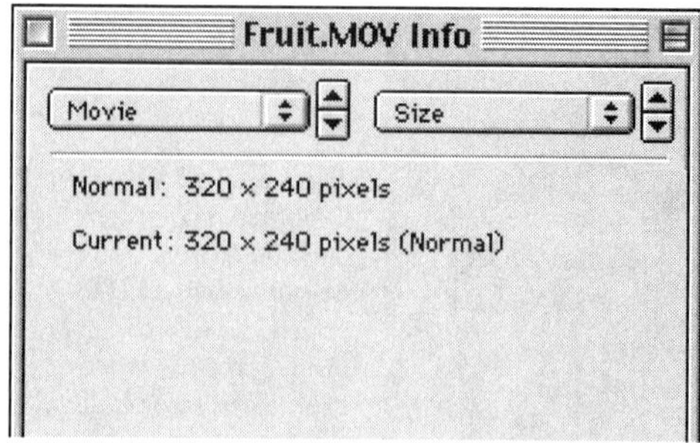

Figure 14.16 The Size panel for the movie displays the movie's width and height. The width for this movie is 320 pixels. The height for this movie is 240 pixels; including the controller, it's 256 pixels.

To determine the dimensions of a movie

◆ In the Info window (accessed by choosing Get Info from the Movie menu), choose Movie from the left pop-up menu and Size from the right pop-up menu.

The Size panel (**Figure 14.16**) tells you the dimensions of the movie (width by height) at its normal size as well as the dimensions at which it is currently set. (The second line will only be different from the first line if the window size has been altered. See *Changing window sizes* in Chapter 2.) The word "none" appears for movies with no visual track.

✔ Tip

- The dimensions listed don't include the height of the controller, which is 16 pixels. To determine the height of the movie including the controller (which you will often need to do), add 16 to the height stated in this panel.

15 Movies on Web Pages: Basics

If you've chosen to put your QuickTime movies on Web pages, you're not alone. There are more QuickTime movies on the Web than any other video format.

In this chapter, we'll start by explaining how QuickTime compares to other Web video choices. Then we'll get into some specifics of how best to prepare QuickTime files for the Web using MoviePlayer.

We'll cover the specific HTML you use to put a movie on a Web page and then show a few special techniques, such as those for *poster movies* (small movies that stand in for larger ones until a user clicks) and *HREF tracks* (text tracks that call up Web pages).

QuickTime compared to other streaming formats

Digital video is starting to become very popular on the Web. Many of the other video technologies—RealMedia, NetShow, and VDOLive, to name a view—are referred to as *streaming* technologies.

What does streaming really mean? While the term has no official definition, to most people it means that the media plays immediately, rather than the end-user having to wait until a file is downloaded.

By this definition, you can make QuickTime files that stream nearly as well as any other technology. QuickTime 3 movies, by default, are saved in a *fast start* format. This means that, although a movie is downloaded into a file, the movie can start playing before the file is completely downloaded. (This technique is sometimes generically referred to as *progressive downloading*.)

The QuickTime plug-in determines when enough of a movie has been downloaded to enable it to play continuously to the end. Movies with very low data rates—such as those that can be achieved with QuickTime's low-data-rate track types, or QuickTime 3's new compressors—can begin playing immediately. Thus, the end-user experience is the same as it is with a RealMedia or other similar file.

The streaming that QuickTime does is called *HTTP streaming*, which differs from *RTP streaming*, used by dedicated media servers. With HTTP streaming, you simply put your movie files on a Web server as you do image files. Movies are downloaded to the user's computer, where the QuickTime plug-in handles the task of playing them. The server-based solutions require special server software, which takes control of sending out streams of media.

An advantage to the scheme QuickTime uses is that if the user wants to replay the data, it doesn't need to be served over the network again; it's sitting there in a file already. With the traditional streaming technologies, if the user wants to replay the data, it needs to come over the network again.

One case where the QuickTime scheme currently can be a problem, however, is that of a movie with a very long duration. This is because there must be room on the viewer's hard drive to store the entire file. The other technologies work by having a server send out the movie data as it is needed; typically nothing is stored on the viewer's computer.

Server-based solutions also excel when there are network slowdowns (since the user's computer and the server can communicate about how the transmission is going and the server can adjust the amount of data being sent), and in situations that call for "live broadcasting" of video. In the future, there will be a version of QuickTime that is server-based; see sidebar, *The future of QuickTime Streaming*.

The future of QuickTime Streaming

Apple is rapidly moving in the direction of a complete client/server solution that has all the advantages of the competing technologies, and then some.

The first thing they're going to release (possibly by the time your read this) is the technology to allow users to view live streams from other sources. There is a standard Internet protocol for doing streaming media called RTP (realtime transport protocol). Apple plans to release a new version of QuickTime 3 that will allow users to view any live RTP broadcast from the Internet in any place they can currently view a QuickTime movie. As a media author, this will allow you to create Web pages or interactive CDs that are designed to showcase live broadcasts.

Later in 1998 or 1999, Apple plans to introduce QuickTime Streaming server technology that will allow you to stream video and audio, just as RealMedia and NetShow do. This will provide advantages in terms of performance and will allow you to broadcast your own live streams. It also means that a file won't have to be downloaded to the viewer's computer.

Making QuickTime movies that stream

If your goal is to create a QuickTime movie that plays immediately without making the user wait, you will need to create a movie with a total data rate that is no greater than the bandwidth of the network connection that you expect the user to have.

If the movie's data rate is higher than the available bandwidth, the user will have to wait until a certain amount of the file has been downloaded before it starts playing. (**Figure 15.1**) For movies with a data rate only slightly higher, this wait may be very short, perhaps no longer than a few seconds; for all intents and purposes this would be considered streaming.

One mistake people make is taking movie files created for CD-ROM and putting them on the Web. Such files have relatively high data rates, and require that the user wait a long time (minutes or even hours) before the movie can start playing.

As we've mentioned previously, getting your movies to have low data rates requires either using low-data-rate track types (music, sprite, 3D, and/or text), or sufficiently compressed video and sound tracks.

If your movie contains low-data-rate tracks, you generally need only to save the file.

If your movie contains video and sound tracks, you'll want to follow the process we described in the previous chapter for compressing video and sound tracks using MoviePlayer's Export command. In the next few pages we'll cover some specific compression choices appropriate for getting those data rates down to desired levels.

Figure 15.1 When a Web movie is being downloaded, the shaded portion of the play bar represents the amount of the movie that has been downloaded. The higher the data rate, the more that needs to be downloaded before the movie will play.

✔ Warning

- It's a bad idea to simply take movies that were originally compressed for CD-ROM and recompress them for the Web. To get the best-looking video, you want to track down the originally captured files (which should have light or no compression), and re-edit and recompress those.

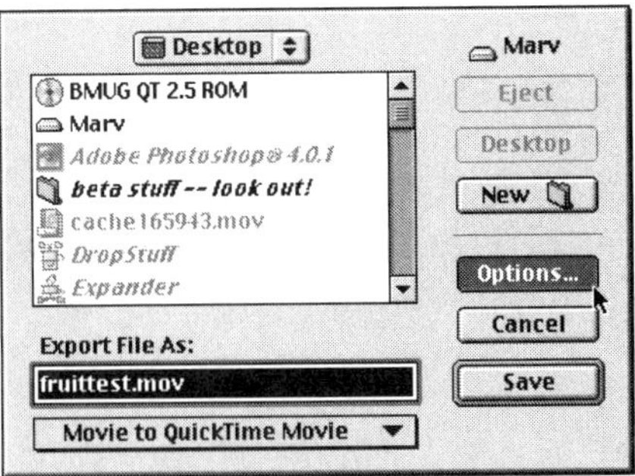

Figure 15.2 Choose Export from the File menu and Movie to QuickTime Movie from the pop-up menu in the Save dialog box, then click the Options button to open the Movie Settings dialog box.

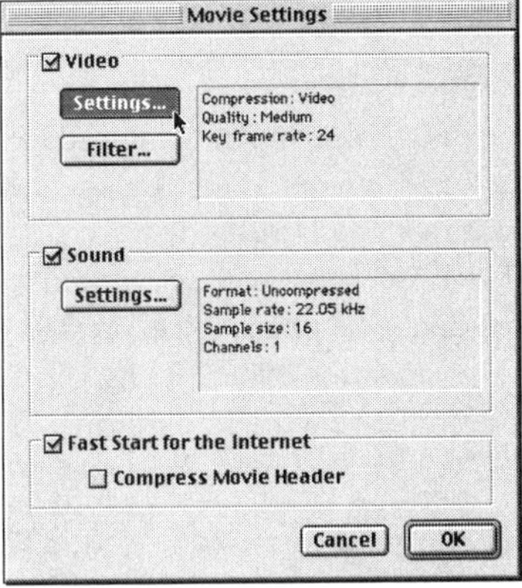

Figure 15.3 Click the top Settings button to open the Compression Settings dialog box.

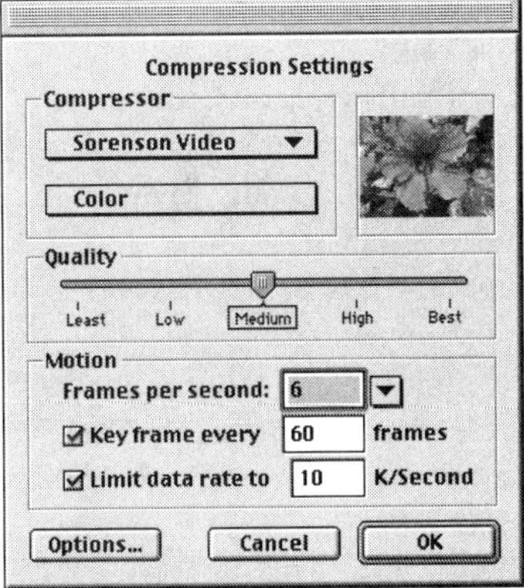

Figure 15.4 The Compression Settings dialog box is where you specify various settings for the video track.

Compressing video for the Web

Unfortunately, it's impossible to provide what everybody wants: a precise recipe for compressing your video for the Web. How you should do it depends on the content of your video, what your personal aesthetics require, who your audience is, and many other factors.

However, we can give you some tips and guidelines that will help you make appropriate choices. (Use this information only as a starting point; even professionals experiment with different combinations of settings until they get the proper balance of data rate, frame rate, and image quality for any particular movie or set of movies playing on the chosen target computers.)

To compress video for the Web using MoviePlayer, you follow the basic steps for exporting (described in the previous chapter) to get to the Compression Settings dialog box; we'll review them here. We'll also comment on each choice that you have to make in that dialog box; recall that other applications provide the same choices, so the information we'll provide here is applicable whether you are using MoviePlayer or another QuickTime application to do the compression.

To access the Compression Settings dialog box

1. Choose **Export** from the File menu, choose **Movie to QuickTime Movie**, and click the **Options** button (**Figure 15.2**).
2. Click the **Settings** button in the Video area of the Movie Settings dialog box (**Figure 15.3**).

   This brings up the Compression Settings dialog box (**Figure 15.4**), where you can choose settings appropriate for Web delivery.

Making Web-appropriate choices in the Compression Settings dialog box

- **Compressor**: In general, the best of the built-in QuickTime compressors for Web video is *Sorenson Video*. This compressor is new to QuickTime 3, and does an excellent job at the very low data rates required for streaming Web delivery. One problem with Sorenson Video is that it doesn't do well on slower computers. (The general rule is that you shouldn't plan to use it for computers with processors that operate at less than 120 MHz; you should test your movie on your target machines if they're even less than 150 MHz.)

  If you know that some of the viewers looking at your Web pages will be using old computers or won't have (and won't go get) QuickTime 3, you may want to choose *Cinepak*. (However, there's a way to create a movie that will work for pre-QuickTime 3 users, but still provide the advanced features of QuickTime 3; see *Alternate Data Rates with MakeRefMovie* in Chapter 16.)

  For computer-generated imagery, if you don't like the results you're getting with Sorenson Video or Cinepak, you may also want to try the *Graphics* compressor or the *Animation* compressor. (The former achieves lower data rates, but only works in 256 colors and decompresses more slowly so may not perform well on very old computers.)

- **Colors**: Some compressors don't give you a choice for the number of colors, but for those that do, we generally recommend choosing the greatest number of colors. Lowering the number of colors generally doesn't lower your data rate enough to warrant the resultant loss in quality. Of course, if your movies only use, say, 256

Estimating target data rates

When you're trying to estimate a good target data rate for your movie you need to be sure you know what units are being used. MoviePlayer reports data rates in bytes, kilobytes, or megabytes per second. Network bandwidths are usually expressed in kilobits per second. A byte is 8 bits. Thus, a 28.8 modem theoretically moves data at 3.6 (28.8 divided by 8) kilobytes per second.

A quick way of estimating a good target data rate in kilobytes is to simply divide the bandwidth by 10 and round down. (Dividing by 10 rather than 8 is faster; plus, it gives you a lower, more conservative estimate that usually ends up being more accurate anyway, since modems rarely reach their theoretical speed.) Thus, if you're creating a movie to be played over 33.6 modems, a good target data rate is about 3 kilobytes per second if you want the movie to start playing just about immediately when the viewer arrives at the Web page. (It may also help you to know that single-channel ISDN lines are 56 kilobits per second, dual-channel ISDN lines are 112 kilobits per second, and T1 lines are 1.5 megabits per second.)

colors, there's no reason to choose a higher number of colors.

- **Quality**: Remember, the higher the quality, the lower the amount of compression, and thus the higher the data rate. We recommend picking a value in the middle of the scale on your first test.
- **Frame rate**: The fewer the number of frames, the lower the data rate. Most current streaming Web video has frame rates of 2 to 10 frames per second. Try a low number to start. To get the best results, use a number that divides evenly into the movie's frame rate before compression. (For example, if your movie currently has 30 frames per second, try 2, 3, 5, 6, or 10.)
- **Key frame rate**: The higher the number here, the lower the data rate. The best choice to make here depends on which compressor you choose. Sorenson Video works best with a key frame rate that's about ten times the frame rate; thus try a key frame every 50 frames if your chosen frame rate is 5. Most Cinepak movies, however, play best with a key frame every second or every two seconds; thus if you have chosen a frame rate of 3, try 3 or 6 in this field, and then experiment with higher numbers.
- **Data rate**: While not all compressors will allow you to set a data rate, both Sorenson Video and Cinepak will. Specifying a number here limits the data rate to that number of kilobytes per second, increasing the amount of compression and thereby lowering the quality if necessary to get to that rate.

  What the right number is depends on the connection speed of your target audience, as well as how much compression your movie can stand. If you're using Cinepak, don't even try to get a data rate low enough for streaming over modem lines;

Can it be smaller?

Remember that if you reduce the window size before you compress you'll get a correspondingly smaller file and lower data rate. While this isn't acceptable for all video clips, it often will help you get a lower data rate while maintaining more of your image and motion quality.

even with quarter-screen movies, about 40 k/sec is as low as you can go if you want something that's recognizable as video. With Sorenson Video, you can usually get data rates that come close to modem bandwidths as long as you have a small frame size and a low frame rate. It's important to realize that the data rate you specify here doesn't include the data rate of your audio.

Spending more to get better results

While the compressors that come with QuickTime are quite good and will be sufficient for most users, those who want the absolutely best-looking video may want to purchase additional compressors. Two to look into today are Sorenson Developer Edition and Cinepak Pro. Each is $500 for unlimited use.

There are also other compressors that you can obtain to use with QuickTime. However, the advantage to Sorenson Developer Edition and Cinepak Pro is that movies compressed with them can play back using the standard Sorenson and Cinepak compressors that all users with QuickTime 3 (or even QuickTime 2, in the case of Cinepak) will have. With other compressors, anyone who views the movie will have to have the compressor you use, or at least a compatible decompressor, installed on their system. Even if you tell them where they can get the necessary decompressor for free, Web users generally don't like having to download and install extra files.

No matter what compressor you use—one that's built into QuickTime, or one of these add-on compressors—you'll get better results if you use Media Cleaner Pro to access the compressor. It has lots of built-in tricks for taking full advantage of the compressors and doing compression in the most optimal ways to maintain image quality.

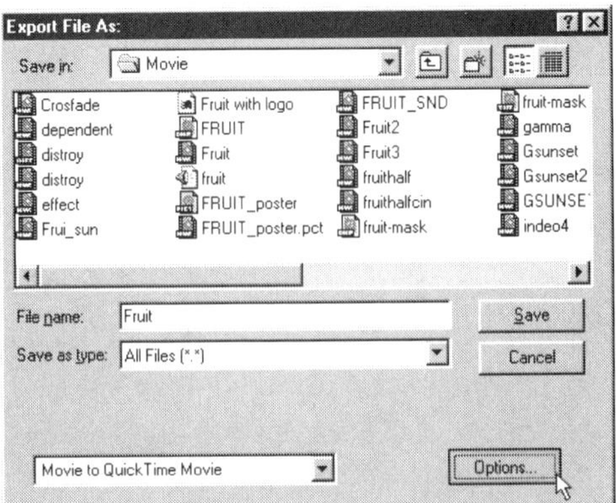

Figure 15.5 Choose Export from the File menu, choose Movie to QuickTime Movie, then click the Options button.

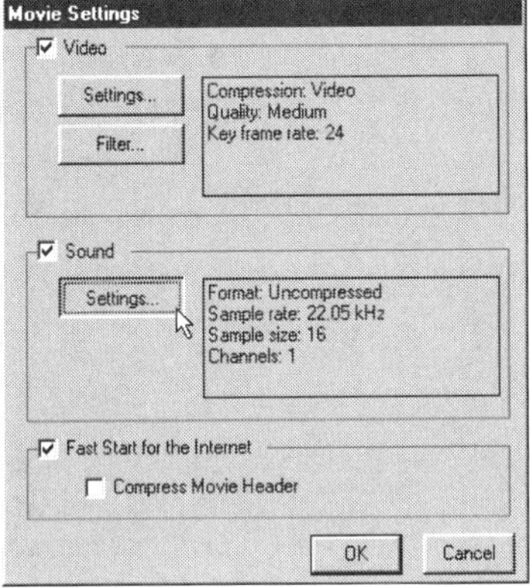

Figure 15.6 Click the Settings button in the Sound area of the Movie Settings dialog box.

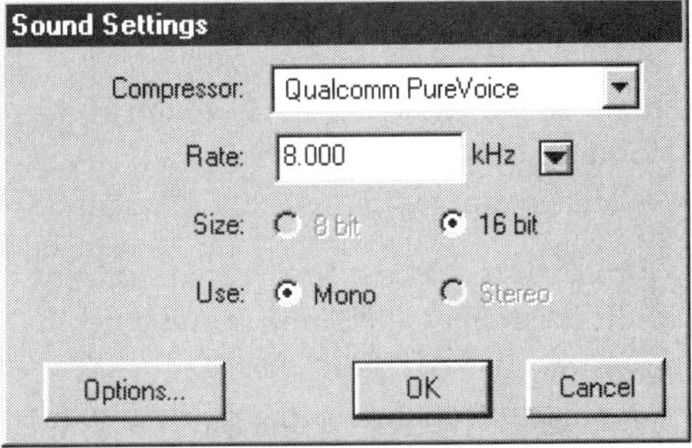

Figure 15.7 Use the Sound Settings dialog box to specify sound settings, including compressor.

Compressing sound for the Web

While sound is not as data-heavy as video, you also will want to compress it appropriately for Web playback.

Here we'll remind you of how to access the Sound Settings dialog box and provide some Web-specific guidance for making your choices. (We covered this dialog box in more depth in Chapter 12.)

To access the Sound Settings dialog box

1. Choose **Export** from the File menu, choose **Movie to QuickTime Movie**, and click the **Options** button (**Figure 15.5**).
2. Click the **Settings** button in the Sound area of the Movie Settings dialog box (**Figure 15.6**).
3. The Sound Settings dialog box appears (**Figure 15.7**), where you can choose settings appropriate for Web delivery.

Making choices in the Sound Settings dialog box

- **Compressor:** Two sound codecs new to QuickTime 3 provide very high compression ratios while maintaining good quality sound. For sound tracks containing only voice, use *Qualcomm PureVoice*. For most other types of sound, use *QDesign Music*. If you believe that some of your viewers won't have QuickTime 3 installed, a good choice is *IMA 4:1*.
- **Rate:** In general, we recommend choosing 8K or 11.025K for the rate.
- **Size:** Choose 8-bit if it's available. Some compressors only work in 16-bit.
- **Use:** Mono is best unless it's crucial that your track play back in stereo.

Professional sound compression

Just as you can purchase professional versions of the Sorenson Video and Cinepak video compressors, you can also buy a professional version of the QDesign Music compressor when you need the very lowest data rates along with high sound quality.

You can also purchase professional software tools for doing QuickTime sound compression. One of these is MacSourcery's BarbaBatch, which provides optimal sound conversion and compression, as well as the ability to process many files at once.

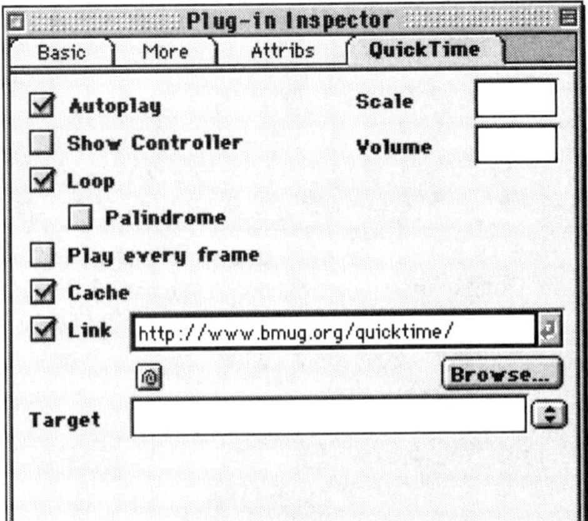

Figure 15.8 GoLive CyberStudio lets you insert a QuickTime movie and then specify settings in this dialog box.

Embedding a QuickTime movie on a Web page

For a QuickTime movie to appear on a Web page, the HTML for the page must include an EMBED tag, which is the standard tag that is used to embed many different types of content on Web pages.

You can either type the EMBED tag yourself or use a WYSIWIG Web authoring tool that supports QuickTime.

When using a WYSIWIG tool you generally insert the QuickTime file (in much the same way that you'd insert a graphic) and then choose specific settings in a dialog box. The EMBED tag is automatically generated; in most cases, you don't even need to look at it if you don't want to. We can't cover the precise methods used in all tools, but see **Figure 15.8** for an example.

Here we'll show you how to write the simplest EMBED tag with only the required parameters; the next page discusses some additional parameters that can be added.

Configuring a Web server for QuickTime

The Web server on which you put your QuickTime movie needs to have a listing for QuickTime files in its MIME types configuration file. Most Web servers at major companies and educational institutions, as well as at most Internet service providers, will have this set correctly already. If your QuickTime movie isn't appearing, and you're sure you typed the EMBED tag correctly, uploaded the file correctly, and have QuickTime correctly installed, there may be a problem with the server not being correctly configured for QuickTime. Contact the webmaster who's in charge of your Web server. They should know what to do, but you can tell them that the MIME type should be "video/quicktime" and the suffix should be "mov".

To write the minimal HTML necessary for embedding a QuickTime movie on a Web page

1. If your movie does not already have a name ending in .mov, rename it so it does.

   The .mov extension is necessary so that servers and browsers recognize the file as a QuickTime file.

2. Place your cursor in the HTML body of the Web page, in the location where you want the movie to appear.

3. Type <EMBED SRC="mymovie.mov", replacing "mymovie.mov" with the location of your movie file. (You can use relative or absolute URLs.)

4. Type a space and then WIDTH=w HEIGHT=h, replacing w with the width of your movie and h with the height of your movie . (See *Checking the dimensions of a movie* in Chapter 14 if you're not sure what these values are.)

5. Type a final > to close the EMBED tag. (See **Figure 15.9** for the full tag.)

When this page is opened in a browser, you'll first see a QuickTime logo (**Figure 15.10**) and then the movie will appear (**Figure 15.11**).

✔ Tip

If you're using a WYSIWYG editor that doesn't have direct QuickTime support, you may find it does have a menu choice that allows you to insert an HTML tag. Netscape Composer, for example, has an HTML Tag command in its Insert menu. When you choose this, a dialog box appears in which you can simply type the EMBED tag as described above. This is simpler than having to switch to editing your HTML source code.

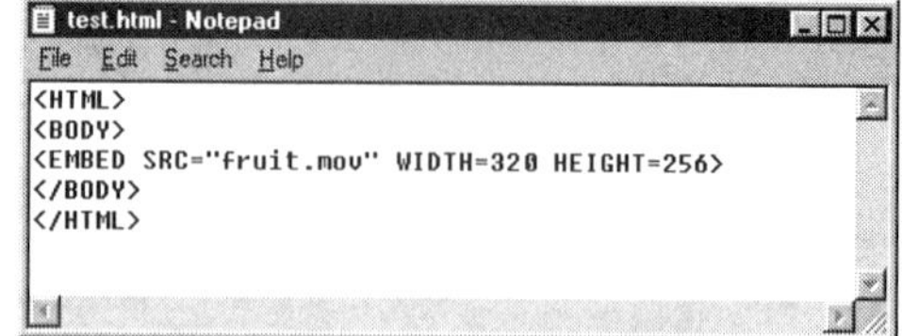

Figure 15.9 When writing your own HTML, use the EMBED tag to insert a movie into a Web page.

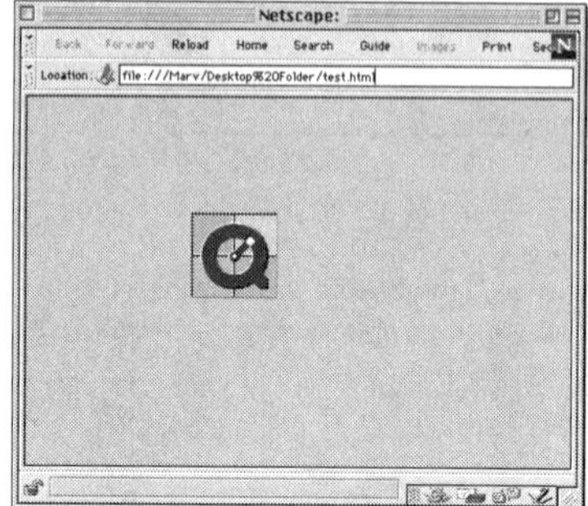

Figure 15.10 The QuickTime logo appears for a second or less...

Figure 15.11 ...and then the movie appears on the page.

Telling your viewers to get QuickTime

While millions of people already have QuickTime and the QuickTime plug-in installed on their computers, it's always a good idea to put something on your Web page or Web site telling them that they'll need QuickTime 3 to play the movies on the page, with a link to http://www.apple.com/quicktime/, where they can get it.

Adding parameters to your EMBED tag

There are other parameters you can use to specify appearance or playback characteristics of your movie. Some, such as **VOLUME**, **LOOP**, and **PLAYEVERYFRAME** merely do things that you can do in MoviePlayer (i.e. change the volume or set the movie to loop or play every frame; see Chapter 3). **PAN**, **TILT**, **FOV**, **NODE**, **CORRECTION**, and **HOTSPOT** are all for QuickTime VR movies, and allow you to specify properties that can also be specified when the VR movies are created. Other parameters have very Web-specific qualities. A complete list is provided in **Table 15.1**, but we'll cover some of the most useful parameters and why you'd want to use them after we show you how to add additional parameters.

Table 15.1

EMBED Tag Parameters for QuickTime Movies

PARAMETER	USE	EXAMPLE
AUTOPLAY	If set to "true", causes movie to start playing when enough data has been downloaded,. If set to "false", movie won't start playing even if browser plug-in is configured to autoplay by default.	AUTOPLAY=true
BGCOLOR	Specifies color in space defined by WIDTH and HEIGHT tags but not taken up by movie. Value is a hexadecimal number.	BGCOLOR = "#FFFFFF"
CACHE	Can be set to "true" (tells browser to cache the movie if possible) or "false" (tells it not to cache the movie). Doesn't work for all browsers.	CACHE = true
CONTROLLER	Indicates whether or not the controller should be shown. Value can be "true" or "false".	CONTROLLER=true
CORRECTION	For QuickTime VR movies. Value can be "none", "partial", or "full".	CORRECTION=none
FOV	For QuickTime VR movies only. Specifies initial field of view.	FOV=60.0
HEIGHT	Required parameter unless HIDDEN is used. Indicates height (in pixels) to be reserved in the document for the movie.	HEIGHT=256
HOTSPOTn	For QuickTime VR movies only. Replace n with ID of hot spot. Value should be the URL of page to load when hot spot is clicked.	HOTSPOT28="http://www.peachpit.com"
HREF	Indicates page to load if movie is clicked. Value should be a valid URL.	HREF="http://www.bmug.org/quicktime"
LOOP	Value can be "true", "false", or "palindrome". Has the same effect as Loop (if set to "true") and Loop Back and Forth (if set to "palindrome") commands in MoviePlayer's Movie menu.	LOOP=true
NODE	For QuickTime VR movies only. Specifies which node of a multi-node movie should open first. Value is an integer less than or equal to the number of nodes in the movie.	NODE=2
PAN	For QuickTime VR movies. Indicates initial pan angle. Value usually can be between 0 and 360, but depends on the movie.	PAN=90
PLAYEVERYFRAME	Value can be "true" or "false". If "true", has the same effect as the Play All Frames command in MoviePlayer's Movie menu.	PLAYEVERYFRAME=true
PLUGINSPAGE	Tells viewers without the plug-in where to go to get it. Value should be set to http://www.apple.com/quicktime.	PLUGSINSPAGE= "http://www.apple.com/quicktime"
SCALE	Scales movie dimensions. Can be set to "tofit", "aspect", or a number.	SCALE = 1.5
TARGETn	Indicates window or frame in which to load URL specified in HREF or HOTSPOT parameters. Leave off the n for an HREF. For HOTSPOT, n should be the same as the following HOTSPOT.	TARGET="_blank"
TILT	For QuickTime VR movies. Indicates initial tilt angle. Value usually can be between -42.5 and 42.5, but depends on the movie.	TILT=15.5
VOLUME	Sets the volume of an audio track. Can be set to a number between 0 and 100.	VOLUME=50
WIDTH	Required parameter. Indicates width (in pixels) to be reserved in the document for the movie.	WIDTH=320

To add additional parameters

1. Insert your cursor before the closing angle bracket in the EMBED tag.

2. Type the parameter name, followed by = (the equal sign), followed by a valid value for that parameter. (Though many browsers can interpret these parameters if there are spaces before or after the =, we recommend not leaving any spaces.) **Figure 15.12** shows the HTML for a QuickTime EMBED tag with additional parameters.

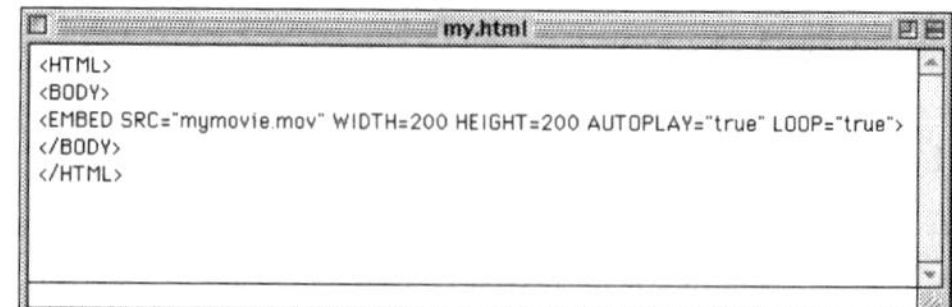


```
<HTML>
<BODY>
<EMBED SRC="mymovie.mov" WIDTH=200 HEIGHT=200 AUTOPLAY="true" LOOP="true">
</BODY>
</HTML>
```

Figure 15.12 Here's an EMBED tag with additional parameters.

Some sample parameters and values and their uses

- AUTOPLAY=true

  This ensures that the movie (as long as it's saved as a fast start movie) will start to play automatically when enough of it has been downloaded for it to play smoothly to the end. (The QuickTime plug-in that is installed with QuickTime 3 is configured by default to play movies automatically regardless of what's in the EMBED tag. However, viewers may have changed this default or they may have an older version of QuickTime; in either of these cases, if you don't include AUTOPLAY=true, the movie will not start to play until the viewer plays it manually.)

- CONTROLLER=false

  This is useful when you don't want a controller to appear for your movies. (The controller appears by default for regular QuickTime movies. It doesn't appear by default for QuickTime VR movies. If you *do* want a controller for VR movies, you'll need to type CONTROLLER=true.)

- BGCOLOR=#000000

  If the HEIGHT and WIDTH parameters specify a height and width that are larger than the actual size of your movie , this

Using HREF links

A less elegant alternative to embedding your movie on a Web page is to use a standard link. On your Web page you'd type something like <A HREF="mymovie.mov"><IMG SRC = "oneframe.jpg"> Click here to play mymovie </A>, replacing "mymovie.mov" with the location of your movie, "oneframe.jpg" with the name of a still image file that you've created to represent the movie, and the text string with whatever text you really want. (You could leave off either the image or the text, if you want.)

When a user who has the QuickTime plug-in installed clicks on the link, a new page opens with the movie on it. Or, if they've configured their browser to use a helper app (like MoviePlayer) to play QuickTime movies, the helper app will open and play the movie.

parameter with this value puts a black frame around the movie on the Web page. #000000 is the hexadecimal value for black. (To identify the hexadecimal value for other colors, see http://www.prgone.com/colors/ for a color to hex table.)

- HIDDEN=true

  This is used for audio-only movies, when you have a background soundtrack that you don't want users to be able to control. The movie downloads and plays, but there's nothing on the page that viewers can see.

- HOTSPOT47="http://www.bmug.org/"

  This would cause the page located at http://www.bmug.org/ to be loaded when a viewer clicks on the hot spot with an ID of 47 in the embedded QuickTime VR movie. (Hot spot IDs are defined when the hot spot is created; you will need to know what these IDs are.) This overrides any URLs already associated with that particular hot spot in the movie. If you want the page loaded into a frame or a window other than the current window, you can use the target parameter with a number identical to the hot spot ID number. (In this case, you could include TARGET47="text" to have the page loaded into a frame called "text.")

- HREF="http://www.apple.com/"

  This would cause the page located at http://www.apple.com/ to be loaded when a viewer clicks in the movie. If you want the page loaded into a frame or a window other than the current window, you can use the TARGET parameter.

✔ Tip

- See http://www.apple.com/quicktime/authors/webmas.html for complete and current documentation of the QuickTime EMBED tag parameters.

Specifying a value for the TARGET parameter

If you want the new page to load in a frame, use the frame's name. The frame's name is specified by the NAME parameter in the FRAME tag in your HTML (e.g. use "text" as the name of your target if the HTML that creates your frame is <FRAME SRC="moreinfo.html" NAME="text">).

Use "_blank" if you want a new browser window to be opened and the Web page to appear in this window. Once a window is opened with this name, you can use the same "_blank" with subsequent URLs to load additional pages into that same browser window.

The TARGET parameter is not specific to the QuickTime EMBED tag. You can find out more about how to specify valid values for the TARGET parameter at http://home.netscape.com/eng/mozilla/2.0/relnotes/demo/target.html.

Creating a small movie to use as a poster movie

One of the new features of the QuickTime plug-in is the handling of *poster movies*. A poster movie is a QuickTime movie with one or a few frames that's meant to stand in for a larger, "full-length" movie; when the poster movie—embedded on a Web page—is clicked, the larger movie file begins to download. (Poster movies with a few frames can still be very small but work better as an enticement than a still image.)

Creating a poster movie is really just a matter of creating a movie containing a subset of the information in the full-length movie. You can use various combinations of copying, pasting, extracting, deleting, exporting, and importing to create this subset of your full movie. We'll show the methods we use most commonly here.

To create a still-image poster movie

1. Make sure that the image you want to use for the poster is visible, and choose Export from the File menu (**Figure 15.13**).
2. Choose Movie to Picture in the pop-up menu at the bottom of the Save dialog box (**Figure 15.14**).
3. You can click the Options button to open a dialog box in which you can choose new compression settings for the image. We generally recommend that you choose PhotoJPEG, since it can compress the image to a very small size. Medium quality is often fine, too. If you don't like the results, you can repeat the process. After choosing your settings, click OK.
4. Click Save.

   The file is exported as a still image.
5. Use the Import command in the File menu (**Figure 15.15**) to turn the still image

Figure 15.13 Position the slider at the image you want as a poster and choose Export from the File menu.

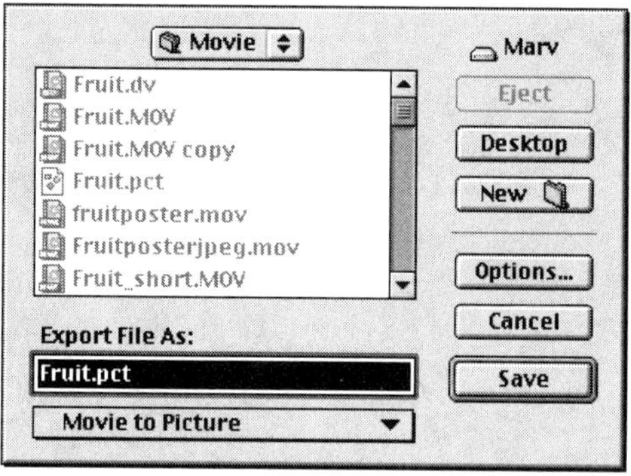

Figure 15.14 Choose Movie to Picture, click the Options button if you want to specify compression settings, and then click Save.

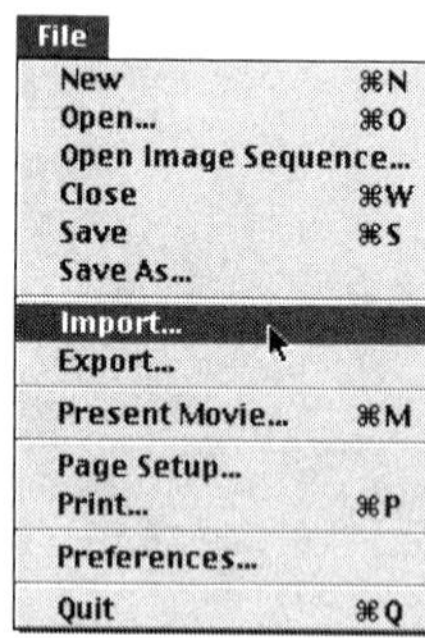

Figure 15.15 Then import the exported still image to create a single-frame movie that can be used as a poster movie.

Figure 15.16 Or, start by copying the frames you want to appear in your poster movie.

Figure 15.17 Paste the frames into a new, empty movie.

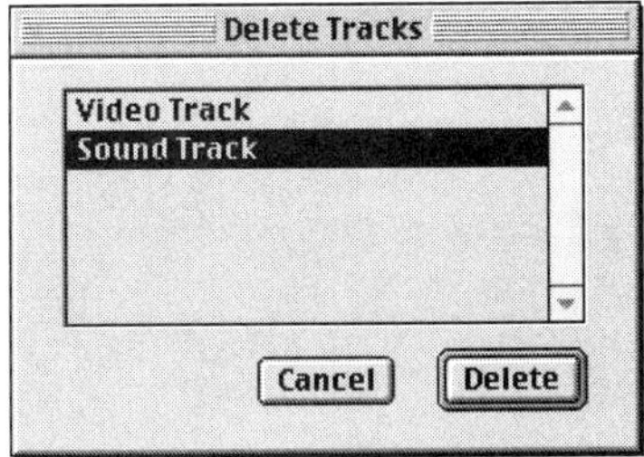

Figure 15.18 Delete tracks that shouldn't be in the poster.

back into a single-frame QuickTime movie. As part of the import process you'll need to provide a name for the new movie file. You should give it a name with a .mov extension. (The process of importing a still image is described more fully in Chapter 8 in *Creating video tracks from a single still image*.)

To create a multiple-frame poster movie

1. Select the frames that you want to use as your poster movie and choose Copy from the Edit menu (**Figure 15.16**).
2. Choose New from the File menu to create a new empty movie file and then choose Paste from the Edit menu (**Figure 15.17**).
3. Use the Delete Tracks command in the Edit menu to delete any audio tracks or other tracks that you don't want to appear in the poster movie (**Figure 15.18**).
4. Save the file as a self-contained file with a .mov extension.

✔ Tips

- The latter method can also be used to create a still-image poster, if you select only a single frame.
- If you like the dynamic nature of a multiple-frame poster, but your movies are QuickTime VR panoramic movies, you may be interested in dynamic thumbnails for VR panoramas. See Chapter 16.

Writing the HTML for a poster movie

Once you have your full-length movie and a corresponding poster movie, you'll need to write your EMBED tag so it all works correctly.

To write HTML that embeds a poster movie

1. Place your cursor in the HTML body of the Web page, in the location where you want the movie to appear.
2. Type <EMBED SRC="myposter.mov", replacing "myposter.mov" with the location of your poster movie file.
3. Type CONTROLLER=false. (You generally don't want the controller to appear for a poster.)
4. Type WIDTH=w HEIGHT=h, where "w" is the width of your full-length movie window and "h" is the height of your full-length movie window. (See *Checking the dimensions of a movie* in Chapter 14 if you're not sure of the width and height of your movie.)

   The reason for specifying the dimensions of the full-length movie is that you need to make space on the page for that movie.
5. Type HREF="myreal.mov", replacing "myreal.mov" with the location of your real movie.

   (If the full-length movie is in a different folder than the poster movie you must specify the path after the HREF relative to the poster movie, not relative to the Web page.)
6. Type TARGET="myself".

   This ensures that the full-length movie appears in the same location on the Web page as the poster movie.

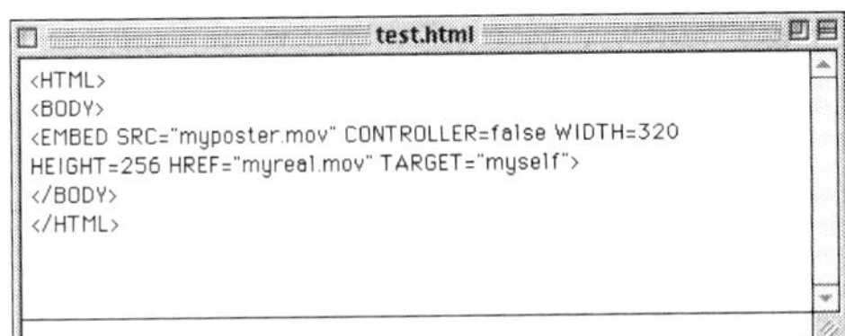

```
test.html
<HTML>
<BODY>
<EMBED SRC="myposter.mov" CONTROLLER=false WIDTH=320
HEIGHT=256 HREF="myreal.mov" TARGET="myself">
</BODY>
</HTML>
```

Figure 15.19 Here's a full EMBED tag for a poster movie.

7. Type the final > to close the EMBED tag. (See **Figure 15.19** for the full tag.)

   When the page with this tag is opened in a Web browser, the poster movie appears. When the poster movie is clicked, it is replaced by the full-length movie.

✔ Tips

- The poster movie will be centered in the space provided by the HEIGHT and WIDTH tags. With no controller, its bottom and top edges won't match those of the full-length movie. If this bothers you, you might want to use image-processing software or MoviePlayer to add to the bottom of the poster image a 16-pixel-high rectangle, perhaps matching the pattern or color of your Web page's background, or perhaps containing text such as "Click to see the movie."
- The full-length movie automatically appears according to the defaults for the EMBED tag parameters (e.g. with a controller for regular QuickTime movies). If you want to change any of these parameters, you'll need to include them in the full-length movie itself, using a tool like the Plug-in Helper, which is described in Chapter 16.

Using HREF tracks to make movies load Web pages

By including a special type of text track, called an *HREF Track*, in your movie, you can have Web pages load at specified times during movie playback.

The simplest form of HREF track is one that loads a Web page into the current browser window if a user clicks at the specified time. There are also variations that allow you to specify another browser window or a frame into which the Web page should load, or to specify that the page be loaded automatically rather than only if the user clicks.

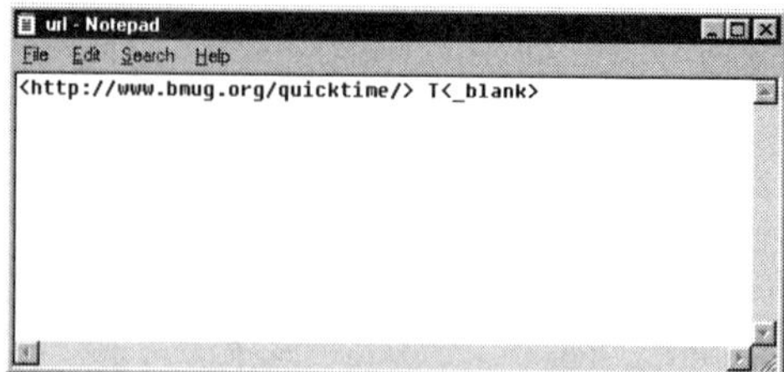

Figure 15.20 In a word processor, type the full URL of a Web page enclosed in angle brackets, followed by "T" and a frame or window name in angle brackets. Then select and copy this text.

To create an HREF track that loads a Web page if a user clicks on the movie

1. In any text editor, type the full URL of the Web page you wish to load, enclosed in angle brackets; for example, <http://www.bmug.org/quicktime/>.
2. If you want the Web page to load in a different window or frame than the one in which the movie is playing, after the closed angle bracket you typed in step 1, type T (which stands for *target*) followed by the name of the window or frame in angle brackets. For example, type T<_blank> to have the URL indicated in step 1 load in an empty browser window (**Figure 15.20**). (See the sidebar *Specifying a value for the TARGET parameter*, earlier in this chapter, for information about how to specify targets.)
3. Select and copy the text you've typed.
4. In MoviePlayer, select the portion of the movie during which you'd like the URL fired if the user clicks, and then hold down the Shift and Option keys (Mac OS)

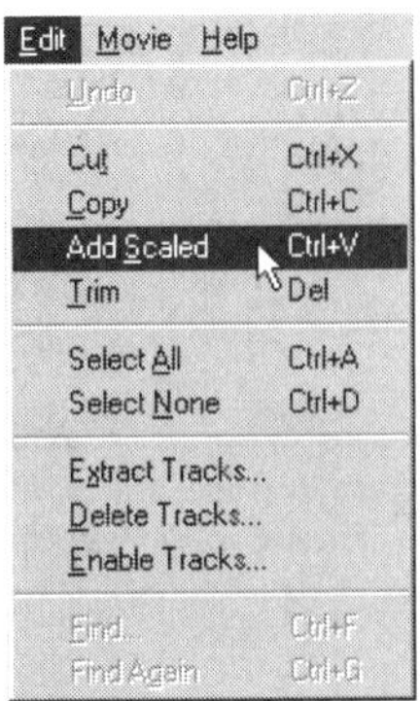

Figure 15.21 Select the portion of the movie during which you wish the URL to be active, then use the Add Scaled command to add the copied text.

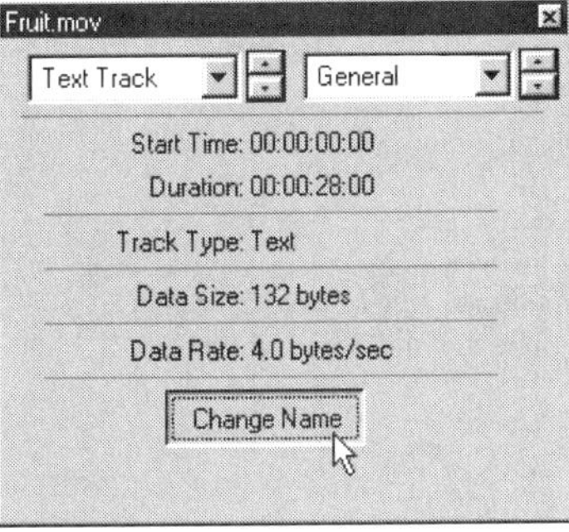

Figure 15.22 Open the General panel in the Info window for the text track you've just added and click the Change Name button.

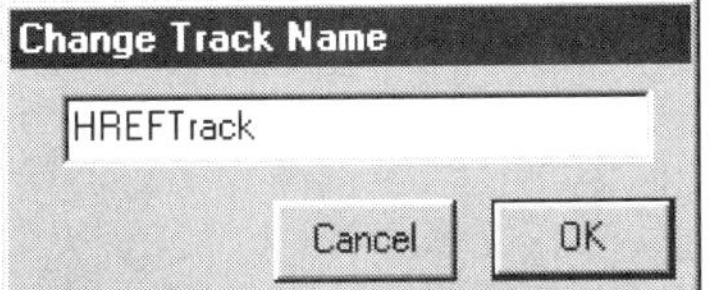

Figure 15.23 Type "HREFTrack" and click OK.

or the **Shift**, **Ctrl**, and **Alt** keys (Windows) and choose **Add Scaled** from the Edit menu (**Figure 15.21**).

5. In the Info window (accessed by choosing **Get Info** from the Movie menu), choose **Text track** from the left pop-up menu and **General** from the right pop-up menu. (If the movie contained a text track prior to adding the typed URL information, the added track will be the last text track in the list.)
6. Click the **Change Name** button (**Figure 15.22**).
7. In the Change Track Name dialog box that appears, type **HREFTrack** and click **OK** (**Figure 15.23**).

   The name of the track, as listed in the left pop-up menu in the Info window, is now "HREFTrack."
8. Unless you want the HREF track to be visible, use the **Enable Tracks** command in the Edit menu to disable the track.
9. Save the file using the **Save As** command and embed it on a Web page as described earlier in this chapter.

To specify that a Web page be loaded automatically

- Follow the steps for creating an HREF track that plays when a user clicks, but put an A at the very beginning of the text that you copy from the word processor (**Figure 15.24**).

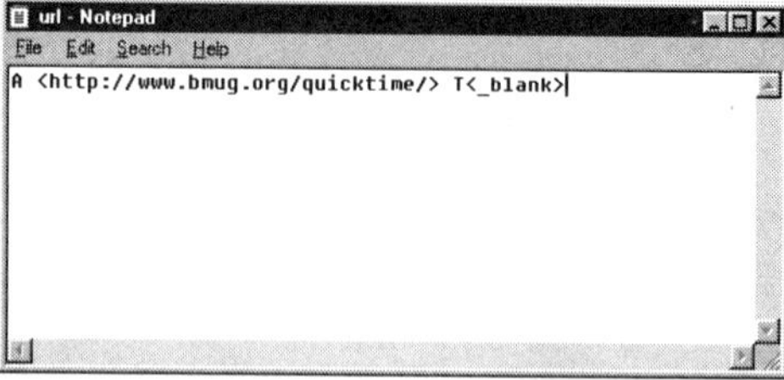

Figure 15.24 You can have the page load automatically, rather than when a user clicks, by putting an "A" before the text string.

✔ Tips

- If you want different URLs fired at different times, rather than individually copying and pasting multiple lines of text you can create a text file with time stamps and import it, as described in Chapter 9. You may want to use the technique described in *Creating a text track that's synched to other tracks* in that chapter to edit the file. **Figure 15.25** shows an example text file with URLs that can be imported.
- When you test your movie containing an HREF track, don't assume that it's not working if the Web page does not load as quickly as you think it should. It may take a few seconds. Be patient.

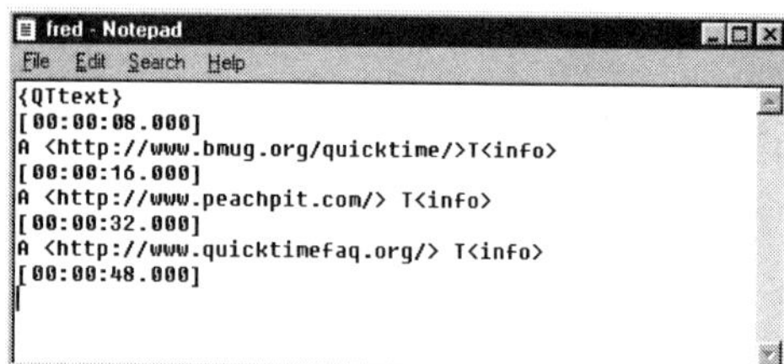

Figure 15.25 If you're going to have multiple URLs, create a text file like this and import it.

16 Movies on Web pages: Advanced

For the most part, we've saved for this chapter the tasks that you can't do with only MoviePlayer and a Web-page creation tool. These tasks require some additional tools, which Apple provides free. (As of this writing, these tools are not yet available on the Windows platform, but it's worth checking for them on Apple's Web site when you read this.)

We'll show you where to get these tools, and then show you what you can do with them: create multiple-data-rate movies, insert Web-specific data directly into movies, and create low-resolution previews and thumbnails for QuickTime VR movies.

Getting important utilities

Apple has made available some special tools that you can use to exploit the capabilities of QuickTime 3. (Many software developers will be supporting these capabilities in future versions of their software, but the free Apple utilities we describe here will serve in the meantime. Be aware that these are unsupported tools.)

To find these tools go to http://www.apple.com/quicktime/developers/tools.html.

On this page (**Figure 16.1**) you'll find a number of tools. While you may be interested in many of them, the ones you should download for the activities in this chapter are:

- MakeRefMovie
- Plug-in Helper
- QTVR Flattener
- QTVR PanoToThumbnail

MakeRefMovie and Plug-in Helper are small applications that you can store anywhere on your hard drive.

QTVR Flattener and QTVR PanoToThumbnail are extensions to QuickTime, and work in conjunction with QuickTime tools such as MoviePlayer that have QuickTime export functionality. Put these extensions in your Extensions folder in your System folder and restart your computer. They will make their presence known when you choose Export from MoviePlayer's File menu: You'll see additional choices for formatting your exported movies in the pop-up menu at the bottom of the Save dialog box (**Figure 16.2**).

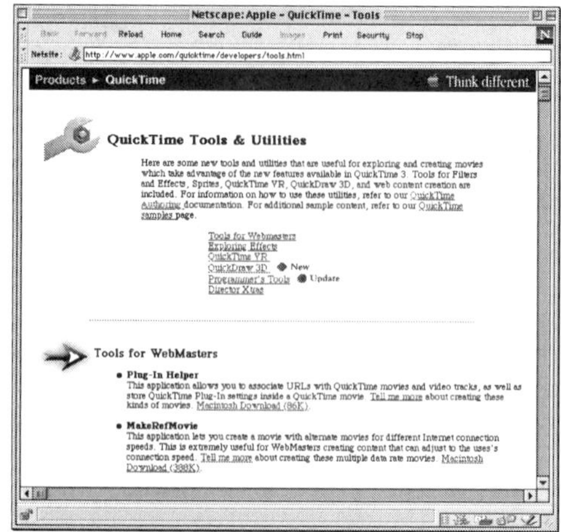

Figure 16.1 Apple's QuickTime Tools page offers a number of free, interesting utilities.

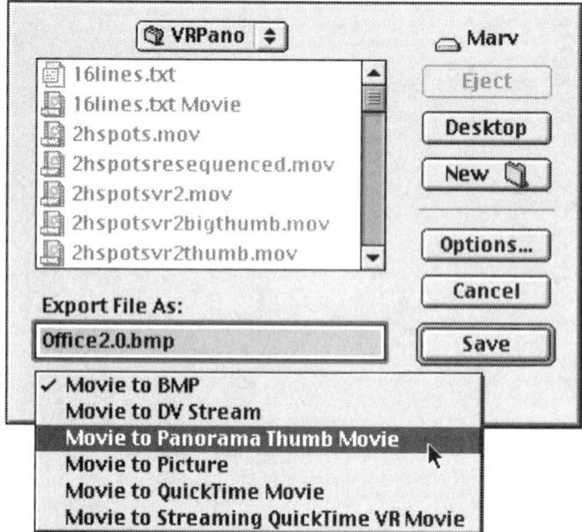

Figure 16.2 You'll find that some of the utilities add extra choices to MoviePlayer's export options for QuickTime VR movies.

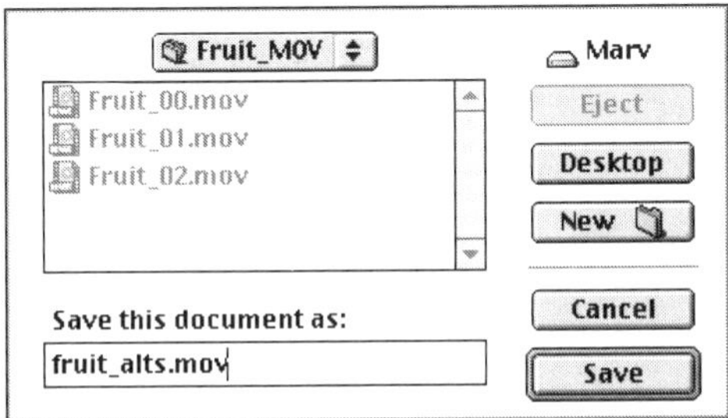

Figure 16.3 When you first open the MakeRefMovie application, you're immediately asked to save the file for your reference movie.

Alternate datarate movies with MakeRefMovie

The QuickTime plug-in has a new feature that allows you to do what is sometimes called *smart streaming*. The general idea is that while Web viewers see only a single movie on your Web page, you actually have, on your Web server, a set of alternate movies; only the one appropriate for the viewer's connection speed, QuickTime version, and installed compressors downloads. You need to first generate the movies with the different specifications. Then you use the MakeRefMovie tool to create the movie (called a *reference movie*) that you'll embed on your Web page; the reference movie contains pointers to the various alternate movies.

To create alternate movies

- ◆ Generate two or more different versions of the same movie, each with a data rate appropriate for some portion of the audience that you want to be able to view your movie. These are your *alternate movies*. Generally, you'll want to create a movie for 28.8 modems, one for a 56K modems, and maybe one for ISDN lines, T1 lines, or faster connections. (See Chapter 15 for guidelines concerning creating movies for these bandwidths.) You may also want to create one that doesn't depend on any QuickTime 3 compressors. (See the sidebar *QuickTime 3-only compressors* for a list.)

To generate a reference movie

1. Put all of your alternate movies into the folder or folders that match the directory or directories where you'll place them on your Web server. (To keep things simple, it's best to put them all in the same folder.)
2. Open the MakeRefMovie application. A Save dialog box appears (**Figure 16.3**).

QuickTime 3-only compressors

- Alaw 2:1
- DV-NTSC
- DV-PAL
- H.263
- Indeo 4.4
- QDesign Music
- Qualcomm PureVoice
- Sorenson Video
- 24-bit Integer, 32-bit Integer
- 32-bit Floating Point, 64-bit Floating Point

3. Enter a name for your reference movie and navigate to the folder that maps to the one on your server where you want the reference movie. (Again, to keep things simple, place it in the same folder that contains your alternate movies.)

4. Click **Save**.

   An empty window appears (**Figure 16.4**).

5. Choose **Add Movie File** from the Movie menu (**Figure 16.5**), and locate one of your alternate-data-rate movies.

6. Repeat step 5 for each of the alternate-data-rate movies, until they are all listed in the window (**Figure 16.6**).

   (Rather than using the Add Movie File command, you can drag files from the Finder directly to this window, or you can use the **Add URL** command from the Movie menu to specify the location of a movie file.)

7. When you add a movie via the Add Movie File command or by dragging it to the window, MakeRefMovie picks a setting in the Speed pop-up menu for that movie.

   If the speed chosen by default for each isn't the connection speed you intended, change it (**Figure 16.7**).

8. If one of your movies is one that you have created specifically to be compatible with versions of QuickTime prior to QuickTime 3, set its speed identical to one of the other movies, select **Last Choice** in its Priority menu and click the **Flatten into Output** checkbox. Set the priority of the movie with the identical speed to **First Choice**. (**Figure 16.8**).

   A movie designated as Last Choice will not be chosen if there are other, higher-priority movies that are appropriate in terms of connection speed and compressors installed on the viewer's computer.

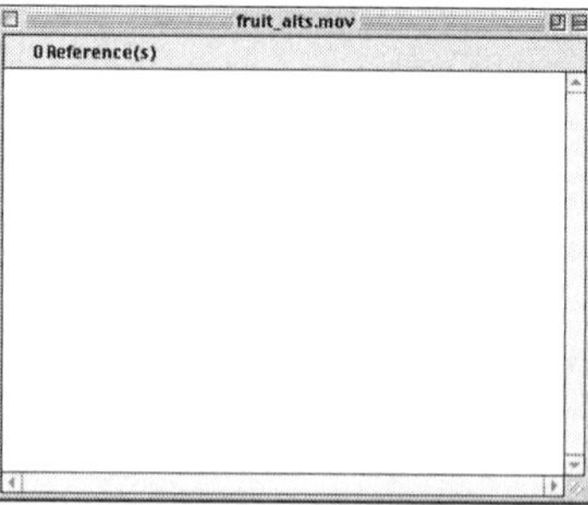

Figure 16.4 At this point, the reference movie has nothing in it.

Figure 16.5 Choose Add Movie File from the Movie menu to add one of your alternate movies to your reference movie.

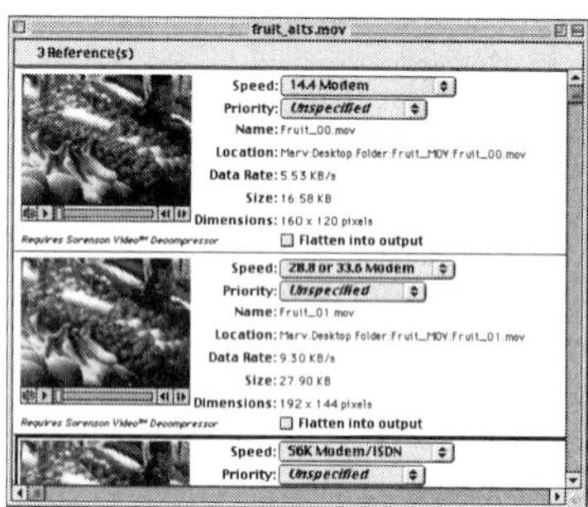

Figure 16.6 As you add your alternate movies, they get listed in the window.

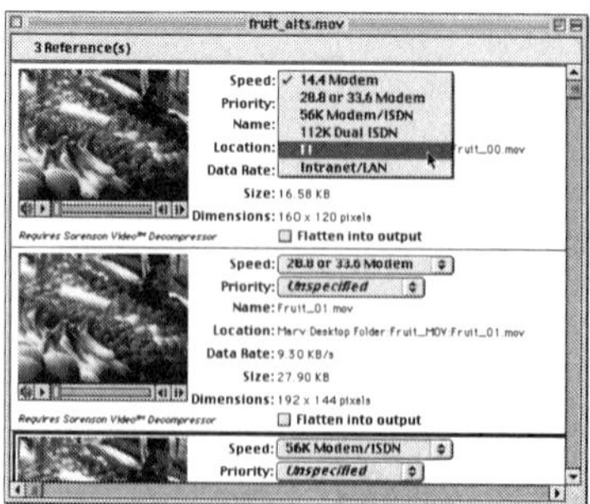

Figure 16.7 Use the Speed pop-up menu to specify the speed at which you intend each movie to be played.

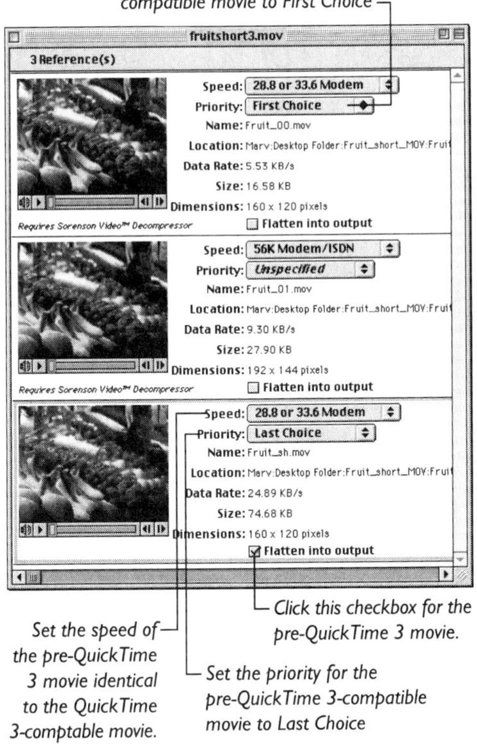

Figure 16.8
Here's an example of the MakeRefMovie window set to include an alternate movie compatible with versions of QuickTime prior to 3.

(The assumption is that the QuickTime 3-compatible movies are always preferable, since QuickTime 3 has improved compression capabilities.) Choosing Flatten into Output causes the reference movie to actually contain the data for this movie; this is necessary since previous versions of QuickTime don't know how to interpret reference movies on Web pages.

9. Choose **Save** from the File menu.
10. Embed the reference movie on your Web page, as described in Chapter 15, *Embedding a QuickTime movie on a Web page*.
11. Make sure to upload the alternate files along with the reference file, placing them in the same directory structure they've been in on your hard drive.

✔ Tip

- If you have Media Cleaner Pro 3.0, we highly suggest that you use it, rather than the above techniques, to create your alternate movies and reference movie. This tool automates the process.

✔ Warnings

- Don't change the names or relative locations of your alternate movies after creating a reference movie. If you do, the reference movie won't be able to locate them.
- Don't edit the reference movie using Movie Player or any other editor.

Plug-In Helper

Plug-In Helper is a tool that allows you to store information that might normally be stored in an EMBED tag directly in the movie itself. You generally want to do this if the movie is not the one embedded on the Web page (e.g. a poster movie calls it). It's also a way to specify default settings for your movie's Web playback characteristics. (Note, however, that if properties set for the EMBED tag contradict the values set by Plug-In Helper, the values in the EMBED tag take precedence.) Plug-In Helper also allows you to specify a URL to go to when a user clicks in the movie.

To use Plug-In Helper

1. Download Plug-In Helper, if you haven't already done so.
2. Double-click on **PlugInHelper** to open the application. (You'll notice that the name of the application file contains no spaces or hyphens.)
3. Choose **Open** from the File menu (**Figure 16.9**) and open the movie in which you want to store plug-in settings.

   The Plug-In Helper window appears (**Figure 16.10**). A preview area located below an Open and an Export button shows your movie. (Don't be concerned if the proportions are not correct; for display purposes, Plug-In Helper squeezes your movie into the space available in the preview area, but it won't save the file this way.)
4. If you want to specify EMBED tag parameters, click the **Add** button in the upper right of the Plug-In Helper window in the area labeled "Movie User Data ('plug')." In the Edit User Data dialog box that appears, type a valid EMBED tag parameter followed by an = (equal sign) and a valid value for that parameter (**Figure 16.11**).

Figure 16.9 Choose Open from the File menu to open a movie in which you want to store plug-in settings or URLs.

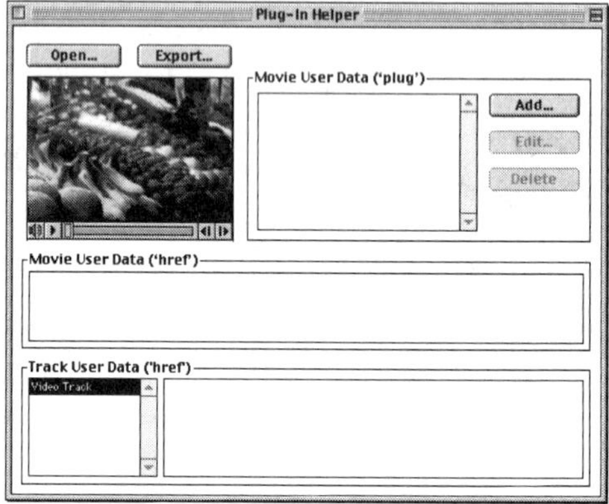

Figure 16.10 The Plug-in Helper window shows your movie in the preview area.

Specifying a URL to go to when the user clicks in a specific video track?

There's a Track User Data ('href') area at the bottom of the Plug-In Helper window. This was included in Plug-In Helper originally so you could specify a URL for specific video tracks. However, with the version available as we write this (1.0d5), this feature is not working. If there are future versions of this tool, this feature may actually be implemented and provide some useful functionality. For example, specifying a URL for a specific video track might be appropriate if a video track contained a logo for a company and you wanted people to go to the company's home page when they click on that logo. Or, you might have side-by-side video tracks and want different pages to load depending on which side they click.

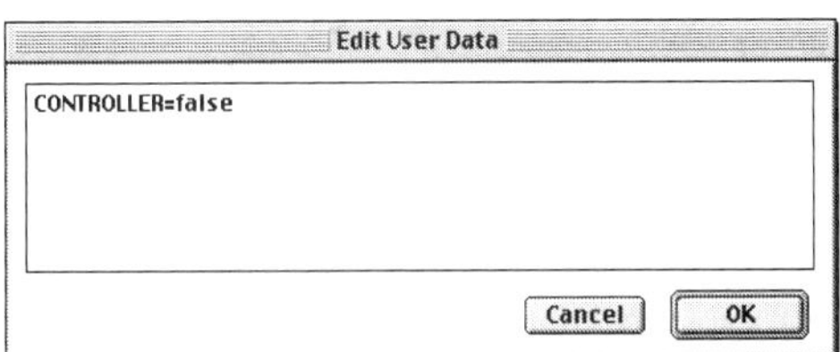

Figure 16.11 Click the Add button in the Plug-In Helper window, and type a valid EMBED tag parameter in the Edit User Data dialog box.

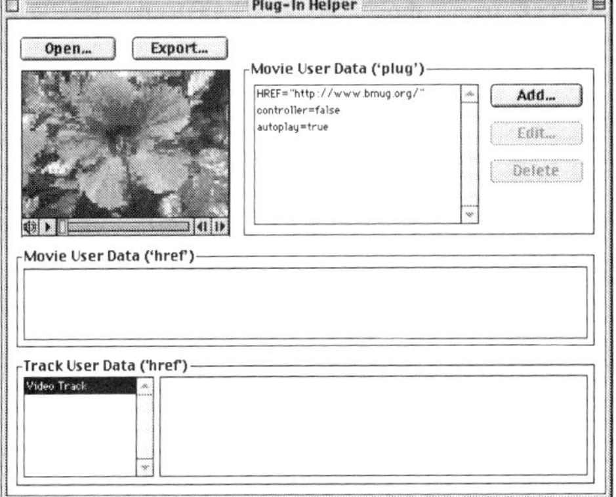

Figure 16.12 You'll see all your properties in the scrolling list in the Plug-in Helper window.

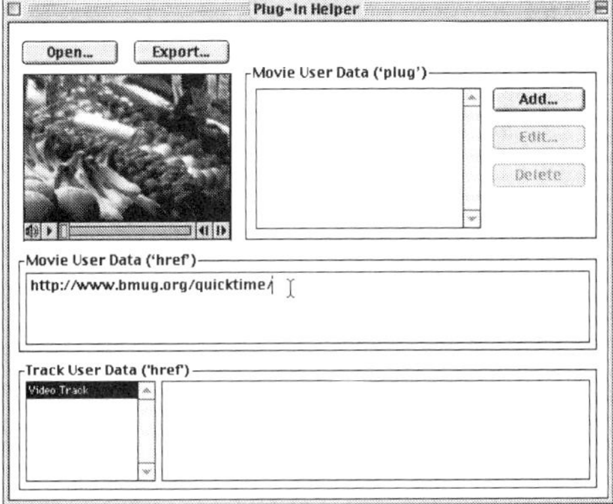

Figure 16.13 Type a URL directly into the Movie User Data ('href') area of the Plug-in Helper window.

Make sure you have *no spaces* on either side of the =.

You can use any valid parameters for the QuickTime EMBED tag, except CACHE, WIDTH, HEIGHT, and HIDDEN. See *Adding additional parameters to your EMBED tag* in Chapter 15.

Click OK or press the Return key when you're done adding the parameter. Repeat this step until you've added each parameter you want included (**Figure 16.12**). Use the Edit and/or Delete buttons to make changes to these parameters.

5. If you want to specify a URL to go to when the user clicks on the movie, type the URL directly in the Movie User Data ('href') area (**Figure 16.13**).

   Typing the URL here provides the same effect as using the HREF parameter in the Movie User Data ('plug') area. The advantage to the latter is that a target window or frame can be specified.

6. Click the Export button.

7. In the Save dialog box that appears, specify a file name (ending in .mov) and location, and click Save.

✔ Tip

- If the Plug-In Helper window is already open, rather than using the Open command in the File menu, you can use the Open button in the upper-left of the window, or drag a movie from the Finder to the preview area.

Creating Streaming VR movies with MoviePlayer and QTVR Flattener

QTVR Flattener's name doesn't tell you much about what it does, which is to create a QuickTime VR movie a viewer can start to explore before it is completely downloaded. These streaming VR movies either have a low-resolution preview that gets replaced by the full-resolution image as it's downloaded (**Figure 16.14**) or are structured in such a way that they are downloaded a vertical strip (or *tile*) at a time (**Figure 16.15**); in either case a viewer can start clicking and dragging in the movie before the full VR movie is downloaded. (If you are also adding settings to your movie using Plug-in Helper, use Plug-in Helper first and then use QTVR Flattener, or the settings may not work.)

Figure 16.14 A QuickTime VR movie with a low-resolution preview shows the full-resolution portions as they're downloaded.

Figure 16.15 QuickTime VR movies can also be downloaded a tile at a time.

To create a streaming QTVR movie

1. If you haven't already done so, download QTVR Flattener, put it in your Extensions folder in your System folder and restart your computer.
2. Open your QTVR movie in MoviePlayer. (Currently, only single-node panorama movies will work.)
3. Choose **Export** from the File menu.
4. In the pop-up menu at the bottom of the Save dialog box, choose **Movie to Streaming QuickTime VR Movie** (**Figure 16.16**).
5. Click the **Options** button.

   A dialog box appears (**Figure 16.17**).
6. If you want your movie to have the tiled effect, make sure the **Create Preview** checkbox is not selected, and then skip to step 10.

   If you want to create a low-resolution preview, click the **Create Preview** check-box to select it.

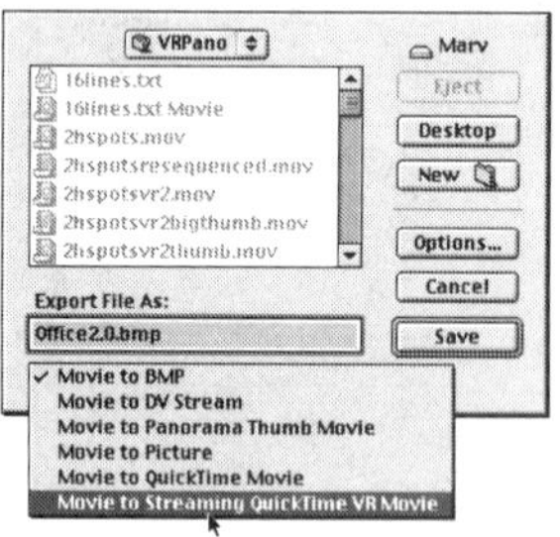

Figure 16.16 To create a streaming VR movie, choose Export from the File menu, and choose Movie to Streaming QuickTime VR Movie in the pop-up menu.

(This choice will only be available if you have installed QTVR Flattener in your Extensions folder in your System folder.)

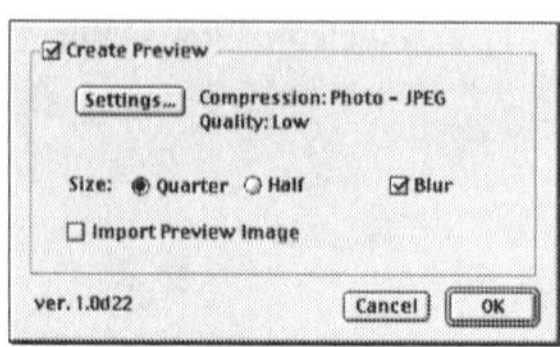

Figure 16.17 After you click the Options button in the Save dialog box, this dialog box appears.

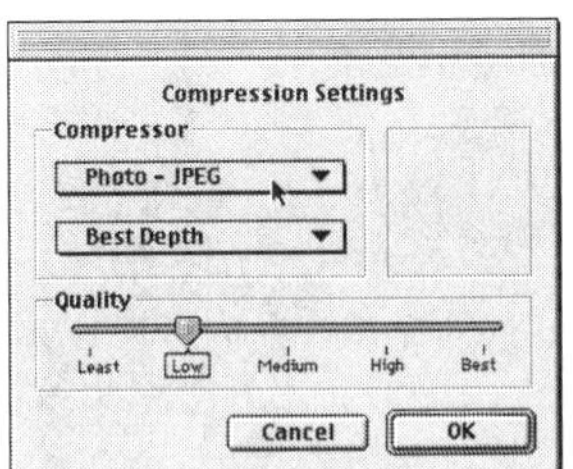

Figure 16.18 Click the Settings button to get a Compression Settings dialog box. Photo-JPEG is usually the best choice.

Figure 16.19 If you don't check the Blur checkbox, the image will be pixelated. (Compare this image to Figure 16.14 and 16.15.)

Preview vs. tiling

Whether you choose to add a preview image or use the tiling effect is essentially a matter of your personal aesthetic preference. The one functional advantage to having a preview is that the viewer can click on hot spots before the movie is completely downloaded; without the preview, viewers must wait until the entire movie is downloaded before the hot spots will work.

7. Though the defaults settings—Photo-JPEG at low quality—work fine for most purposes, if you want to change the compression settings for the preview that will be created, click the **Settings** button.

   A Compression Settings dialog box appears (**Figure 16.18**). Good compressors to choose for this purpose are **Photo-JPEG** or **Sorenson Video**, since they can achieve the highest compression ratios. (The Read Me file that is currently downloaded with this tool says that the only choices that will work are Component, Graphics, Motion JPEG, None, Photo-JPEG, Planar RGB, and Video but we've found that Sorenson Video works just fine.)

   When you're done choosing your settings, click **OK** to return to the previous dialog box.

8. To get the smallest and fastest-downloading preview, choose the **Quarter** radio button for Size. (This will create an image with one-quarter the resolution of the image in the movie; Half creates an image with half the resolution. The lower the resolution, the more pixelated the preview image will be.)

9. Check the **Blur** checkbox if you want the image to be blurry (**Figure 16.19**) rather than pixelated.

10. Click **OK**.

11. Give the file a new name, specify a location, and Click **Save**.

There's no way to remove or change the information added with QTVR Flattener, so make sure not to overwrite your original file.

This movie, if embedded on a Web page, will either show the low-resolution preview or show a tile at a time while the movie is being downloaded.

Creating panorama thumbnails with QTVR PanoToThumbnail

Poster movies (which we covered in the previous chapter) are a nice way to provide a preview of a full-length movie. Another method, for QuickTime VR panorama movies, involves creating a *thumbnail*, or miniature self-playing version of the full panorama (**Figure 16.20**), which can be placed on a Web page .

The tool you'll use, QTVR PanoToThumbnail, currently works only with single-node movies created with QuickTime VR 2 (the version that's installed with QuickTime 3).

To create a thumbnail version of a QuickTime VR panorama movie

1. If you haven't already done so, download QTVR PanoToThumbnail and put it in your Extensions folder in your System folder.
2. Open your QuickTime VR single-node panorama in MoviePlayer.
3. Choose Export from the File menu.
4. In the pop-up menu at the bottom of the Save dialog box, choose Movie to Panorama Thumb Movie (**Figure 16.21**).
5. Click the Options button.
   A dialog box appears (**Figure 16.22**).
6. We've found that the default settings—Photo-JPEG compression at Low quality, with a height of 64 pixels, Auto width, 10 frames, and a frame rate of 10 frames per second—work quite well, but you can change any of these, if you'd like. (Clicking the Settings button gives you access to a standard Compression Settings dialog box in which you can change the compressor, color depth, and quality.)

Figure 16.20 A thumbnail version of a panorama, particularly if it's self-playing, can be a great enticement for people to explore your panorama.

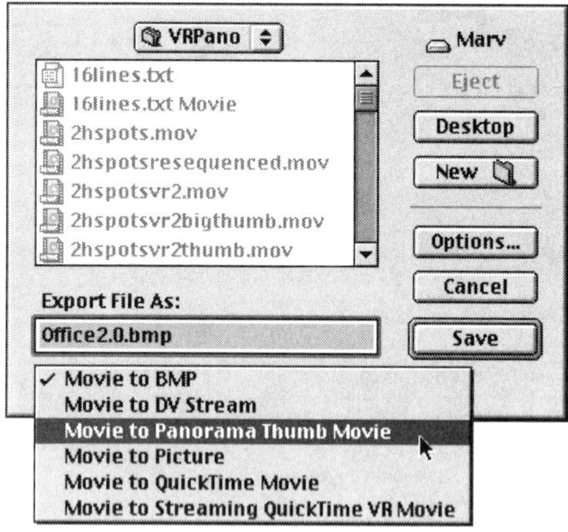

Figure 16.21 If QTVR PanoToThumbnail is installed in your Extensions folder, the Movie to Panorama Thumb Movie choice is available when you choose Export from the File menu.

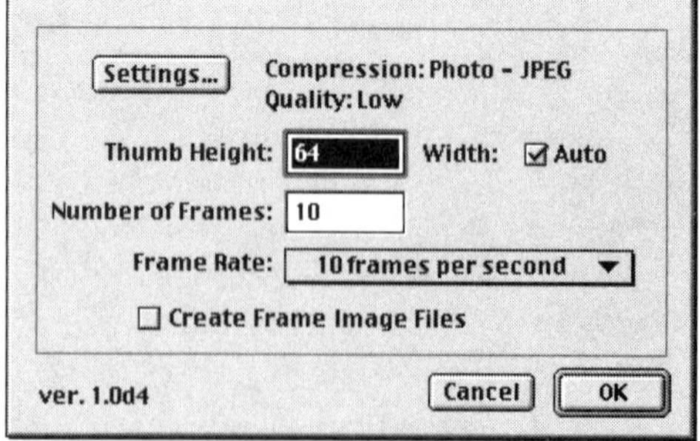

Figure 16.22 The default settings for the thumbnail produce good results.

7. Click **OK** to return to the Save dialog box, then click **Save** to begin exporting the file.

   You can embed the exported file on a Web page as you would any QuickTime file.

✔ Tip

- If you want to make a thumbnail for a QuickTime VR 1.0 movie, you'll need to first convert it to a VR 2.0 movie. You can easily do this with the QTVR Converter utility, located on the same Web page as the other tools we've covered in this chapter. Put it in your Extensions folder, restart, and when you choose **Export** from MoviePlayer's File menu, you'll find an additional option in the pop-up menu: **Movie to QuickTime VR Movie 2.x**.

17 Movies on CD-ROM, Kiosk, and Videotape

While vast numbers of people distribute QuickTime movies on the Internet and World Wide Web, QuickTime is also the best choice for CD-ROM, an excellent choice for video kiosks, and even useful for producing traditional videotape.

In this chapter, we'll cover the basics of preparing QuickTime video for CD-ROM and kiosk; the issues are quite similar. (Be sure to also read Chapter 14, which covers issues common to all delivery platforms.)

We'll also talk about incorporating QuickTime movies into media presentations created with multimedia tools and what licensing requirements there are for distributing QuickTime.

Finally, we'll explain some techniques for putting QuickTime movies onto standard analog videotape or the new Digital Video tapes.

Overview of issues regarding compression for CD-ROM and kiosk

For CD-ROM and kiosk video you generally don't need to get data rates anywhere near as low as those for Web playback, since you don't have the same bandwidth constraints. For 2x CD-ROM (the low end of what's currently available), the data transfer speed is 300 kilobytes per second; movie data rates can approach 200 kilobytes per second—tens to hundreds of times the practical data rates for streaming Web video. Hard drives (on which you may store video for a kiosk) can transfer data at multiple megabytes per second.

For many people, these higher data rates open the door for larger frame sizes, even full-screen. On the other hand, you may not necessarily want to take advantage of the maximum possible data rate, since you still have the problem of the total data size of your movie running up against the storage limits of your chosen medium. You also may not need to take advantage of such high data rates, since compressors like Sorenson Video provide high quality at lower data rates.

As with Web video, we can't give you any specific recipe for preparing QuickTime video for CD-ROM or kiosk. You'll need to experiment until you get the best combination of settings. However, we'll give you some ideas about where to start your experimentation.

Setting up a kiosk

There are different ways you can go when setting up a kiosk; the compression choices you make depend on the way you've set up the kiosk.

If you don't want to spend much money, you can use any old computer, and choose one of the standard video compressors included with QuickTime.

However, there are some video cards that do compression and decompression using specialized hardware; because they contain a dedicated chip for doing the compression and decompression and do not rely on the computer's processor, they can deliver more video to the screen faster, allowing for full-screen, full-motion video. The compressor you choose will be a proprietary compressor that works specifically with that card; it will be installed when you install the software for the card. (Most of these cards are based on a Motion JPEG compressor, and are often referred to as M-JPEG cards.)

An in-between solution is to use one of the third-party (software-only) compressors described in the sidebar *Video compressors you can buy*, later in this chapter. Since you're setting up the playback computer, you simply need to make sure that the appropriate codec is installed.

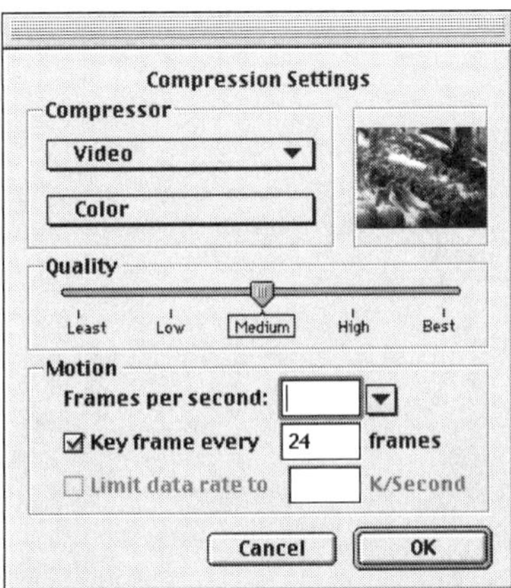

Figure 17.1 You make compression choices in the Compression Settings dialog box.

DVD

DVD (an acronym that actually doesn't stand for anything, but which many people think stands for "Digital Versatile Disc") is the next-generation compact disc. It can store as much as 17 gigabytes of data on a disc that looks just like a compact disc (which holds only 650 megabytes).

There are several different forms of DVD, just as there are different forms of compact discs. *DVD-ROM* discs are like CD-ROM discs; both hold data just as hard drives and other storage devices do. Since QuickTime movies are just files, they can be put on DVD-ROM discs as part of a standard multimedia production. (Related to DVD-ROM are *DVD-R*, which is recordable, and *DVD-RAM*, which is recordable and erasable.)

DVD-Video discs are meant to replace laser-discs. They play in DVD players that people connect to their TVs. They also play on computers that have DVD drives along with the necessary decoding hardware and/or software. In the future you'll be able to use QuickTime to display and, in certain cases, edit the video on DVD-Video discs.

Video compression choices

When you compress your video for the higher data rates possible with CD-ROM or a hard drive, the choices you make in the Compression Settings dialog box (**Figure 17.1**) will be somewhat different than they are for Web delivery. (See Chapter 14 for information on how to access this dialog box.)

- **Compressor:** Of the codecs included with QuickTime, you are again probably going to choose between Cinepak and Sorenson Video. Since Sorenson Video gives you better quality at lower data rates, you can put more hours of video on a single CD-ROM or hard drive with Sorenson Video than you can if you use Cinepak to achieve similar quality. However, remember that Sorenson Video doesn't play well on slower computers (those running at less than 150 MHz). Thus, for CD-ROMs that you need to target at the lowest common denominator, Cinepak may be a better choice.
- **Colors:** As with any other delivery method, you should normally choose the highest possible number of colors unless your video really requires the lower bit-depth..
- **Quality**: You can probably leave the quality slider at its default position for your first test. (Remember that the higher the quality, the better the image will look, but the less compressed the movie will be.)
- **Frame rate**: If your video has a high frame rate, even as high as 30 frames per second, it's reasonable to keep the same frame rate; don't enter a value in this field, and the frame rate will be left alone. However, high frame rates result in high data rates; if you want a lower frame rate (perhaps because you're willing to sacrifice motion quality for image quality or frame size), pick a value that is a fraction of your original frame rate.

- **Key frame rate:** As with Web video, the compressor and the frame rate chosen determine what's a good number to enter here. For Sorenson Video, it's recommended that you start with a number here ten times the frame rate. For Cinepak, start with a number one or two times the frame rate.
- **Data rate**: If this field is enabled, you can enter a target data rate in kilobytes per second. If you're compressing with Cinepak, you generally want to pick a high value, to ensure decent quality. The highest number you should enter depends on the speed of the slowest drive that you expect your movie to be played from. For movies to be played on 2x CD-ROM drives, 180 is usually a safe maximum value. For 4x CD-ROMs, a value of 300 is a good place to start. If you're targeting even faster CD-ROM drives or hard drives for kiosk use, you can pick a higher value here, but it may work best to simply turn this choice off; let the other variables determine the data rate, and don't try to limit it here. If you're using the Sorenson Video compressor, you can get very good quality at much lower data rates; we recommend starting with a number below 100, regardless of the speed of your target drive.

Windows only?

One additional compressor choice, if you are developing on a Windows computer and intend the movie to play back only on Windows computers, is Indeo 4. It also requires more powerful computers to play back, however.

Video compressors you can buy

As with Web video, there are additional codecs you can purchase that can be used to compress QuickTime movies, often resulting in better-looking video. Sorenson Developer and Cinepak Pro, described in Chapter 15, are two choices. Others include Eidos Escape (from Eidos Technologies) and TrueMotion (from Duck Corporation). Your viewers will also have to have the coresponding decompressor, but this is less of an issue than it is with Web video. For CD-ROM, you include the decompressor on the disc—users don't generally have a problem if this extra file is installed during the installation process. For kiosks, you simply install the decompressor on the hard drive.

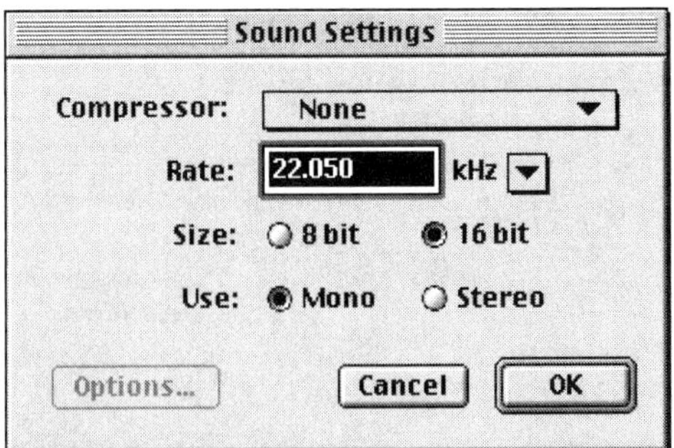

Figure 17.2 The Sound Settings dialog box is where you specify sound settings.

Sound compression choices

When you're preparing movies for CD-ROM or kiosk, you can also be somewhat more liberal in the choices you make in the Sound Settings dialog box (**Figure 17.2**).

- **Compressor:** In most cases, IMA 4:1 is a good choice. It provides very good sound quality. Data rates aren't as low as those for the new QuickTime 3 codecs, Qdesign Music and Qualcomm PureVoice, but since you're not compressing for the Web, getting those ultra-low data rates isn't as important.
- **Rate:** Here also you may want to try settings that give you better quality, rather than going for the lowest number. A good place to start is 11.025 kHz for voice and 22.050 kHz for music.
- **Size:** 16-bit audio will sound better than 8-bit audio. The IMA 4:1 compressor and others only work in 16-bit anyway.
- **Use:** You generally don't need to use stereo unless your original source is stereo and it's important for your presentation to have stereo sound.

Overview of authoring and presentation tools' support for QuickTime

Though MoviePlayer works just fine as a way to play movies on CD-ROM or hard drive, most people want to use QuickTime movies as part of a larger presentation that includes other media, such as text and graphics. And while you can certainly accomplish this by creating a Web page (as described in Chapter 15), you generally have more control and flexibility if you use some kind of presentation or authoring tool.

On the Macintosh, just about all presentation tools (like PowerPoint), as well as multimedia authoring tools, include QuickTime support —ranging from simply allowing you to put a QuickTime movie in the presentation, to providing extensive methods for interactively controlling the movie. On Windows computers, QuickTime 3 support is not yet the norm; only a select set of tools (Macromedia Director among them) provide this capability. We expect this to change soon, however. (Many tools do support older versions of QuickTime.)

In this chapter, we'll summarize the QuickTime support available in Macromedia Director (since it's the most popular authoring tool available) and HyperCard (since it offers the most extensive support for QuickTime). **Table 17.1** lists some other tools that support QuickTime.

Table 17.1

Some Authoring Tools That Support QuickTime

Tool	Authoring Platform*	Company	Web address
Director	Mac/Windows	Macromedia	http://www.macromedia.com/software/director
HyperCard	Mac	Apple	http://www.apple.com/hypercard
SuperCard	Mac	IncWell	http://www.incwell.com
PowerPoint	Mac/Windows	Microsoft	http://www.microsoft.com/powerpoint
HyperStudio	Mac/Windows	Roger Wagner Publishing	http://www.hyperstudio.com
ClickWorks	Mac	Pitango	http://www.pitango.com/
ToolBook	Windows	Asymetrix	http://www.asymetrix.com/
Authorware	Mac/Windows	Macromedia	http://www.macromedia.com/software/authorware
MovieWorks	Mac	Interactive Solutions	http:www.movieworks.com/
MetaCard	Windows (also Unix)	MetaCard Corporation	http://www.metacard.com
Special Delivery	Mac	Interactive Media Corp.	http://www.imcinfo.com

*The information in this table is accurate at the time of writing. Some products may have added support for additional platforms since the time of writing.

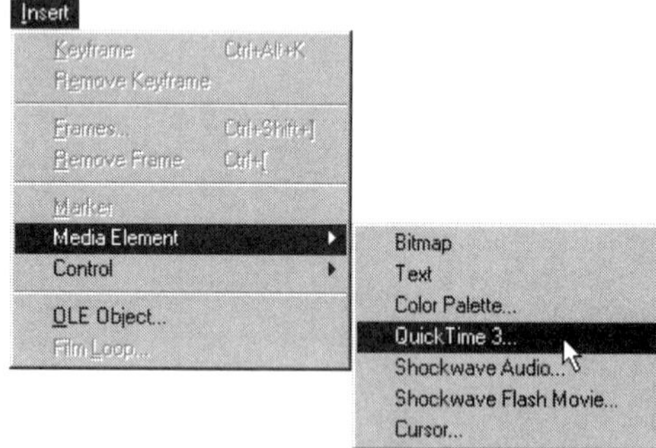

Figure 17.3 In Director 6.5, choose Media Element, then choose QuickTime 3 from the Insert menu.

QuickTime in Macromedia Director

It's easy to include QuickTime and QuickTime VR movies in projects created with the current version of Macromedia Director, 6.5. You use the Insert menu, choosing Media Element, then QuickTime 3 (**Figure 17.3**). A dialog box appears in which you select a movie (by clicking either a Browse button, to select one on your local computer, or an

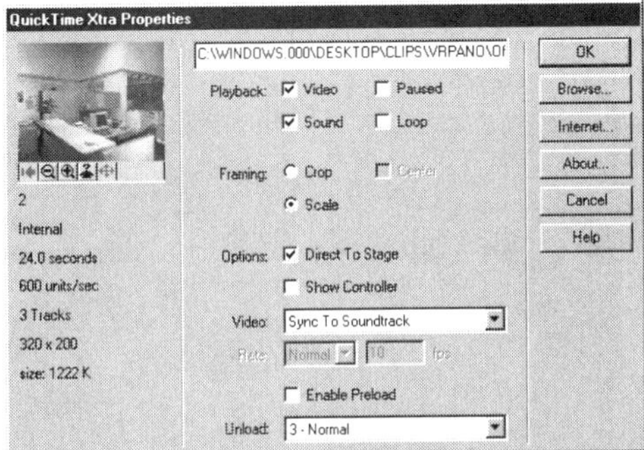

Figure 17.4 In Director's QuickTime Xtra Properties window, pick a movie and specify settings.

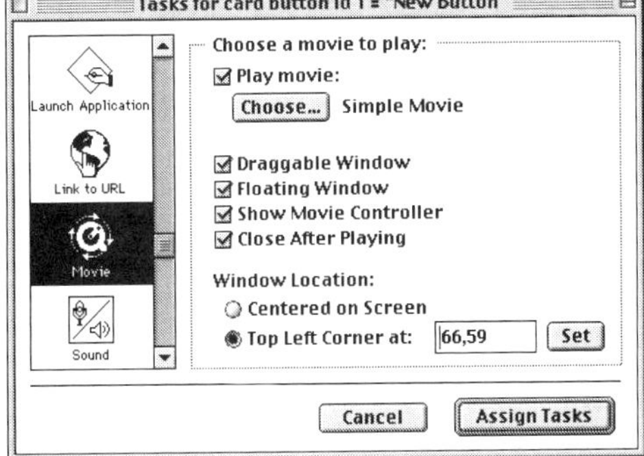

Figure 17.5 You can attach a Movie task to a button in a HyperCard stack.

Internet button, to type the URL for one on the Internet) and specify various settings for the movie (**Figure 17.4**). The movie gets added to the Cast window, and can then be included in your presentation, just like any other media element. In addition, Director's scripting language, Lingo, contains some commands that can be used to control the movie interactively, such as those for enabling and disabling tracks, starting and stopping the movie, reading the text in a text track, changing the volume of an audio track, and controlling the view in a VR movie. One drawback to Director is that, on the Mac, for both authoring and playback it requires a PowerPC processor for complete QuickTime 3 support.

QuickTime in HyperCard

HyperCard is currently a Mac-only application. A movie can be added to a HyperCard stack in a number of ways; one of the easiest is to add a button to a card, click the Task button in the button's Info window, and assign a Movie task (**Figure 17.5**).

In the current version of HyperCard (2.4), there are a huge number of scripting elements for controlling and testing just about every aspect of a movie's appearance and behavior. Using HyperTalk (HyperCard's scripting language) you can do many of the things you can do to a movie in MoviePlayer, and some that you can't. Some examples include exporting a movie, finding text in a text track, rotating and skewing a movie, specifying actions to occur when the movie reaches a certain point, specifying a graphics mode and transparency color, accessing copyright information, specifying a language for a track, and moving sprites in a sprite track.

Licensing requirements for distributing QuickTime

You can distribute QuickTime movies (as long they're yours) without asking anyone's permission or paying anyone anything.

However, typically when you create any kind of disc for distributing your movies, you want to include the QuickTime software, in case the user doesn't have QuickTime or has an older version of QuickTime that won't show your movies to their best advantage.

If you want to distribute QuickTime to anyone, you must get permission from Apple. The terms of Apple's QuickTime software distribution agreement are found at http://developer.apple.com/mkt/registering/swl/agreements.html#QuickTime.

In essence, what these say is that to distribute QuickTime 3 you must include Apple's QuickTime installer on your disc and use it during your install process. You have a choice of installers: There's one that will cost you nothing, but it puts an ad promoting QuickTime Pro on the desktop (which users can easily delete). There's another that won't install an ad, but you'll need to pay a fee of $1 per unit that you distribute. Both of these install only the Standard edition of QuickTime. Distributing QuickTime Pro (which costs end-users $30), costs $2 per unit.

✔ Warning

- We are authors, not lawyers. If you are worried about signing legal documents that you don't fully understand, you should talk to a lawyer.

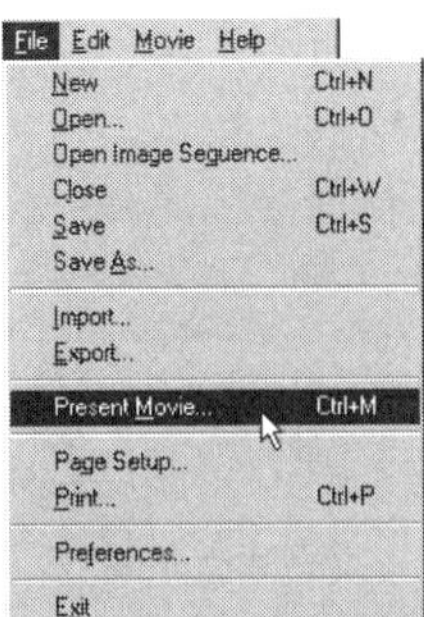

Figure 17.6 Choose Present Movie from the File menu.

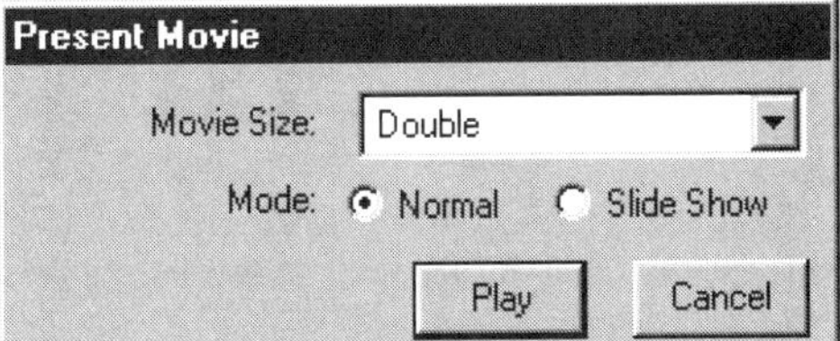

Figure 17.7 Choose Normal as the mode, pick a size, then press record on your VCR and click Play in the Present Movie dialog box. As long as the video from the computer is going into your VCR, the movie will be recorded to tape.

✔ Note

- If you have high-resolution movies, you've probably made them with a hardware and software digital video solution that should also be used for doing the output.

Outputting to analog videotape

What if you create a QuickTime movie that you want to distribute to people who don't have computers that can play QuickTime movies? Outputting to videotape may be the solution.

You need to have extra hardware in (or added to) your computer in order to turn what's in your computer, the QuickTime movie, into something that can be understood by a videotape machine. In general, the hardware you need is referred to as *video-out*. Some computers have video-out capabilities built in. Many inexpensive video cards also have this feature. Once you have this hardware installed and configured properly—read the user manual for the computer or card—you can use the Present Movie command in MoviePlayer.

To output a movie to videotape

1. Open the movie in MoviePlayer.
2. Choose Present Movie from the File menu (**Figure 17.6**).

   The Present Movie dialog box appears (**Figure 17.7**).
3. Choose a size appropriate for your movie. (You may need to test to see which size setting provides the optimal combination of performance, visual quality, and size. For 320-by-240 movies, Double often works well. If your movie is smaller than 320-by-240, you may have a hard time getting full-screen video that looks good and plays well.)
4. For mode, choose Normal.
5. When you have appropriate settings, press record on your VCR, then click Play in the Present Movie dialog box.

Exporting a video track as DV

DV (short for "Digital Video") is the format that many manufacturers are using in their new DV camcorders. (In Chapter 8 we discussed how you can open DV files.) If you want to output your QuickTime movie to a DV tape rather than to analog tape, you'll have to follow different steps. Since DV is a digital format, you can export the movie in DV format, then copy the movie from your computer to your DV camcorder or DV video deck.

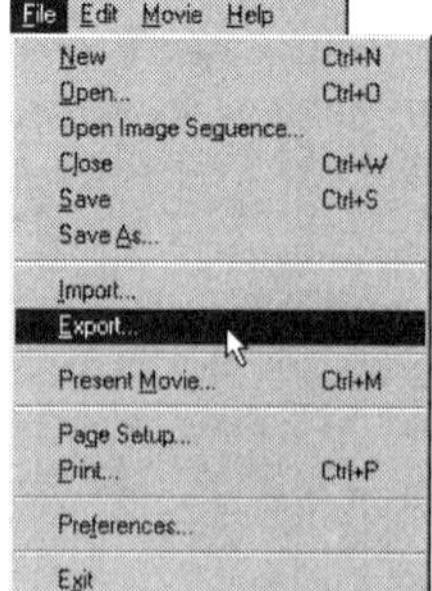

Figure 17.8 Choose Export from the File menu.

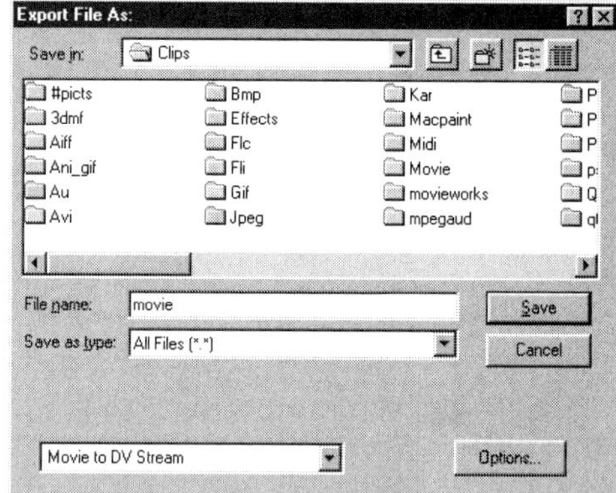

Figure 17.9 Select Movie to DV Stream and click the Options button.

To export a video track in the DV format

1. Choose Export from the File menu (**Figure 17.8**).
2. Choose Movie to DV Stream in the pop-up menu at the bottom of the Save dialog box (**Figure 17.9**).
3. Click the Options button.
4. In the DV Settings dialog box (**Figure 17.10**), select either NTSC or PAL format for your video. (NTSC is the standard in the US and Japan; PAL is the standard in most of Europe.)
5. If you are using a consumer DV camera, leave the Locked checkbox unselected. (Locked audio is only appropriate for some professional variants of DV.)
6. Click OK.
7. Click Save.

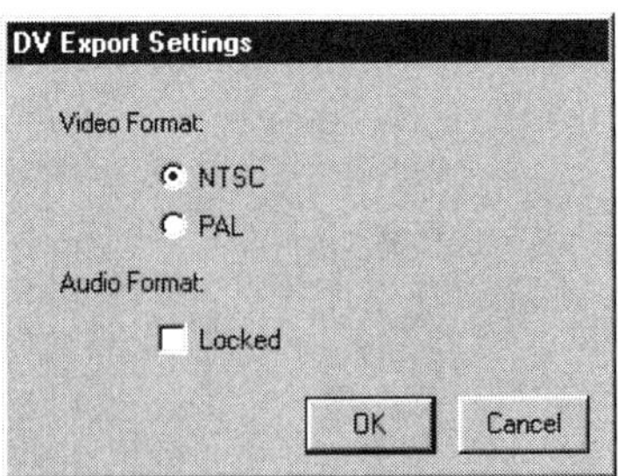

Figure 17.10 Choose your settings in the DV Settings dialog box.

✔ Warnings

- Movies exported as DV streams always scale to the standard DV size (720 x 480 pixels), so your movie will be distorted if the proportions aren't right.
- Not all QuickTime track types can be exported in the DV format. Audio-only movies don't export. Sound tracks do export as long as they're accompanied by a visual track. Currently, music tracks don't export at all. 3D and Sprite tracks do export OK, but, of course, if it's an interactive (wired) sprite track, none of the interactivity is exported. You can't export any kind of MPEG track.

Moving a DV file to a DV device

You'll need to have an additional card (and accompanying software) for your computer to move files between your computer and DV device. Follow the instructions that come with this product.

A

Mouse and Keyboard Tricks

Tables A.1 and A.2 list various keyboard and mouse actions that perform useful functions in MoviePlayer. We've mentioned many of these previously in the book, but they are consolidated here for your convenience. (We haven't listed the keyboard equivalents that appear in MoviePlayer's menus.) These will all work in MoviePlayer; many will work in other QuickTime-savvy applications, too.

Table A.1

Mac OS Mouse and Keyboard Shortcuts and Enhancements

SHORTCUT/ACTION	WHAT IT DOES
Control + Step buttons	Show scratching slider
Control + Play button	Play all frames
Option + right Step button	Jump to end of movie or end of selection
Option + left Step button	Jump to beginning of movie or beginning of selection
Option + drag size box	Scale to next "good" size
Shift + drag size box	Scale movie disproportionately
Option + Volume Control button	Turn audio on/off
Up or Down Arrow keys	Raise or lower volume
Left or Right Arrow keys	Step back or advance one frame
Return or Spacebar	Play if paused; pause if playing
Command + . (period)	Stop playing
Double-click movie image	Play
Single-click playing movie image	Stop playing
Shift + double-click movie image	Play the movie backward
Shift + Volume Control button	Overdrive audio
Shift + pointer over image in VR movie	Zoom in
Ctrl + pointer over image in VR movie	Zoom out
Option + pull down Edit menu	Trim replaces Clear, Add replaces Paste
Shift + Option + pull down Edit menu	Add Scaled replaces Paste
Control + Paste, Add, or Add Scaled*	Bring up Text Import Settings dialog box or Compression Settings dialog box.
Option + click image sample in Compression Settings dialog box	Zoom in
Shift + Option + click image sample	Zoom out

*When pasting or adding text copied from editor or graphic copied from graphics application.

Table A.2

Windows Mouse and Keyboard Shortcuts and Enhancements

SHORTCUT/ACTION	WHAT IT DOES
Alt + Step buttons	Show scratching slider
Ctrl + Alt + right Step button	Jump to end of movie
Ctrl + Alt + left Step button	Jump to beginning of movie
Ctrl + Alt + drag size box	Scale to next "good" size
Shift + drag size box	Scale movie disproportionately
Ctrl + Alt + Volume Control button	Turn audio on/off
Up or Down Arrow keys	Raise or lower volume
Left or Right Arrow keys	Step back or advance one frame
Enter or Spacebar	Play if paused; pause if playing
Double-click movie image	Play
Single-click playing movie image	Stop playing
Shift + double-click movie image	Play the movie backward
Shift + Volume Control button	Overdrive audio
Shift + pointer over image in VR movie	Zoom in
Ctrl + pointer over image in VR movie	Zoom out
Ctrl + Alt + pull down Edit menu	Trim replaces Clear, Add replaces Paste
Shift + Ctrl + Alt + pull down Edit menu	Add Scaled replaces Paste
Alt + Paste*	Open Text Import Settings dialog box or Compression Settings dialog box
Ctrl + Alt + click image sample in Compression Settings dialog box	Zoom in
Shift + Ctrl + Alt + click image sample	Zoom out

*When pasting text copied from editor or graphics copied from graphics program.

MOUSE AND KEYBOARD TRICKS

Configuring QuickTime

B

When you first install QuickTime, it is configured according to some default settings. These usually work just fine, but you can change your configuration if you need to. This is done via two separate windows: the QuickTime Settings control panel and the QuickTime Plug-in Settings dialog box. We'll cover both of these windows in this appendix.

Using the QuickTime Settings Control Panel

The QuickTime Settings control panel (which we briefly introduced in Chapter 1 and have used in a few other places in the book) has a number of panels. Most do not affect MoviePlayer and most do not need to be changed, but here's a summary of them all.

Autoplay (Mac OS only)

This panel **(Figure B.1)** specifies what happens when certain volumes or discs appear on your desktop.

If you have a PowerPC, we recommend that you leave the Enable CD-ROM AutoPlay option unchecked, because of a new virus, called the AutoStart virus that can infect your system when this is checked.

Connection Speed

Choose the speed of your Internet connection here **(Figure B.2)**. The speed chosen will be used when you come to a page that has a reference movie (see Chapter 16).

File Type Associations (Windows only)

This panel **(Figure B.3)** is used to indicate whether or not you want QuickTime applications (like MoviePlayer, Plug-in, and PictureViewer) to open various types of files.

Select this checkbox if you want your audio CDs to play from start to finish when inserted.

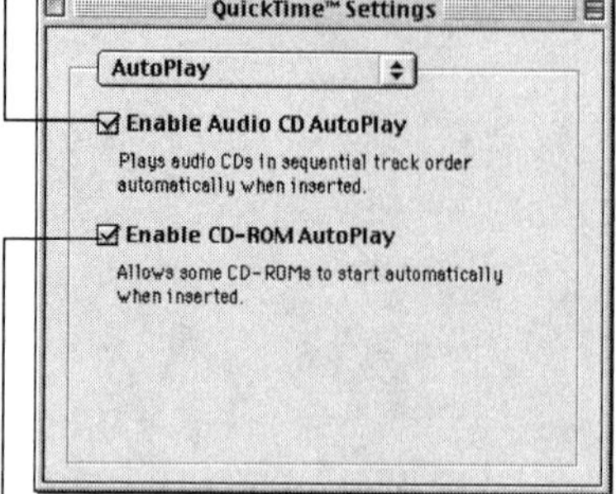

Select this checkbox only if you don't mind if programs on certain CDs (designated as autoplay by their creators) to start automatically.

Figure B.1 Autoplay panel

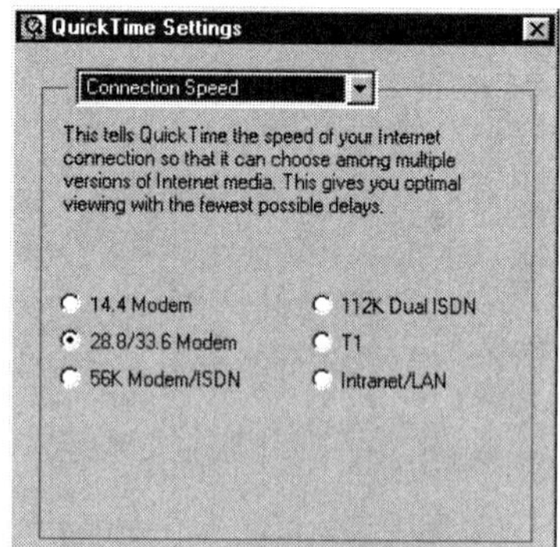

Figure B.2 Connection Speed panel

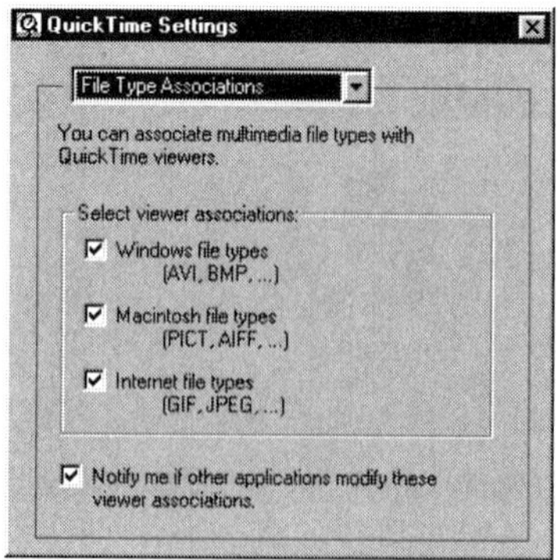

Figure B.3 File Type Associations panel

Click here to enter an access key that you've been given.

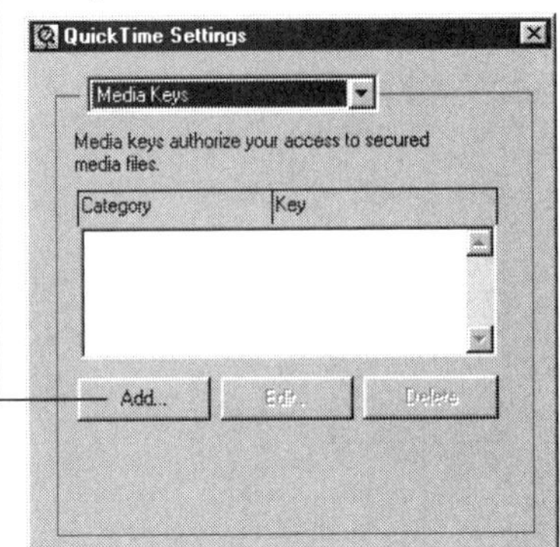

Figure B.4 Media Keys panel

Select a synthesizer in this list.

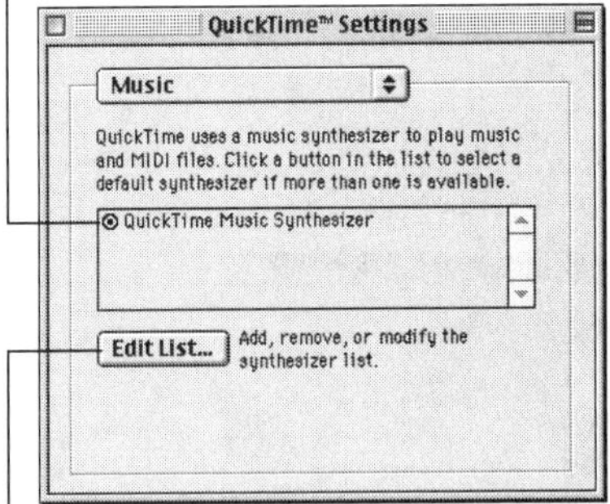

Click here to change the choices available in the list above, e.g. to add your hardware synthesizer.

Figure B.5 Music panel

Click here if you want your Mac OS machine to use DOS file extensions to determine what application should be used to open a file.

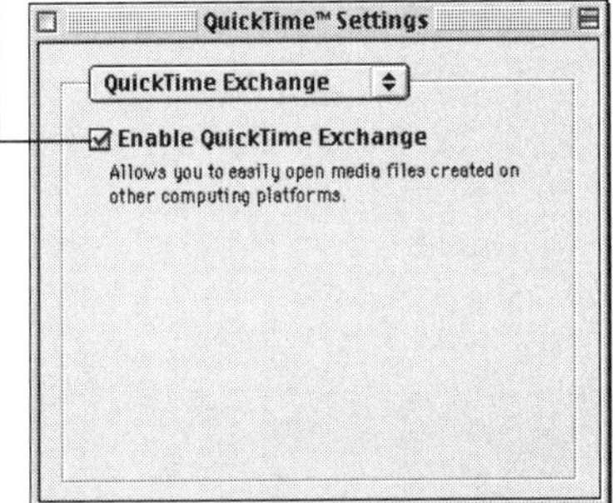

Figure B.6 QuickTime Exchange panel

Media Keys

Some movies can be encrypted. In order to play back the movie, you need to have an access key, which you enter in this panel **(Figure B.4)**.

Music

If you have a hardware MIDI synthesizer, register it on this panel **(Figure B.5)**. (See Chapter 13 for more details.)

QuickTime Exchange (Mac OS only)

The Mac OS usually recognizes files by *filetype* (a piece of information stored with the file). QuickTime Exchange **(Figure B.6)** enables the Mac OS to recognize standard DOS file-name extensions (e.g. ".bmp" or ".wav") if there is no filetype.

Registration

This panel **(Figure B.7)** is used to enable QuickTime Pro (see Chapter 1).

Sound In (Windows only)

This panel **(Figure B.8)** is used when you're capturing audio for QuickTime movies and you have more than one audio input.

Click here if you've purchased QuickTime Pro already and have registration information to enter.

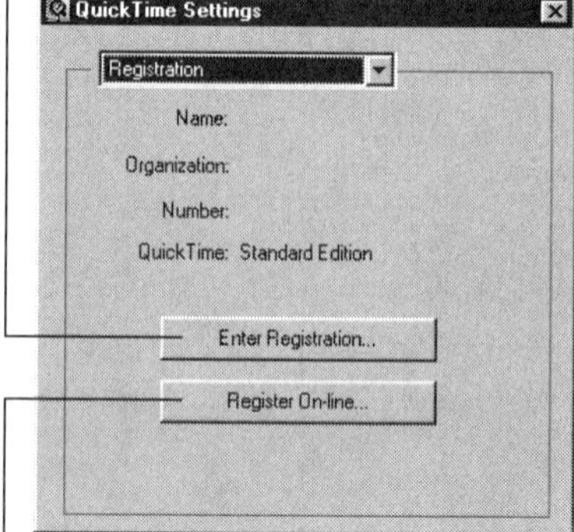

Click here if you want to load a Web page with information about purchasing QuickTime Pro.

Figure B.7 Registration panel

Select the audio input you want QuickTime to "listen to" when recording audio.

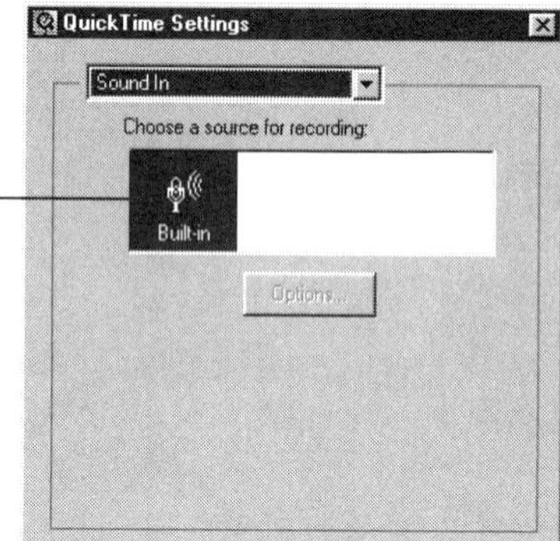

Figure B.8 Sound In panel

Windows computers may have multiple devices for playing back sound. If your system is DirectSound compatible, choose DirectSound. WaveOut is the lowest common denominator.

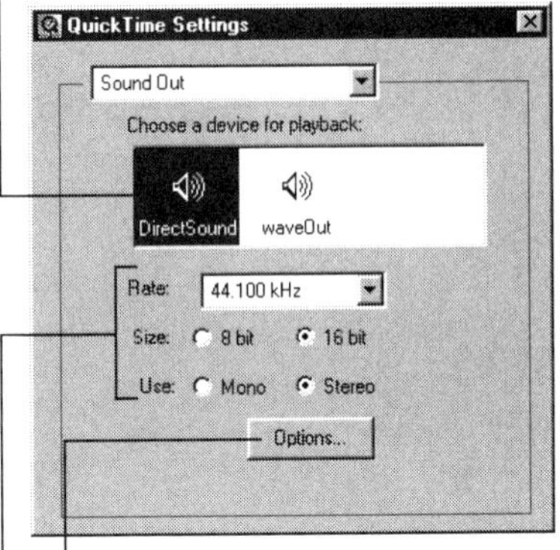

This button may be available for certain audio playback devices. Click it to change additional settings particular to the device.

Set these to the highest values possible in order to make sure that files are played back at their highest quality.

Figure B.9 Sound Out panel

This is the slowest but most compatible method for Windows to draw graphics on your screen.

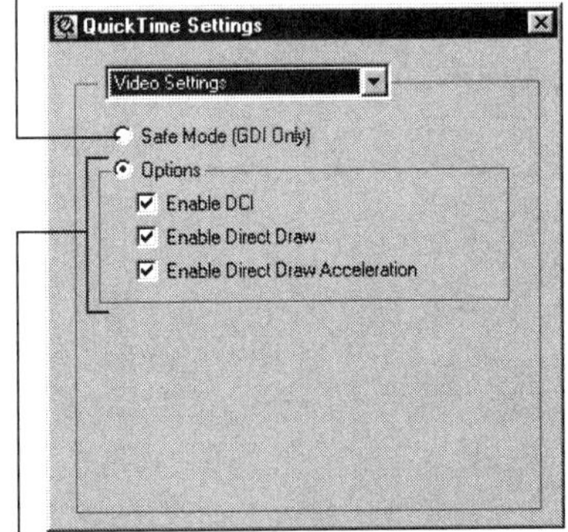

These options will provide better playback performance. Only deselect them if you believe they're not compatible with your graphics card.

Figure B.10 Video Settings panel

Sound Out (Windows only)

Use this panel **(Figure B.9)** to specify sound playback characteristics.

Video Settings (Windows only)

The settings here **(Figure B.10)** determine how QuickTime works with your video display system.

✔ Tip

- For the best QuickTime playback performance under Windows, you'll need the current version of DirectX . You can get this at http://www.microsoft.com/directx/download.asp. You'll also want to get the current DirectDraw and DirectSound drivers for your video and sound cards. (You can find these at http://www.download.com. Choose **Drivers** from the Categories list. To locate a sound driver, choose **Sound & Multimedia** in the Subcategories list. To locate a video driver, choose **Display & Video** in the Subcategories list.)

Using the QuickTime Plug-in Settings dialog box

Movies on Web pages have an extra button in the controller, a downward-pointing triangle at the far right side. Clicking and holding this button reveals a drop-down menu. Choose **Plug-in Settings** to open the QuickTime Plug-In Settings dialog box **(Figure B.11)**.

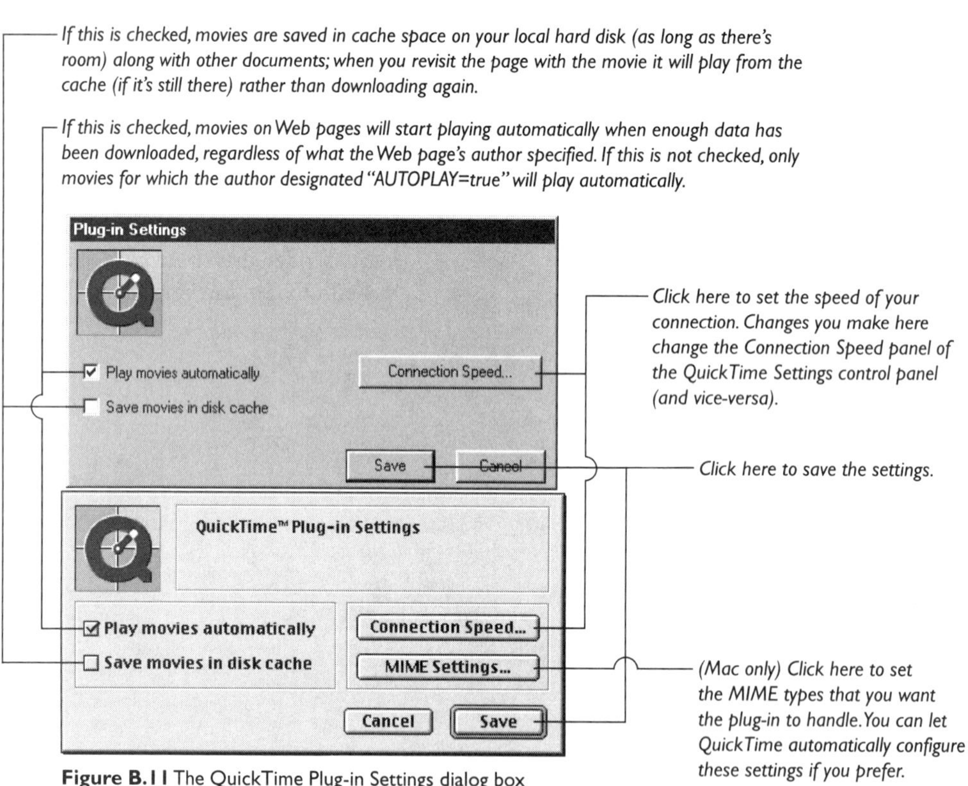

Figure B.11 The QuickTime Plug-in Settings dialog box

RESOURCES

In this appendix we list vendors and products mentioned in this book along with URL's, followed by a select group of informational Web resources.

Apple Computer Inc.

QuickTime and MoviePlayer
1-888-295-0648 (to order QuickTime Pro)
http://www.apple.com/quicktime/

HyperCard
http://www.apple.com/hypercard/

Apple MIDI manager (unsupported)
ftp://ftp.info.apple.com/Apple_Support_Area/Apple_Software_Updates/US/Macintosh/Unsupported/MIDI_Management_Tools_2.0.2.sea.bin

Sprite Export Xtra, Plug-in Helper, MakeRefMovie, QTVR Flattener, QTVR PanoToThumbnail, 3D Movie Maker
http://www.apple.com/quicktime/developers/tools.html

MacSourcery

BarbaBatch
http://www.macsourcery.com

Strata Inc.

Strata VideoShop 4.0/3D
http://www.strata3d.com/html/videoshop.html

Macromedia

Director
http://www.macromedia.com/software/director/

Terran Interactive

Media Cleaner Pro
(can also purchase Sorenson Video Developer Edition and QDesign Music Codec Professional Edition here)
http://www.terran.com

Adobe Systems

Premiere
http://www.adobe.com/prodindex/premiere/main.html
Photoshop
http://www.adobe.com/prodindex/photoshop/main.html

Opcode/Gibson

OMS (Open Music System)
http://www.opcode.com/oms/

Mark of the Unicorn, Inc.

Free MIDI
http://www.motu.com/english/software/freemidi/fmdist.html

Electric Cafe

ModelShop
http://www.eleccafe.com/

Lightwork Design

QD3D Plug-ins
http://www.lightwork.com/qd3d/

Viewpoint Datalabs

(check in the future for plug-ins for QuickDraw 3D)
http://www.thinkfish.com/

GoLive

CyberStudio
http://www.golive.com/

Pangea Software

3DMF Optimizer
http://www.realtime.net/~pangea/

Lari Software

Electrifier Pro

http://www.larisoft.com/Products/ElectrifierStudio/

Totally Hip Software

WebPainter

http://www.totallyhip.com

Paceworks

ObjectDancer

http://www.paceworks.com/products/objectdancer.html

Sorenson Vision

Sorenson Video Developer Edition

http://www.s-vision.com/products/sorensonvideo/SorensonVideo.htm

Compression Technologies Inc.

Cinepak Pro

http://www.cinepak.com/

QDesign

QDesign Music Codec Professional Edition

http://www.qdesign.com/

Eidos Technologies

Eidos Escape

http://www.eidostechnologies.com

Duck Corporation

TrueMotion

http://www.duck.com

Codec Central

Lots of info on compressors

http://www.codeccentral.com

Judy and Robert's Little QuickTime Page

A weekly infomation page by the authors of this book

http://www.bmug.org/quicktime

QuickTime FAQ

Frequently Asked Questions about QuickTime

http://www.quicktimefaq.org

QuickTime and MoviePlayer Pro 3: Visual Quickstart Guide Web Site

Companion site to this book

http://www.peachpit.com/vqs/movieplayer

INDEX

Note: *Page numbers in italic denote screens.*

Numbers

3D Movie Maker, associating tween tracks with 3D objects with, 134
3D movies, effect of Step buttons on, 27
3D tracks
- changing texture mapping for, 135–136
- changing the renderer for, 137
- creating dynamic, 134
- creating from a 3DMF file, 134
- creating with texture maps, 136
- determining if an object has a texture map, 135

3DMF file, creating a 3D track from, 134

A

About QuickTime, checking QuickTime version with, 3
Add Annotation dialog box, 65
- adding text to copyright information in, 68

Add command, adding new data to a movie with, 76
Add Scaled command, adding new data to a movie with, 77
AIFF file format, 14
Alignment options, Text Import Settings dialog box, 119
alpha channels, creating tracks with, 97
Alpha Gain filter, 175
alternate movies, creating, 203
animated GIF files
- creating video tracks from, 112
- format, 14

Animation video compressor, QuickTime 3, 104, 184
annotation data
- adding, 64–65
- changing, 66
- deleting, 66
- that movies can contain, 64

Annotations panel, 65
- changing copyright information in, 68

Anti-Alias check box, Text Import Settings dialog box, 119
Apple Computer
- methods for getting QuickTime program from, 6
- QuickTime Tools page, 202
- saving QuickTime movies from their Web site, 10

AU file format, 14
audio CD file
- creating a sound track from, 151
- format, 14

audio compressors, included with QuickTime 3, 146
audio level
- changing for movies, 31
- overdriving, 32

audio tracks
- adding still images to, 141
- adding new to a video file, 140
- changing the default volume and balance of, 143
- playing when the movie is in the background, 142
- working with, 139–143

authoring tools, with QuickTime support, 218–219
Auto-Size options, Text Import Settings dialog box, 119
AVI files
- creating video tracks from, 112
- format, 14
- possible problems with, 112

B

Back button, QuickTime VR, 43
background color
- changing for a sprite track, 133
- changing for an imported text track, 119

balance, changing in an audio track, 143
bandwidth, 168
BarbaBatch sound compression software, 188
black-lining technique, turning off in MoviePlayer, 115
Blur filter, 175
BMP file format, 14
BMP video compressor, QuickTime 3, 104
bytes, 169

C

captions, adding to VR movies, 99
CD-ROM
  movies on, 213–223
  overview of compression issues for, 214
  sound compression choices, 217
  video compression choices, 215–216
Change Track Name dialog box, 199
Chapter List button, Movie controller, 38
Chapter List Maker program, 126
chapter lists
  tools for creating, 126
  using, 38
Choose Filter dialog box, 174–175
Choose Language option, Movie menu, 23
  setting up alternate language tracks with, 82
Choose Movie Language dialog box, 23
Cinepak Pro video compressor, advantage of, 186
Cinepak video compressor, QuickTime 3, 104, 184
Clear option, Edit menu, 60
Clear Preview button, in Preview panel, 69
CNN Video Vault Web site, for downloading QuickTime movies, 10
codecs. *See* video compression; *individual compressor names*
color
  changing background of a sprite track, 133
  making transparent in a track, 95
  setting options in video compressors, 184
Color Picker dialog boxes, 95
Color Style filter, 175
color table
  adding custom to a movie, 100
  products for creating custom, 100
Color Tint filter, 175
ColorSync filter, 175
combining two movies, 59
Component Video compressor, QuickTime 3, 104
composition (dither copy) mode, Graphics Mode panel, 96
Compression Settings dialog box, 106–107
  accessing, 183
  making Web appropriate choices in, 184
  video compression choices in, 215–216
Compressor option, Sound Settings dialog box, 147
compressors-decompressors (codecs). *See* video compression
controllers, movie. *See* movie controllers
Convert button, Open dialog box, 13, 13–14
copy modes, Graphics Mode panel, 96
copying movie data, 52
copyright information
  changing, 68
  showing for movies, 20
creating
  a picture-in-a-picture effect, 93
  a still image file from any movie image, 101–102
  video track from a single PICT file, 111
  video track from a single still image, 110
  video tracks from a sequence of still images, 109
  video tracks from non-QuickTime animation and video files, 112
  video tracks from PICS animation files, 113
cutting movie data, 53

D

data rates
  checking, 169
  estimating target, 184
  settings for video for Web pages, 185–186
  sound track, 146
  understanding, 168
  video track, 104
data size
  checking, 169
  understanding, 168
DeBabelizer, 100
Delete Tracks dialog box, 79
deleting
  parts of a movie, 60
  portions of text from a text track, 128
  tracks from movies, 79
desktop virtual reality. *See* QuickTime VR movies
difference frames, 105
Digital Video (DV)
  exporting a video track as, 222–223
  popularity of on Web, 180
digitized sound, understanding the characteristics of, 146
Direct X version 3.0, Windows system software, 5
DirectDraw drivers, for Windows systems, 5
DirectSound drivers, for Windows systems, 5
dither copy mode, Graphics Mode panel, 96
Don't Auto-Scale option, Text Import Settings dialog box, 119
Double Size option, Movie menu, 18
double-sized movies, saving, 170
downloading, QuickTime movies, 10
drag-and-drop editing, Mac OS, 62–63
Drag Zoomed Object button, 45
dragging, a movie window to optimal size, 18
Drop Shadow option, Text Import Settings dialog box, 119
DV files
  creating video tracks from, 112
  format, 14
DVD discs, types of, 215
DV-NTSC/DV-PAL video compressors, QuickTime 3, 104
dynamic 3D tracks, creating, 134

E

Easy Open control panel, opening non-QuickTime files with, 16
Edge Detection filter, 175
Edit Annotation dialog box, 66

Edit menu
  Enable Tracks command in, 80
  Extract Tracks command in, 80
  selecting and deselecting movie data from, 48
editing
  canceling a selection, 48
  drag-and-drop in Mac OS, 62–63
  movies with MoviePlayer, 47–74
  selecting a portion of a movie, 48
  selecting all the data in a movie, 48
EMBED tag, 189
  adding parameters to, 191–192
  parameters for QuickTime movies, 191
  sample parameters and values and their uses, 192–193
  writing the minimal HTML for embedding a QuickTime movie on a Web page, 190
Emboss filter, 175
Enable Tracks command, Edit menu, 80
exiting, slide-show mode, 30
exporting
  a movie image as a PICT or BMP, 101–102
  a text track with text descriptors and time stamps, 123–124
  a video track in the DV format, 222–223
  MoviePlayer movies as QuickTime movies, 171–173
  to other formats with MoviePlayer, 2
Extract Tracks command, Edit menu, 176
Extract Tracks dialog box, removing tracks from movies with, 78

F

fast start format, 170
  QuickTime 3 movies saved in, 180
file dependencies, checking, 74
file formats, compatible MoviePlayer, 14
Fill Screen option, Movie menu, 18
Film Noise filter, 175
filters
  applying, 174
  samples of, 175
finding, text in a text track, 130
FLC/FLI files
  creating video tracks from, 112
  format, 14
flipping, a track's image, 89
font, changing in a text track, 128
Font options, Text Import Settings dialog box, 119
font size, changing in a text track, 128
font style, changing in a text track, 128
Format panel, checking sound track characteristics in, 148
FPS (frames per second), 37
frame by frame movie presentation, 30
frame rate
  checking for movies, 37
  picking in Image Sequence Settings dialog box, 109
  settings for video compressors, 185
frame size, checking your movies, 178
frames. *See* key frame; difference frames

G

General Convolution filter, 175
General MIDI specification, 158
Get Info option, Movie menu, 21
GIF file format, 14
Go To Poster Frame option, Movie menu, 67
graphics
  adding a small from another application to a movie, 114
  pasting from a graphics application into a movie, 56
  replacing a sprite's with another QuickTime track, 132
Graphics Mode panel, copy modes in, 96
Graphics video compressor, QuickTime 3, 104, 184

H

H.263 video compressor, QuickTime 3, 104
Half Size option, Movie menu, 18
hot spot pointers, 42–43
hot spots, finding and using in QuickTime VR movies, 42–43
HotBot search engine, finding QuickTime movies with, 10
HREF links, using instead of EMBED tags, 192
HREF tracks, 179
  specifying that a Web page load automatically, 200
  using to make movies load Web pages, 198–199
HSL Balance filter, 175
HTML
  writing minimal for embedding QuickTime movies on Web pages, 190
  writing to embed a poster movie, 196–197
HTTP streaming, 180
HyperCard, in QuickTime, 219
HyperTalk scripting language, 219

I

Image Sequence Settings dialog box, 109
images, adding to existing movies, 114
importing
  from other formats, 2
  music from an audio CD to a sound track, 151
  non-QuickTime movie files, 15–16
Info window in MoviePlayer, opening, 21
Instrument Picker dialog box, changing instruments in a music track with, 160–161
Intel Indeo Video Interactive video compressor, QuickTime 3, 104

J

JPEG/JFIF file formats, 14

K

karaoke files
converting to QuickTime, 159
creating a music and text track from, 159
filename extension, 157
importing into movies, 157
key frame, 105
key frame rate, settings for video compressors, 185
keyboard and mouse trick, 225–227
KeyedText option, Text Import Settings dialog box, 119
kilobytes (k), 169
kiosk. *See* video kiosk

L

languages
choosing for playback of movies, 23
setting up alternate for tracks, 82
specifying for a track, 83
licensing requirements, for distributing QuickTime, 220
logos, adding to VR movies, 98–99
looping a movie, 33

M

Mac Control Panels folder, QuickTime setting icon on, 3
Mac OS
drag-and-drop editing, 62–63
hardware and software requirements for running QuickTime, 5
installing QuickTime 3 on, 7
mouse and keyboard shortcuts and enhancements, 226
MacSourcery's BarbaBatch sound compression software, 188
Make movie self-contained radio button, Save As dialog box, 73
MakeRefMovie utility, 202
creating alternate movies with, 203
generating a reference movie with, 203–205
Mask panel, masking a visual track with, 91
Media Cleaner Pro (Terran's), 100, 126
processing movies for final delivery with, 168
MediaCity, Web site address for downloading QuickTime movies, 10
megabytes (MB), 169
memory, loading tracks into, 86
MIDI (Musical Instrument Digital Interface) files
converting to QuickTime, 158
exporting a QuickTime music track as, 165
filename extension, 157
general specification for, 158
importing into movies, 157
MIDI synthesizer, playing music tracks through, 163–164
M-JPEG cards, 214
Mono setting, Sound Settings dialog box, 147
Motion JPEG A video compressor, QuickTime 3, 104
Motion JPEG B video compressor, QuickTime 3, 104
Motion JPEG video cards, 214
mouse and keyboard tricks, 225–227
.mov filename extension, saving movies on a Mac with, 170
Movie Controller, MoviePlayer
adding visual tracks to QuickTime VR movies with, 98
height of, 178
movie controllers, 17
movie data
copying, 52
cutting, 53
pasting into a movie, 54–55
pasting into a newly created movie, 58
pasting into other applications, 54
selecting and deselecting, 48
movie files, saving, allowing dependencies, 72
Movie FPS, checking, 37
movie image, exporting as a PICT or BMP, 101*102
Movie Information dialog box, 20
Movie Settings dialog box, 172–173, 173
movie tracks, determining which are in a movie, 22
movie window
changing proportions of in Windows, 19
methods for changing size, 18
MoviePlayer
added functionality in Pro edition, 2
advantages of exporting movies as QuickTime movies, 171–172
Apple utilities for, 202
basic movie editing, 47–74
basics, 11–23
compatible file formats, 14
compressing video for the Web with, 183
creating a picture-in-a-picture effect, 93
drag-and-drop editing in Mac OS, 62–63
exporting movies as QuickTime movies, 171–173
exporting to other formats with, 2
flipping a track's image, 89
Info window, 21
making a color in a track transparent, 95
masking a visual track in, 91
methods for changing window size, 18
masking a visual track, 91
movie controllers, 17
opening Info window in, 21
opening non-QuickTime files, 13–14
opening QuickTime movies, 12
playing visual tracks side-by-side, 92
playing and pausing all open movies in, 35
playing sound from all open, 35
preparing QuickTime files for the Web with, 179–200
relayering tracks in, 94
repositioning a track's image, 90
resizing a track, 90
rotating a track's image, 88, 90
setting audio to play when movie is in background, 142
skewing a track image, 90

INDEX

Standard versus Pro editions, 2
using as a sound conversion utility, 156
when not to export movies as QuickTime movies, 171
working with visual tracks in, 87–102
movies
adding a custom color table to, 100
adding images to an existing, 114
adding new audio to a video file, 140
adding new data to, 76–77
adding small amounts of text to, 129
applying filters to, 174
basic editing of, 47–74
changing audio level for, 31
changing copyright information in, 68
changing the duration of a track, 81
changing window size, 18
checking the dimensions of, 178
checking the frame rate of, 37
checking the frame size, 178
choosing a language for playback, 23
choosing size of when presenting, 29
combining two, 59
copying movie data, 52
compressing only selected tracks in, 176–177
creating new and pasting movie data into, 58
cutting movie data, 53
deleting parts of, 60
deleting tracks from, 79
delivery basics, 167–178
designating a set of alternate tracks for, 84–85
disabling and enabling tracks, 80
exiting slide-show mode, 30
exporting as QuickTime movies, 171–173
extracting a single track from, 78
frame by frame in slide-show mode, 30
getting information about, 21
getting samples of from Apple Web site, 10
getting time-related information about, 51
importing MIDI files into, 157
jumping to beginning of a selection, 28
jumping to end of a selection, 28
keeping a portion of and deleting everything around it, 60
loading tracks into memory, 86
looping or playing backward, 33
muting the audio, 31
on Web pages, 179–211
opening non-QuickTime, 13
opening QuickTime, 12
outputting to analog videotape, 221
overdriving the audio in, 32
pasting movie data into, 54–55
pausing, 26
playing, 26, 33
playing all frames in, 34
playing audio when in background, 142
playing only what is selected, 50
preparing for distribution, 167–178
presenting one frame at a time, 30
presenting to play automatically, 29
quickly moving around in, 28
removing a single track from, 78
replacing a section of with data from another, 61
saving, 72
saving double-sized, 170
saving for distribution, 170
scaling a track to a specific duration, 81
searching for text in a text track, 130
selecting and deselecting data in, 48
setting a preview for, 69
setting up tracks with alternate languages, 82
showing copyright information for, 20
stepping through frame by frame, 27
stopping presentation before the end of, 29
varying the playback rate of, 36
MPEG audio tracks
creating from an MPEG sound file, 115–116, 152
working with, 139–143
MPEG files
creating MPEG tracks from, 115–116, 152
formats, 14
multinode movie, 42
music tracks
changing instruments in, 160–161
converting from MIDI files, 158
converting to sound tracks, 155
creating from a karaoke file, 159
exporting QuickTime as MIDI files, 165
playing through a MIDI synthesizer, 163–164
substituting your own custom instrument sounds in, 162

N

node, 42
non-QuickTime movie files, 13–14
converting, 15–16
creating video tracks from, 112
importing, 15–16
opening with Easy Open control panel, 16
saving, 15

O

object VR movies, 39
manipulating objects in, 41
objects, moving zoomed in, 45
Open dialog box, 14–14
Open Image Sequence option, File menu, 109
OpenDML file format, 14
opening
Image Sequence Settings dialog box, 109
Info window for a movie, 21
non-QuickTime movie files, 13–14

INDEX

QuickTime movie files, 12
Size Panel in Get Info window, 88
overdriving audio level, 32

P

panorama VR movies, 39*40
parameters
adding to EMBED tag, 191–192
samples with values and their uses, 192–193
specifying a value for a TARGET, 193
Web site address for EMBED tag documentation, 193
pasting
graphics from a graphics application into a movie, 56
movie data into a movie, 54–55
movie data into a newly created movie, 58
text from a word processor into a movie, 57
Pause button, Movie controller, 26
pausing a movie, 26
Photo JPEG video compressor, QuickTime 3, 104
Photoshop file format, 14
PICS animation file, creating a video track from, 113
picture-in-a-picture effect, creating, 93
PictureViewer, enhanced features in Pro edition, 2
PICT file, creating a video track from a single, 111
Planar RGB video compressor, QuickTime 3, 104
Play All Frames option, Movie menu, 34
play bar, Movie controller, 28
Play button, Movie controller, 26
Play Selection Only option, Movie menu, 50
playback rate, varying for movies, 36
playing movies, 26, 33
Plug-in Helper utility, 202
specifying a URL to go to when user clicks a specific video track, 206
using, 206–207
PNG file format, 14
poster movies, 179
creating a multiple frame, 195
creating a still-image, 194–195
writing HTML that embeds, 196–197
poster setting, 67
Preferences dialog box, MoviePlayer, 142
premul black alpha channel mode, 97
premul white alpha channel mode, 97
premultiplied alpha channels, 97
Present Movie dialog box, 29, 30
presentation tools, with QuickTime support, 218–219
preview
removing, 70
setting for movies, 69
setting using data from other movies, 71
viewing current, 70
Preview panel, Clear Preview button in, 69
previewing versus tiling movies, 209
Pro Player Edition, checking for in Registration panel, 4
progressive downloading, 180

Q

quality settings, for video compressors, 185
QDesign Music compressor, 188
QTVR Flattener utility, 202
using with MoviePlayer to create streaming VR movies, 208–209
QTVR PanoToThumbnail utility, 202
creating panorama thumbnails with, 210–211
QuickDraw GX file format, 14
QuickTime
audio compressors included with version 3, 146
authoring and presentation tool support for, 218–219
basics, 1–10
configuring, 229–234
configuring a Web server for, 189
converting MIDI files to, 158
cost of different versions, 6
creating MPEG tracks from MPEG files in, 115–116
determining what version you have, 3–4
exporting a music track as a MIDI file, 165
getting version 3, 6
hardware and software requirements for, 5
in HyperCard, 219
in Macromedia Director, 218–219
installing version 3, 7
licensing requirement for distributing, 220
methods of getting to the Upgrade to QuickTime 3 Pro Web page, 8
movie controllers, 17
MoviePlayer as part of, 1
MoviePlayer compatible formats, 14
playing movies, 25–38
presentation tools with support for, 218–219
Standard versus Pro editions, 2
telling viewers to get it, 190
transitional edits, 55
upgrading to Pro version, 8
versus other streaming formats, 180–181
video compressors in version 3, 104
QuickTime movies
advantages of exporting MoviePlayer movies as, 171–172
downloading, 10
embedding on a Web page, 189
making movies that stream, 182
outputting to analog videotape, 221
playing, 25–38
preparing for the Web with MoviePlayer, 179–200
QuickTime Music Synthesizers dialog box, 163–164
QuickTime Plug-in Settings dialog box, configuring QuickTime in, 234
QuickTime Settings control panel, 163–164
configuring QuickTime in, 230–233
QuickTime VR movies
adding tracks to, 98

adding visual data to, 98–99
creating panorama thumbnails with QTVR PanoToThumbnail utility, 210–211
effects possible by adding data to, 99
finding and using hot spots in, 42–43
interacting with, 39–46
looking around in panorama, 40
manipulating objects in object movies, 41
presenting, 46
stopping presentation of, 46
zooming into, 44
zooming images out, 44
QuickTime VR controller, 17

R

Rate option, Sound Settings dialog box, 147
reference movie, creating, 203–205
Registration panel, 4, 232
registration code
entering, 9
for upgrading to Pro version of QuickTime, 6, 8
Renderer panel, changing the renderer for a 3D track in, 137
renderer plug-ins, availability of, 137
Replace option, Edit menu, 61
replacing, a section of a movie with data from another, 61
repositioning tracks, 90
resizing tracks, 90
resources guide, 235–237
RGB Balance filter, 175
rotating
a track's image 90 degrees, 88
tracks, 90
RTP (realtime transport protocol) streaming, 180–181

S

sample rate, setting in Sound Settings dialog box, 146, 147
Save As dialog box, 72–73
Make movie self-contained radio button, 73
Save normally (allowing dependencies) radio button, 72
Save normally (allowing dependencies) radio button, Save As dialog box, 72
saving
a movie file so it is self-contained, 73
converted non-QuickTime movie files, 15
double-sized movies, 170
movie files, allowing dependencies, 72
movies for distribution, 170
QuickTime movies from Web pages, 10
search engine, HotBot, 10
Select All option, Edit menu, 48
Select Override Track dialog box, 132
selections, jumping to, 49
Set Poster Frame option, Movie menu, 67, 68
Set Preview to Selection button, in Preview panel, 69
Set Track Alternate dialog box, designating a set of alternate tracks in, 84–85
Set Track Language dialog box, specifying the language of a track in, 83
SGI file format, 14
Sharpen filter, 175
Show Copyright option, Movie menu, 20
changing information, 68
Show Hot Spots button, 42
Size option, Sound Settings dialog box, 147
Size panel, Get Info window, 88
checking the dimensions of a movie in, 178
skewing, tracks, 90
slide-show mode, 29–30
slider bar, Movie controller, 28
smart streaming, 203
Sorenson Developer Edition, advantage of, 186
Sorenson Video compressor, 184
sound
compressing for the Web, 187
understanding the characteristics of digitized, 146
sound compressors, professional versions available, 188
sound conversion utility, using MoviePlayer as, 156
Sound Designer file format, 14
sound file
converting to a different format, 156
creating a sound track from, 149
sound level
changing in movies, 31
overdriving, 32
Sound Settings dialog box
changing sound tracks characteristics in, 153–154
compressing sound for the Web in, 187
converting a music track to a sound track in, 155
making choices in, 188
options in, 147
sound compression choices in, 217
sound tracks
changing the characteristics of, 153–154
checking characteristics of, 148
converting a music track to, 155
creating from an audio CD, 151
creating from sound files, 149
creating from a System 7 sound file, 150
data rates, 146
working with, 139–143
SoundBlaster-compatible sound card, for Windows computers, 5
spatial compression, QuickTime 3, 104–105
Sprite tracks, 131–133
attaching a graphic or video sequence to, 132
changing the background color of, 133
replacing a graphic with another QuickTime track, 132
Standard Edition, checking for in Registration panel, 4
Standard MIDI Import Options dialog box, 158
still image file
adding to an audio track, 141

creating from any movie image, 101–102
Step buttons, Movie controller, 27
Stereo setting, Sound Settings dialog box, 147
stopping, a movie presentation before it reaches the end, 29
straight alpha channel mode, 97
streaming technologies, versus QuickTime, 180–181
streaming VR movies, creating with MoviePlayer and QTVR Flattener, 208–209
Style options, Text Import Settings dialog box, 119
System 7 sound file
creating a sound track from, 150
substituting for an instrument in a music track, 162
system requirements, hardware and software, 5

T

Targa file format, 14
target data rates, estimating, 184
TARGET parameter, specifying a value for, 193
temporal compression, QuickTime 3, 104–105
text
adding small amounts to a movie, 129
Anti-aliasing, 128
changing features of when importing, 119–120
deleting portions of from a text track, 128
pasting from a word processor into a movie, 57
replacing existing in text tracks, 127
text color, changing for an imported text track, 119
text descriptors
exporting a text track with, 123–124
using to specify text appearance in individual frames, 122
Text Export Settings dialog box, 123–124
text file, creating with text descriptors and time stamps, 123–124
text frames, specifying duration and appearance of, 121
Text Import Settings dialog box
options in, 119
creating a music and text track from a karaoke file, 159
text tracks, 117–130
changing font, size, and style of text in, 128
changing text already in, 127
creating by importing text files, 118
creating from a karaoke file, 159
creating one that's synched to other tracks, 125–126
deleting portions of text from, 128
exporting with text descriptors and time stamps, 123–124
searching for text in, 130
specifying duration and appearance of individual frames created, 121
specifying appearance of when importing, 119–120
texture maps
changing for a 3D track, 135–136
changing images mapped onto 3D objects with, 135–136
creating 3D tracks with, 136
thumbnails, creating, 210–211
TIFF file format, 14
tiling versus previewing movies, 209
Time panel, Info window, 51
time stamps
alternate ways to specify, 121
exporting a text file with, 123–124
using to specify a duration for individual frames of text, 121–122
tools, for advanced tasks for movies on Web pages, 201–211
track names, 76
track type, determining when name doesn't match type, 22
tracks
adding new to movies, 76–77
blending, 96
changing the duration of, 81
changing the layer of, 94
combining with the Add and Add Scaled commands, 76–77
compressing only selected using MoviePlayer, 176–177
deleting, 79
designating a set of alternate, 84–85
determining which are contained in a movie, 22
disabling, 80
enabling a disabled, 80
extracting from movies, 78
flipping, rotating, resizing, and skewing, 88–90
loading into memory, 86
making a color transparent in, 95
making partially transparent, 96
masking a visual, 91
putting visual side by side, 92
relayering, 94
returning to the beginning size and orientation, 90
scaling to a specific duration, 81
setting up with alternate languages, 82
Sprite and 3D, 131–137
video and MPEG, 103–116
working with, 75–86
working with visual, 87–102
transitional edits, 55
Trim option, Edit menu, 60
tween tracks, for animating objects in a 3D track, 134

U

Undo command, 53
unlock code
entering, 9
for upgrading to Pro version of QuickTime, 6, 8
Use option, Sound Settings dialog box, 147
utilities, getting important from Apple Web site, 202

V

version number, checking system for, 3–4
video compression
choices in Compression Settings dialog box, 215–216
determining how a track was compressed, 108

for the Web, 183–186
making Web appropriate choices, 184–186
products available to purchase, 216
setting in the Compression Settings dialog box, 106–107
understanding, 104–105
Video compressor, QuickTime 3, 104, 184, 203
video filters, 175
video kiosk
movies on, 213–223
overview of compression issues for, 214
sound compression choices, 217
video compression choices, 215–216
VideoShop application, 134
visual data, adding to QuickTime VR movies, 98–99
visual tracks
creating from a sequence of still images, 109
creating from a single PICT file, 111
creating from a single still image, 110
creating from DV files, 112
creating from FLC/FLI files, 112
creating from non-QuickTime animation and video files, 112
creating from PICS animation files, 113
data rate of, 104
deleting audio that extends beyond the end of, 140
determining how they were compressed, 108
exporting as Digital Video (DV), 222–223
masking, 91
placing side by side, 92
working with in MoviePlayer, 87–102
Volume Control button, Movie controller, 31
volume, changing default in audio track, 143
VR movies, adding logos to, 98–99

W

Web
compressing sound for, 187–188
compressing video for, 183–186
popularity of Digital Video (DV) on, 180
Web authoring tool, 189, 190
Web pages
advanced tasks for movies on, 201–211
basics of movies on, 179–200
embedding a QuickTime movie on, 189–190
settings for video data rates, 185–186
using HREF tracks to make them load, 198–200
writing the HTML for embedding a movie on, 190
Web server, configuring for QuickTime, 189
window sizes
advantage of reducing before compression, 185
changing, 18–19
Windows Control Panel folder, QuickTime icon in, 3
Windows operating systems
hardware and software requirements for, 5
installing QuickTime 3 on, 7
mouse and keyboard shortcuts and enhancements, 227
WYSIWYG Web authoring tool, 189, 190

Y

Yahoo, finding QuickTime movies in Web site, 10

Z

Zoom buttons, 44
zooming, QuickTime VR movies in and out, 44